Information Technol
Legal and Comme

CW00408970

AUSTRALIA
Law Book Co.
Sydney

CANADA and USA
Carswell
Toronto

HONG KONG
Sweet & Maxwell Asia

NEW ZEALAND
Brookers
Wellington

SINGAPORE and MALAYSIA
Sweet & Maxwell Asia
Singapore and Kuala Lumpur

Information Technology Transactions: Legal and Commercial Strategies

Duncan Cornell Card

UK Editor: Mark O'Conor

THOMSON

SWEET & MAXWELL

First published in 2002 by
Thomson Canada Ltd
Published in 2005 by
Sweet & Maxwell Limited of
100 Avenue Road London NW3 3PF
www.sweetandmaxwell.co.uk
Typeset by Servis Filmsetting Limited, Manchester
Printed in England by Ashford Colour Press, Gosport, Hants

A CIP catalogue record for this book is available from the British Library

ISBN 0421 895403

This book is dedicated to my grandmother, Marian Pringle Cameron

Table of Contents

Foreword to the UK Edition

"The level of awareness [needed] to solve a problem is greater than the level of awareness that created the problem." —Albert Einstein

This book is designed to increase the reader's awareness of certain business, legal and regulatory issues in order to avoid, mitigate and solve problems that commonly arise in technology transactions. Always with a focus on getting the deal done, this book recognises and addresses the challenges that project executives face when charged with the task of structuring, planning, negotiating and implementing a technology transaction on time, on budget and with operational success that minimises risk.

For the most part, the lessons that this book painlessly teaches are lessons that others have painfully learned. This book could not have been written without the benefit of such experience and the wisdom of those who lived to tell their transactional tales.

The author's greatest hope is that this book and its lessons will contribute to the awareness necessary to facilitate transactional success through simple management strategies, innovative commercial solutions, respect for each participant's interests, and practically managed business and legal risks.

Since first publishing the book two years ago, I have had the opportunity to present the book's strategic approach on how to avoid or minimise the causes of IT transactional risk to many legal and IT business conferences, and I have used the book to develop several IT procurement courses across Canada. Perhaps the most important response I have had to the book is how very similar risk-management mistakes are across all industrial sectors and jurisdictions of IT users. IT use and management is truly international, and IT commerce has common bonds of structure and strategy around the world, from Santa Clara to Tokyo, from Houston to Hong Kong, and from Toronto to London.

One of the most important themes, and consistent imperatives, in this book is that collaboration among those with IT transaction experience and expertise will always lead to better commercial outcomes than when transaction owners engage in projects alone.

A fine example of this truth lies in the UK edition of this book. Mark O'Conor, a partner and commercial IT lawyer at the prestigious firm of Bird & Bird, has done a superb job of adapting my many checklists, commercial options and transactional strategies from the North American IT market to UK, European and wider international contexts. This collaboration has resulted in a much improved work that truly addresses the transactional demands of UK and international IT markets.

In the light of this, I am extremely pleased that an edition of my book is being released in the United Kingdom to assist practitioners and commercial decision-makers towards an increased transactional level of awareness.

Duncan Cornell Card
Toronto
September, 2004

Author's Acknowledgments

The first people to thank for their contributions to the creation of this book might be surprised to know the truly essential role that they played throughout this project: Geoffrey Bell, Q.C., for imparting his superlative standards of professional excellence and devotion to advocacy; David Gordon, for his wise counsel to "read it again"; The Hon. William Graham, M.P., Minister of Defence (Canada), for sharing his internationally respected commitment to professional leadership and advanced legal education; and, Warren Seyffert, Q.C., for sharing his genius for converging business and law to achieve client success.

I am indebted to, and wish to express my sincere gratitude to, my colleagues at Ogilvy Renault for their support of this project, and for their commitment to leading the legal profession in the emerging and developing IT-law needs of its clients, and, in particular, my partners Daniel Paul, Jim Riley, Andrew Fleming, Mark Hayes and Dany Assaf.

I deeply appreciate the tremendous work that Nadia Bastin invested in the preparation of this book's original manuscript, its proofreading and its revisions. I am especially indebted to those in London who have worked so very hard to prepare the UK Edition of this book. They have been led by the internationally respected commercial IT lawyer, Mark O'Conor of Bird & Bird; his colleague, Katie Rushton, assistant solicitor specialising in tax, worked on the tax section in Chapter 3. Julian Chase at Sweet & Maxwell has demonstrated both vision and boundless energy to expedite the UK Edition of this book to market, and I am very grateful to him for both his enthusiastic support and his exceptional management of this project.

Most importantly, I wish to thank my wife, Jenny, for her encouragement and patience while I disappeared to our den to write for too many hours at a time.

About the Author

Duncan Cornell Card is one of Canada's leading information technology and e-Business lawyers. Duncan's technology practice focuses on strategic commercial transactions, including facilities management and outsourcing services, data management and protection, technology procurement transactions including licensing, enterprise software projects, commercial and corporate joint ventures, e-commerce and internet business strategies and commercial structures, "offshore" and international transactions, technology intensive "turn key projects", and all related technology development and commercialisation transactions. Duncan is a partner at the prestigious Canadian law firm, Ogilvy Renault.

Duncan is included in Lexpert/American Lawyer's annual ranking of the top 500 of all lawyers in Canada for the last seven years, where he is also cited in the 2004 edition as one of Canada's three "Most Recommended" Computer/IT Law lawyers (the highest ranking in Lexpert Magazine's independence professional survey results). He has also been cited as one of the top internet lawyers in the world in the independent *International Who's Who of Internet and E-Commerce Lawyers (UK)*, as one of the world's leading technology lawyers in Euromoney's Guide to the *World's Leading Technology, Media & Telecommunications Lawyers*, and as one of the world's leading e-Business lawyers by Euromoney Magazine's *Euromoney Directory of e-Business and Finance* (London, June 2001). He appears in *Mondaq Business Briefing*, one of the world's leading online collection of professional business advisors.

Duncan graduated from Queen's University in Canada as the Gold Medallist in Sociology with an Honours (*Magnum Cum Laude*) in 1979; Queen's University and the London School of Economics and Political Studies with his LL.B. law degree in 1982; the Academy of International Law at The Hague with a Certificate (International Law) in 1982; and the University of Toronto with his LL.M. graduate law degree (International Trade Law) in 1987. Duncan was called to both the Ontario, Canada Bar and the Bermuda Bar in 1984.

From 1988–1990, Duncan was Corporate Counsel at BCE PubliTech, a subsidiary of BCE Inc., Canada's then largest corporation. In addition to having acted as a director for Warner Communications companies in Canada, Duncan has served as a director of GlobeNet Communications and as a director of FinancialCAD Corporation. Duncan is currently a director of Capital G Corporation, which owns one of Bermuda's largest banking and financial services enterprises. Duncan is currently an elected member of the Board of Trustees, Queen's University in Kingston.

Duncan provides internationally recognised leadership through many industry and professional affiliations, including the Retail Council of Canada's e-Business Committee; founding member of the Technology Industry Committee, The ADR Institute of Ontario, Inc.; the Toronto Computer Lawyers Group; the Computer Law Association (US); and as a Canadian correspondent for Globe Business Publishing's *World e-Business Law Report* in London, UK. He is a member of the board of directors of the Canadian Information Technology Law Association, and a member of: the Computer Law Association (US); the American Bar Association's Science and Technology Committee; the International Bar Association's Intellectual Property and Entertainment, and International Computer Technology Law Committees.

Duncan is a frequent author and speaker on topics related to technology law and transactions. He taught the Cyberlaw Course in the Faculty of Law at Queen's University in Kingston in 2001, and he taught the Graduate Law Program (LL.M.) (Intellectual Property Licensing Transactions) at Osgoode Hall Law School, York University in Toronto in 1999. Although this is Duncan's first book, since 1990, he has published or presented over 180 papers and articles concerning technology transactions and e-Business commercial and legal issues. Duncan has appeared as an "on-air" legal affairs resource for CityTV in Toronto, and his articles have appeared in the Santa Clara University Law School's *Computer and High Technology Law Journal, Computing Canada, CIO Canada, The Globe & Mail's Report on Business Magazine, Bottom Line Magazine* and the *Canadian Computer Law Reporter*.

Revised and updated by D. C. Card, July 26, 2004
For S&M "UK Edition"

Preface

"In the way of the warrior, it is essential to do it right from root to branch. If you do not understand the root and the branch, there is no way for you to know your duty."—Thomas Cleary, *Code of the Samurai*[1]

This book has been written for anyone who has responsibility for the development, creation, implementation, acquisition, management or commercial use of information technology. It is designed as a guide and primer for the most important management, commercial, legal and strategic issues that you need to know for involvement in a technology transaction. The transactions that you will most commonly use this book for assistance with include the following:

(a) technology services:
- acquisition, procurement,
- installation, testing,
- ASP services,
- joint ventures,
- benchmarking, performance audits,
- maintenance,
- call centres,
- network monitoring,
- co-branding strategies,
- outsourcing services,
- consulting services,
- research and development,
- data management,
- security services,
- data warehousing,
- software design and development,
- disaster recovery and back-up services,
- strategic alliances,
- distribution, reseller, VAR, sales and marketing,
- support,
- e-business hosting,
- systems integration,
- enhancement and customisation services,
- teaming arrangements,
- facilities management,
- telecommunication and ISP,
- testing, prototyping and beta-testing,
- business process re-engineering;

(b) hardware:
- acquisition, procurement,

---

[1] Thomas Cleary, *Code of the Samurai: A Modern Translation of the Bushido Shoshinshu* (Tuttle, Boston. Copyright, © 1999), p.7.

- leasing,
- assembly, OEM arrangements,
- marketing representative,
- component manufacturing,
- network infrastructure,
- development,
- research and development,
- distribution and sales channels,
- turn-key systems;

(c) software:
  - acquisition, procurement,
  - firewall,

- Application Service Provider ("ASP"),
- integration, interface,
- assignment, conveyance and sale,
- networking,
- collaboration,
- research and development,
- data management,
- security access systems,
- encryption,
- systems engineering,
- enterprise solutions, ERP, CRM, etc.,
- technology transfer, licensing.

This book is not a detailed and comprehensive treatise on everything you need to know about the technology transactions that you will engage in, nor is it intended to be an exhaustive review of all the issues addressed; it could never stand as a definitive work on all the many topics touched on within it. Instead, its comprehensive review of technology transaction issues is intended to provide the essential points of reference to describe how the various pieces of a transaction fit together, and to help you determine which issues are relevant to your particular transaction. From the very beginning of the planning and needs recognition process, to preparing for the negotiation of a transaction, through to the contracting and effective management of the transaction, the topics and issues identified in this book are intended as a comprehensive reference tool to assist you in structuring, planning for, negotiating, executing, and managing your technology transactions from start to finish.

However, with such a condensed explanation of otherwise complicated commercial, management and legal considerations, an important cautionary reminder is always necessary. Once the task of preparing an annotated checklist of transaction issues and related management strategies is created, the simple and direct way in which the issues and strategies are presented may make it all too tempting for readers simply to stand back and judge that each of the issues presented is painfully obvious and trite. However, based on my experience of how often so many such "obvious" issues are absolutely forgotten, or even ignored, you might wisely reserve your judgment on that score. Despite their seemingly obvious nature, even the most prudent and best intentioned managers can easily be overwhelmed by the complicated logistics, detailed commercial issues, financial considerations, administrative concerns, inevitable legal complications and management challenges of a technology transaction—all of which require immediate attention. That is why this book should be considered as a handbook, a reference resource, and a management guide to mission critical issues that can all too easily slip through the cracks of any technology transaction.

If there is one theme that is common across this book's chapters, it is early planning and preparation. From that fundamental cornerstone of transaction success, to the specific and detailed commercial issues that will arise in the course of most technology transactions, this book is about getting the deal done in the most efficient, and risk-managed, way possible. Far too many transactions either never quite take off, go sideways until they are abandoned, or even crash and burn, and so this book identifies the most common and frequent causes of transaction mishap, and then reverse-engineers these causes into practical commercial, management and legal strategies to manage the risks involved.

Realistic business judgment is key. Not every risk can be avoided, and impractical attempts to do so could easily interfere with the business transaction itself. Managing the most worrying risks with the right strategies is about balance, and it is about the quality of commercial judgment that results from many years of experience. By recognising and addressing those potential (and frequently occurring) commercial and legal issues as early as possible in the planning and organisation of the transaction, the better able you will be to find that balance and exercise sound commercial judgment to get the deal done.

Perhaps the most important message that this book contains is that there is a direct and proportional relationship between the things you should do to manage the proposed transaction effectively, and the chances that your project will be successful, with minimal disputes and with well managed (if not mitigated or avoided) risks. As discussed throughout this book, perhaps the most worthwhile activities you can undertake to promote the success of your transactions directly derive from an understanding of what the most common risks are for the delay or failure of technology projects. Many such hazards can indeed be efficiently managed during the planning phase of almost any technology transaction.

As you read this book, several fundamental principles will become evident. These principles are guiding maxims on which most, if not all, technology transactions should be based. Though the principles emerge in different ways throughout this book, they may be summarised in the following way:

- if you cut too many corners in building a square, you will end up with a circle;

- build the deal to last from the beginning using several important commercial strategies;

- build the deal with professional advisors in order to keep other professional advisors away from the project after it closes—pay them now, so you do not have to pay them much more later;

- understand in realistic and practical terms what the risks are for the project, and face those risks with practical business and legal strategies;

- use balance and judgment to interpret the advice your professional advisors give you and engage advisors who speak your language—often, complicated problems can be entirely side-stepped with a simple commercial rather than legal solution.

To provide guidance towards finding the right "risk–reward" balance to get the deal done, and to help you exercise commercially-relevant judgment concerning the most appropriate commercial and legal strategies for technology transactions, the book is organised around five key stages that reflect the chronological life of most technology transactions:

   I. The Preparation and Planning Phase

  II. The Preliminary Steps of Engagement

 III. Strategies and Negotiation of Key Business and Legal Issues

 IV. Risk-Management Strategies

  V. Transaction Balance and Judgment

Each of the stages, in turn, has a series of intermediary activities that are essential for the proper management of the transaction process. These issues are presented as a checklist at the beginning of each chapter for ease of reference, since the book has been designed as a technology transaction reference workbook for ongoing consultation.

Chapter 1

The Preparation and Planning Phase

"The general who wins a battle makes many calculations in his temple before the battle is fought. The general who loses a battle makes but few calculations beforehand. Thus, do many calculations lead to victory, and a few calculations to defeat. . . . It is by attention to this point that I can foresee who is likely to win or lose."—Sun Tzu, *The Art of War*, "Laying Plans"[2]

1.0 Checklist I: Preparing for the transaction

1.1 Assembling the right team
  ☐ Internal resources
    ○ Managers/executives
    ○ Employees
    ○ Affiliated company
    ○ Internal team composition
  ☐ External resources
    ○ Information technology consultants
    ○ Financial consultants
    ○ Legal services
    ○ Incumbent information technology providers
    ○ Public relations
1.2 Identify knowledge assets
  ☐ Knowledge-asset management
  ☐ Knowledge-asset valuation
    ○ Market valuation
    ○ The whole-problem solution
    ○ Work in progress
    ○ Clear chain of title
    ○ Protection of knowledge assets
1.3 The business case
  ☐ External advisors
  ☐ Needs assessment
  ☐ Business vision
    ○ Objective
    ○ Specific requirements
  ☐ Not a project plan
  ☐ Not an information technology comparative evaluation
1.4 Participant selection
  ☐ Know the participant(s)
    ○ Financial information
    ○ Corporate information
    ○ Human resources
    ○ Customer relations
    ○ Supplier information
    ○ Ambit of operations
    ○ Governance and management
    ○ General market intelligence

[2] Part I, "Laying Plans", Sun Tzu, *The Art of War*. Edited by James Clavell (Dell Publishing, a division of Bantam Doubleday Dell Publishing Group, Inc., Copyright © 1983).

- ☐ The selection process
  - ○ Multi-source selection
  - ○ Sole-source selection
- ☐ Technology requirements
- ☐ Operational/business requirements
- ☐ Financial impact
- ☐ Human-resource impact
- ☐ Industry norms and competitive analysis
- ☐ Solution alternatives
- ☐ Business-case relevance

1.5 Transaction due diligence
- ☐ Governance
  - ○ Corporate authority
  - ○ Corporate approvals
  - ○ Management authority
- ☐ Third-party obligations
  - ○ Shareholder agreements
  - ○ Financial documents
  - ○ Commercial arrangements
  - ○ Confidentiality obligations
  - ○ Miscellaneous obligations
- ☐ Intellectual property rights
  - ○ Identifying the intellectual property
  - ○ Three key issues
  - ○ Intellectual property creation and ownership
  - ○ Ownership—registration searches
  - ○ Intellectual property commercial rights
- ☐ Regulatory issues
  - ○ Industry regulation
  - ○ Capital market regulation
  - ○ Commercial regulation
  - ○ Trade associations
- ☐ Technology standards and performance
  - ○ Operational/technical specifications
  - ○ New or proven technology
  - ○ Performance record
  - ○ Business environment demonstrations
  - ○ Standards compliance
  - ○ Tax/customs
  - ○ Electronic records and evidential weight
- ☐ Participant references
  - ○ Supplier references
  - ○ Financial references
  - ○ Customer references
  - ○ Strategic alliance references
  - ○ Competitive references
- ☐ Dispute history
  - ○ Labour disputes
  - ○ Commercial alternative dispute resolution
  - ○ Claims and demands
  - ○ Litigation
  - ○ Judgments and orders

Successful technology transactions are like icebergs. Only 10 per cent of the transaction is in public view; the other 90 per cent is hidden in the planning and preparation that other participants in the transaction will never see. However, although the other participants to the transaction may not actually witness your planning and preparation, they will certainly see the quality and depth of your devotion to organisation when it comes to the ease with which you will lead your transaction through its various phases.

The planning phase of the technology transaction is both the most important stage in determining its success and, all too often, the most frequently ignored and neglected. In my experience, that neglect arises for many reasons. Sometimes it arises from a lack of experience concerning what steps can actually be taken to improve one's commercial position, and sometimes it is the result of unreasonable and artificial time constraints that are imposed on those who are responsible for leading the transaction; often, the two factors are linked. It may also arise because of one's reliance on the other participants to plan and organise the transaction, and it can also arise from good old-fashioned blind faith that everything will work out for the best. However, I believe that the most common reason for the failure of participants to plan and prepare for a transaction properly is simply because many technology transaction managers and participants do not fully understand and appreciate that most of the reasons for subsequent transaction failure, delay and dispute can be identified, addressed, managed and, often, entirely avoided, through diligent planning and organisation during the preparation stage of the transaction.

When transaction managers deconstruct or reverse-engineer what the most likely risks of failure and delay are for the proposed project, they will readily appreciate that many, if not most, of those risks of failure or delay can be directly identified, mitigated and possibly even avoided by undertaking the appropriate planning and preparation activities. In my experience, these are:

1. the alignment of executive management ownership and responsibility—even if the transaction is delegated from top-level executives to operational managers, the ultimate supervision and informed management control of the transaction must come from a senior executive level. In Europe, this has developed into the concept of "stakeholder buy-in", whereby projects in both the public and private sector live or die by whether or not the relevant people are behind the project and sufficiently kept involved as the project progresses;

2. identifying the right team of internal and external people, who have the experience and expertise to plan, organise, negotiate, implement and manage all aspects of the technology transaction through all of its stages;

3. investing the time and resources to gain complete and accurate knowledge of both your own technology operations, requirements and related business circumstances, and all of the relevant attributes of the other project participants;

4. preparing a thorough and cogent business case for the technology transaction, complete with all of the information and analysis that executive management will require both to understand and approve the transaction; and

5. investing the time and resources that are necessary to plan and organise yourself, including reasonable and relevant due diligence enquiries, to formulate your commercial interests, technological requirements, risk tolerance and legal concerns before you commence the transaction.

Planning and preparing for a technology transaction comprises a suite of activities, all of which are interrelated and each of which will affect the other activities. If you do not have the appropriate internal and external team assisting you on the transaction, then it will be more difficult to execute the business case. If you lack

3

vital information about the other participants, then the business case may not be accurate. If you have not ensured that there are no regulatory impediments to the transaction, then the best transaction team and all of the information-gathering activities in the world will not help. And, if there are significant parts of the planning and preparation activities that are forgotten or ignored, perhaps due to artificial time restraints, then there may be aspects of the transaction's risk that you will not be able to identify and which may remain beyond your management and control.

Assembling the right team

1.1 Many technology transactions are complicated by the fact that they are consortia transactions that require the collaboration of many participants. Not only do many transactions involve multiple participants, including consultants, numerous technology providers, subcontractors and their related companies, but they require a broad and varying array of experience and expertise across many disciplines. An international computer systems integration, or outsourcing, transaction can easily involve expertise in computer hardware and software, facilities management, business process re-engineering, asset transfers, telecommunications, networking infrastructure, international tax, accounting, electronic record maintenance, immigration, employee transfers and human-resource management, various legal areas of expertise, project management and expertise concerning whatever regulatory constraints or restrictions might apply.

When composing your transaction team, remember that most technology transactions require adult supervision. Considering the way in which many failed transactions are staffed, technology projects would benefit from package labelling, perhaps requiring the following warning label to be posted on the wrapping of a technology transaction:

> "WARNING: Untrained personnel must not be left alone with this technology transaction. The operation of this transaction by untrained personnel may be injurious to the health of the organisation and cause irreparable harm. Adult supervision required."

Whether as a collection of internal contributors or as an array of external advisors, it is essential to identify and organise the personnel resources that are required for the project early in the transaction planning process.

Internal resources

1.1.1 You should identify the internal resources you will require to plan, prepare for, negotiate, document, implement and manage the performance of the transaction as soon as possible. Those will likely include:

Managers/executives

1.1.1.1   Who will lead and manage the transaction and report to the organisation's executive management or board of directors?

Employees

1.1.1.2   All assigned employees should have the appropriate knowledge, experience and skills that the particular project requires (*e.g.* a colleague from finance and a colleague familiar with the current IT architecture will often be useful members of the team. See below for further consideration of these points). Be sure you know whether or not your internal staff are employees or independent contractors. Many technology departments and enterprises have hired personnel as independent contractors whom the organisation generally refers to and treats as "employees". However, the implications for any misunderstanding in that regard may have very serious consequences for tax liabilities, ownership of intellectual property and for the protection of your confidential information.

Affiliated company

1.1.1.3   Consider whether or not any of your organisation's affiliated companies have information that is required for the transaction, and related experience or expertise. Frequently, related companies have valuable planning experience that they can contribute.

Internal team composition

1.1.1.4   (a) *Business*—The internal team, first and foremost, requires business leadership. More than any other single aspect of a technology transaction (including, the technology itself), all the specialised interests involved in the transaction should be fundamentally directed toward achieving the transaction's overall business objective. The narrow delegation of the project's management to persons who may have a personal vested interest in the outcome (*e.g.* who will be entitled to a bonus if the transaction closes), or who may only be interested in a particularly narrow aspect of the overall project (*e.g.* marketing, financial or technological), may lend to a skewing of the transaction away from the balanced, broader business priorities of the organisation. In my experience, most successful technology transactions are led by a business person who is capable of balancing and co-ordinating all of the distinct organisational interests towards the overall best interests of the organisation. (b) *Finance*—As Chapter 3 of this book illustrates, there are a myriad of financial issues concerning technology transactions that go far beyond pricing issues. The person who manages those financial issues will have to be very skilful in evaluating the financial impact that negotiation and constantly changing commercial arrangements will have on the transaction's business case. Obviously, your financial manager should be supported throughout the transaction with accurate and current information concerning relevant market research, tax issues and any other financial circumstances of the proposed transaction.

(c) *Information technology*—It is hard to imagine how any technology transaction could be successful without the direct participation of a senior technology manager.[3] Unless a senior technology manager is involved with a transaction from the outset, the project may run the risk of serious delays and perhaps failure. It is best if this leadership is provided early in the planning stages of the proposed transaction, and certainly when the business case is being formulated. The continuity of such leadership will be required throughout the entire transaction process.

(d) *Human resources*—Perhaps one of the most neglected participants in the management of a technology transaction are human-resource managers. Whether to help acquire specialised technology expertise, undertaking employee due diligence or security clearances, considering confidentiality agreements, the implications of relevant legislation such as the Acquired Rights Directive (implemented and known colloquially as TUPE in the UK), transfer employees, or revising or reallocating employees' work assignments, there is a tremendous wealth of experience and judgment that your human-resource managers can bring to the project.

(e) *Legal/regulatory*—There are many reasons why your internal legal staff should be involved as soon as possible when planning the transaction.

First, as this book illustrates, the best-managed technology transactions occur where the intersection of business and law is recognised and respected. Your internal legal advisors will know a great deal about both your business and the applicable legal challenges. Your lawyers will also have an in-depth understanding of the regulatory issues that you live with on a day-to-day basis, and which may have a direct impact on the proposed transaction.

Secondly, although it can drive business people to distraction from time to time, lawyers are nonetheless trained to be organised. Technology transactions that would otherwise be frantic and chaotic end up benefiting greatly from organisational discipline. That is a very necessary skill to move the transaction forward, and to keep all the commercial, technological and legal issues organised and on track.

Thirdly, in-house legal counsel is often the hub for the various divisions of your

---

[3] This is a deceptively obvious point. There are many technology-dependent transactions within otherwise sophisticated businesses where the CIO or senior manager of MIS are not consulted in the early stages of the transaction, even where the transaction will have a significant impact on the business. For example, situations often arose in the early days of e-business and internet-based operations in bricks and mortar businesses where projects were spearheaded by sales and/or market departments, or by other operations teams, who frequently did not fully involve technology managers early in the planning process of business initiatives. See Shane Schick, "IT Department Excluded from Strategic Decisions", *Computing Canada Magazine*, Vol. 28, Issue 10, May 10, 2002, p.8. *www.itbusiness.ca*.

enterprise's organisation and administration. Because in-house legal counsel are so often central to activity for transaction management and administration, they can readily co-ordinate all the other organisational interests in the transaction process. In my experience, in-house legal counsel provide one of the few corporate management services that deals directly with all of the business' other corporate services on a day-to-day basis, including sales and marketing, operations, human resources, finance and even the board of directors.

Lastly, if your in-house legal counsel does not have any specialised legal knowledge or transactional experience concerning technology projects, they are likely to be the most appropriate people to work with and supervise the specialised external legal advisors that you may retain—thus saving business managers' time and money through such a value-added management role.

(f) *Common organisational perspective*—If the members of each participant's transaction team do not have a common organisational perspective on the project, then the proposed transaction may face the risk of failure because the participants were not able to forge a common business objective and shared commercial goal. As a hypothetical example, imagine four participants who are interested in creating a buying group to establish an online exchange to purchase volume-discounted office software products. However, in the course of preparing for the transaction, each of the four participants selects internal teams with entirely different transactional interests and organisational perspectives. One participant sends its team of procurement managers; the next participant sends its e-commerce and online business strategy team; the third participant sends its information technology experts; and the fourth participant, who would ultimately like to sell the exchange at a profit, sends its investment managers. The danger of selecting internal teams that may reflect the narrow interests of each participant (but that will not have a common perspective concerning what is necessary to move the project forward) is that participants will work at cross purposes, have competing interests and agendas, and run the risk of failing to structure and implement a commercial enterprise that will achieve the business case. Such a fragmented array of cross-purpose interests could very easily be the fatal fault line in any technology project. Ideally, you should therefore ensure that each participant's internal team comprises all of the skills and perspectives to promote the successful accomplishment of the project's business objectives.

External resources

1.1.2 It is important to recognise that technology transactions are extremely specialised. In many ways, they are very distinctive commercial transactions. There are a broad range of complex, mission critical or "enterprise" technology transactions that will not arise more than once or twice in the course of a business manager's career. It is most likely that the larger and more complex the transaction is, the less experience and expertise that you will have internally to plan for, negotiate, implement and manage the transaction. Perhaps the best illustration of this arises in large and sophisticated technology transactions, such as when a corporation acquires an enterprise-wide application solution, or even outsources part or all of its information systems requirements to a facilities management service provider. In such situations, a participant's executives may only experience one or two such transactions in their entire career, whereas external advisors who specialise in such projects may successfully engage in many each year.

Therefore, you should assess your internal team's expertise and experience, and then determine whether or not those skills are adequate for the proposed transaction. The strategic benefits that may be secured by retaining external advisors can occur in a wide range of technology transactions, whether due to the size of the expenditure, onerous time constraints, its operational importance, potential risks or liabilities, or the project's uniqueness. Although specialist and experienced external resources and advisors can play an extremely valuable role in any technology transaction, their involvement is all about proportion and balance—and in reaching such a balance by realistically and honestly assessing your organisation's internal limitations and skills gaps. Procuring the right external resources can mean the difference between project success and failure, but you have to strategically plan for the deployment of those resources early in the preparation of the transaction.

Information technology consultants

1.1.2.1   There is a broad range of IT industry consultants available to assist you. Many of those consultants have come from in-house IT or management information system (MIS) departments, or they may practise as business consultants with a specialised focus on the IT sector. You may also consider retaining specialised consultants who focus their practice on the specific type of transaction that you are considering. For example, many international providers of enterprise software systems will provide a list of consultants whom they have authorised to configure and implement their software products. In addition, there are consulting firms (large and small) that specialise in particular types of software systems, systems integration and/or large outsourcing transactions. Perhaps most importantly, IT consultants who have worked on a wide range of the transaction types that you may be considering may also have up-to-date knowledge of industry norms and business practices for such transactions which you may wish to consider as you prepare for the project.

Financial consultants

1.1.2.2.   Often, IT consultants and related business consultants will be in a position to provide you with helpful financial information and advice concerning the proposed transaction. However, you may also wish to consider involving your own accountants and auditors in such issues because of their knowledge of your business (and perhaps even of your current technology infrastructure and costs). Other financial advisors who can add significant value as you prepare for the transaction include: your insurance advisors; accounting firms that specialise in tax and other related issues common to the IT industry; and financial research services that can assist you with price benchmarking or cost-comparison activities, as well as helping to draft the appropriate service-level regime with its related deductions regime (should the levels fail to be reached).

Legal services

1.1.2.3 Without in any way diminishing the important role that in-house legal counsel should play in the course of planning and managing the proposed transaction, external legal advisors may contribute very specialised expertise in several areas that complement both the commercial and legal knowledge of your internal team. Of course, the more specialised and experienced your external legal advisors are, the more they will understand your commercial and technology objectives, and the more they will be able to add significant value at each stage in the transaction process. In addition to the benefits of accumulated commercial experience and knowledge of relevant business norms, there are a wide range of very specialised legal issues that a lawyer whose practice is devoted to commercial technology transactions can assist your team to address and resolve.

For example, it is extremely likely that the following legal issues will arise: (i) contract preparation and negotiation; (ii) human resources; (iii) immigration; (iv) tax; (v) public-sector procurement, regulatory constraints or requirements; (vi) privacy concerns; (vii) electronic records requirements; (viii) electronic evidence issues; (ix) internet legal issues, intellectual property, dispute resolution, export control restrictions; and (x) IT industry-specific risk-management issues.

Incumbent IT providers

1.1.2.4 Providers of IT, data or telecommunications products and services will often also offer to provide you with related consulting and advisory services. As a matter of project planning, such technology providers will offer their services to help participants *(i.e.* prospective customers) to identify and organise technology needs, operational requirements, potential due diligence concerns and even to help participants better define their business and technology requirements. Such engagements may take a wide forms of structure, including consulting arrangements, or even just as a part of the technology provider's marketing and sales activities. Obviously, the issue of consulting independence will arise in situations where the advisors have a vested interest in a particular outcome or participant decision, such as the participant selecting a particular business case direction or a specific type of technology transaction. However, such conflicting interests are usually quite obvious and less complicated to manage where such conflicts are recognised and factored into the decision-making process.

Public relations

1.1.2.5 Many technology transactions require professional planning concerning government management, media and public relations. Where the proposed transaction will have a material impact on your organisation's public relations or requires governmental or regulatory approvals, it may be very beneficial to seek the advice of professional public-relations experts early in the planning process. From media communications to public-policy lobbying, the message that you may wish to communicate in connection with the project may be quite different from your business's day-to-day public-relations requirements. In my experience, the avoidance of public-relations problems requires early and proactive planning. Once a controversial issue has become a public-relations or reputation problem, it can often be beyond the management, repair or damage control of even the most skilful and experienced public-relations manager.

Identify knowledge assets[4]

1.2 It is important for all managers of businesses engaged in technology transactions to understand and appreciate the types of knowledge assets that their enterprise relies upon for its success and viability. Since most technology transactions will involve some form of knowledge-asset design, development, creation, use, application, transfer (whether by license or otherwise), reproduction, communication, commercial exploitation or management, you should identify all of the knowledge assets upon which the project's success will depend.

Knowledge-asset management

1.2.1 Your business's knowledge assets may take a variety of forms. They may be tangible or intangible. They may exist in material form or they may only exist electronically or digitally. They may be created by people or by machines, and they may not even be expressed yet—existing only as ideas, concepts, knowledge, experience or as discussion topics. But all such knowledge assets may be your property, confidential information or intellectual property, and they may play a vital role in the success of the transaction. Such knowledge assets might include:

[4] The term "knowledge assets" is intended to go beyond traditional "intellectual property" in recognition of all the property, trade secrets, and competitive advantages that your business may require, but which are not otherwise included in the narrow and traditional legal meaning of intellectual property. For a discussion concerning the limitations of industrial laws to the knowledge economy, see D. Card, "Outmoded Laws Pose Dangers to International Electronic Commerce", *IP Worldwide*, June 1995, The New York Law Publishing Company, Premier Issue.

Tangible:
- artistic works (painting, music, graphics, choreography);
- information/data;
- charts;
- integrated circuit topography;
- customer lists;
- laboratory reports;
- designs (industrial or other);
- photographs;
- development notes;
- recordings (sound/audio);
- diagrams;
- schematics;
- documentation, reports;
- software;
- drawings;
- supplier lists;
- formulae;
- systems architecture;
- the shape or structure of an object;
- trade names;
- trademarks or logo.

Intangible (except where otherwise physically manifest):
- concepts;
- integrity/reputation;
- experience;
- know-how;
- goodwill/brand awareness;
- methodologies;
- ideas;
- business processes;
- information (trade secrets);
- software "look and feel";
- innovations;
- management systems.

Statutory protection for some knowledge assets:
As regards legislative protection for knowledge assets, there is a wide range of statute and regulation both at the local level within the UK and at a European level. To list every potential one would not be useful, but the following are arguably the most relevant to information technology transactions.
- The Copyright Designs and Patents Act 1988;
- The Companies Act 1985;

- The Data Protection Act 1998;
- The Patents Act 1977;
- The Trade Mark Act 1994;
- The Copyright and Rights in Databases Regulations 1997;
- The Semiconductor Products (Protection of Topography) Regulations 1987.

Knowledge-asset valuation

1.2.2 Most technology transactions require an understanding of the commercial or capital value of the knowledge assets that are required for the project. There are many ways to value knowledge assets, though each method of valuation may be specific to each type of knowledge asset. Indeed, there are books and articles that have been published on the topic of technology and intellectual property valuation,[5] and such helpful literature may provide you with assistance in that specific aspect of project planning and preparation.

Because asset valuation may be an important part of the transaction, you will want to include the relevant asset-valuation experts on your team. In my experience, knowledge-asset and intellectual-property valuation may be more of an art than a science, but there is some consistency to the criteria that are often relied upon in those endeavours. However, it is important to remember that no single source or methodology can provide a completely reliable, accurate—or even reasonable—valuation. It is most often the case that the following approaches are used in combination with each other, as the circumstances of any given transaction requires.

---

[5] Some of the most helpful work that I have relied upon in understanding, addressing and dealing with knowledge-asset valuation and related pricing structures in the context of technology transactions include the following: Tom Arnold, "100 Factors Involved in Pricing the Technology Licensing" in *Licensing Law Library, 1988, Licensing Law Handbook* (Clark Boardman Co. Ltd, New York); Joseph K. Andonian, "New Method to Determine Royalty Rates", *Les Nouvelles*, Licensing Executives Society, June 1, 1991; Daniel M. McGavock, David A. Haas and Michael P. Patin, "Factors Affecting Royalty Rates", p.107 (hereinafter "McGavock *et al.*, 'Factors', *Les Nouvelles*, June 1992"); Joseph R. Wager, "Valuation Fallacies; A Better Way", *Les Nouvelles*, Licensing Executives Society, September 1994; Stefano Sandri, "Methodology Approach to Evaluation", *Les Nouvelles*, Licensing Executives Society, December 1995; John T. Ramsey, *Technology Transfers and Licensing* (Butterworths Canada Ltd., Toronto, 1996), Chap. 2, entitled "Valuation", pp.7–19; F. Michael Hruby and Mark Lutz, "Model Helps Set Value of Technology", *Les Nouvelles*, Licensing Executives Society, March 1997; Stephen A. Degnan and Corwin Horton, "A Survey of Licensed Royalties", *Les Nouvelles*, Licensing Executives Society, June 1997; Paul R. Betten, "Valuing Upfront License Fees", *Les Nouvelles*, Licensing Executives Society, Vol. XXXV, No.1. March 2000, pp.40–43; Richard Razgaitis, *Early-Stage Technologies: Valuation and Pricing* (John Wiley & Sons, Inc., September 1999).

Market valuation

1.2.2.1 Two of the most important mechanisms to determine the value of knowledge assets are historical and current market activity.

(a) *Historical*—What is the past and comparative market activity for the technology? You should secure media and industry information concerning industry practices, recent transactions, bankruptcy cases and other reported commercial transactions which could provide excellent comparative information. Furthermore, relevant industry trade associations, professional advisors such as accountants and consultants, government records and public filings may also provide valuable comparative information.

(b) *Current*—There are several possible ways to determine the current value of a knowledge asset, including: (i) going to those in the industry who would potentially "pay the price" and ask them for their views on current value—in a sense, to solicit a value from the market that would reasonably be expected to participate in such a transaction; obviously, seeking the views of industry participants on such sensitive matters in the planning phase of the project may have commercial risks and disadvantages; (ii) determining present value by auctioning the knowledge asset in a multiple-participant bid-and-tender process, especially where the value of the knowledge asset can be isolated from the overall value of the technology transaction; (iii) calculating the cost for another person to create the knowledge asset, including management, labour, all applicable overhead expenses that generally accepted accounting principles (GAAP) would reasonably recognise; (iv) calculating knowledge-asset value in terms of possible revenue generation, or profitability if commercially exploited; and (v) valuing the knowledge asset through comparative-pricing modelling, market-demand research or even initially launching the knowledge asset in test markets. Most valuation methodologies will, to a greater or lesser degree, be related to ratios among various market and financial variables, such as creation costs, capital investment, maintenance or support overhead, revenues, profitability, operating and maintenance expenses, average time after which such knowledge assets become obsolete, elasticity of market demand and the impact of volume production on production or delivery costs.

The whole-problem solution

1.2.2.2 Does the knowledge asset solve or address the whole of a particular problem, or only part of a problem? If the knowledge asset is a stand-alone work that provides a solution that does not require any other goods or services to function, it may have greater value.

Work in progress

1.2.2.3 Is the knowledge asset finished, or is it still in development? Arguably, the further along the knowledge asset is in design, development and creation, the more valuable it will be (and the easier it may be to determine its market value). The knowledge asset may also have greater value if it has been tested, verified and even commercially implemented. Uncertainty concerning the knowledge asset's concept, design, existence and even its ultimate development may reduce its value to the proposed project. All too often, companies do not take this important issue into account, and attempt to disclose or even commercially exploit under-developed knowledge assets. Premature commercialisation of a knowledge asset can have a detrimental impact on valuation, especially where there are operational or functional problems that may be associated with the product or service long after those problems have been resolved.

Clear chain of title

1.2.2.4 A clear chain of title for the ownership of the knowledge asset may increase its commercial value. In the same vein, if the paper trail for the creation, development or acquisition of the knowledge asset is complete and accurate, then that may also improve the commercial value of the knowledge asset. Conversely, any uncertainty concerning title may diminish its commercial value, depending upon the nature and extent of any such controversy. For example, where there are creators who did not waive their moral rights or transfer their ownership rights in the work, if there is litigation concerning its ownership, if the work is subject to a claim of breach of confidentiality, or if the development records and creation paper trail is weak, with many gaps and omissions, then such ownership risks and additional costs associated with establishing ownership may greatly reduce the knowledge asset's value.

Protection of knowledge assets

1.2.2.5 There are several aspects of knowledge-asset protection that may enhance its value. Some are very technical legal protections and some are just common sense. But if the knowledge asset has not been protected from unauthorised use or access by others, it may have lost its uniqueness and thus its competitive advantage.

(a) *Legal protection*—Knowledge assets may be protected by a wide range of statutes and by the common law. In various ways, intellectual-property law provides the owners of knowledge assets with a certain degree of monopoly protection to use and commercially exploit those assets. Therefore, if the exclusivity and competitive advantage of the knowledge asset can be legally protected, such as through copyright, trade marks or patents, their value may be directly enhanced. Enquiries into the nature and extent of such protection will often require the assistance of legal advisors who specialise in intellectual-property law.

(b) *Physical security*—To what extent has access to the knowledge assets been restricted and controlled by physical security measures? These may include controlling access to premises, vaults or secure rooms, restricted access on a need-to-know basis, security guards, network security, firewalls, encryption systems, surveillance cameras, pass codes, sign-in registers and visitor passes, and biometric identification measures. This can also include mechanisms for indelibly marking the asset itself with some sort of mark of ownership. Digital watermarking (whereby ownership details are added to the valuable digital asset itself) can prove to be a useful adjunct to the legal protection discussed above. Copyright law in England makes it an infringement of copyright to attempt to remove such marks and moves at a European level could also impose criminal penalties for so doing.

(c) *Human resources*—What personnel background checks and screening have been used to control access to the knowledge assets? What is the history of employee interference with the business's knowledge assets, including theft, unauthorised access or sabotage? Is there an employee assistance programme that will help the company to avert the most common reasons for employee misadventure, such as family problems, anger management, substance abuse, mental illness or financial troubles?

(d) *Knowledge-asset management programme*—Many organisations have implemented formal knowledge-asset (or intellectual-property) management programmes, whereby those assets are identified, assessed, recorded, physically protected, legally protected and managed in accordance with a stipulated management policy and formal administrative infrastructure. Arguably, the value of knowledge assets may be positively affected if they have been created, managed and legally protected within a formal asset-management regime.

The business case

1.3   In my experience, this may be the most neglected aspect of planning a technology transaction. There are several aspects of a transaction that are fundamental to most organisations and which should be included in most project assessments, technology-requirements analysis and as a fundamental part of the strategic business planning for technology transactions. For each of these aspects of planning, there are many important attributes of a thoroughly formulated and properly constituted technology transaction business case—with almost as many books that explain how business cases should be prepared and presented. However, some of the most frequently neglected aspects of preparing a business case for a technology project are discussed in this section.

External advisors

1.3.1 There are several important factors to why you will most likely want to involve external advisors to formulate the business case. Although your internal team is experienced in planning and preparing for "ordinary course of business" transactions and projects, technology transactions will often create commercial, organisational and management demands that are outside the realm of their experience. In addition, if the problems or objectives that the technology transaction is facing are mission critical, if the proposed project will require a substantial investment, if the transaction is unique or particularly creatively formulated, or if there are complicated industry issues (*e.g.* regulatory, tax, legal, administrative or technological issues), then you should consider involving specialist external advisors to help you formulate a business case.

Needs assessment

1.3.2 Far too frequently, business managers proceed with a technology transaction solely on the basis that, superficially, they understand that a technology solution is required to resolve a particular business "problem". If transaction decisions are made without a thorough and detailed understanding of your current circumstances, then the business case will not be able to describe your project's needs and requirements fully. The old adage, "You don't know where you're going until you know where you've been", applies to almost all technology transactions. You should thoroughly understand (and ensure that the business case accurately reflects) your specific circumstances before you can formulate a strategic vision of where you want to go.

In most cases, the preparation of the business case will require an understanding of: (i) the day-to-day business operational and technology performance requirements; (ii) your current IT costs, efficiencies, and inefficiencies; (iii) the technology support role that your employees currently perform; (iv) all of the components of your existing technology and telecommunications infrastructure, (v) your technology support and maintenance records, including all operational failures and deficiencies, together with service incidents and results; and (vi) the impact (at all levels) that your existing technology infrastructure is having on your organisation.

Business vision

1.3.3 The business case is above all a vision statement of where your organisation wants to go and what the specific requirements are for getting there.

Objective

1.3.3.1 The business case should describe the business objective that you want the technology transaction to achieve and the vision of where you want to end up. The objective should describe your intended business destination—not just financial or technological objectives. Although your overall business vision and objective may include destination requirements related to administration, operations, security, market advantage, technological innovation, personnel and management, the business case should describe in some detail the desired commercial results of the project.

Specific requirements

1.3.3.2 The business case should also provide you with a "how to get there" blueprint of strategy, cost/investment, management, transactional process, and very detailed and specific operational and functional requirements (even specifications) that the transaction is to achieve. In addition to the budget analysis, the personnel-resources allocations and all the other required business case contents, you should ensure that you have a very specific and comprehensive understanding of what you need the technology to do and exactly how (in terms of operational and business results) the creation, acquisition, implementation or use of the proposed technology must perform to achieve the commercial objective described in the business case.

Not a project plan

1.3.4 Having just described the business case as the fundamental vision statement for the proposed project, to be expressed in terms of both your current circumstances and all of the technology requirements and strategic steps to achieve your goal, it is hard to explain why so many managers confuse the business case with a "project plan". Where the former is a statement of project vision, the latter is a statement of the commercial and administrative steps that will be implemented to achieve that objective. As the project's commercial or transactional circumstances change through the course of the transaction (and they will—often), the project plan will need to be revised. If the business case can be described as the war plan, then project plans are the battle plans for each specific transaction that will be implemented to achieve the overall business objective. In fact, the success of the business case may depend upon the project plan, though the two should never be confused. A project plan (however well it is prepared) cannot be a substitute for the business case, which explains and justifies the overall business goal that you want to achieve.

Not an information technology comparative evaluation

1.3.5 If possible, every project plan should include a comparative evaluation of possible alternative technologies and transactions. However, the conclusions of such an evaluation (*i.e.* why a particular technology or transaction should be adopted) should not be confused with or considered a substitute for a project plan—and it should certainly never be relied upon as a substitute for the business case.

Situations will arise in which it will be very tempting to simply move an intuitively assessed technology problem forward by contacting prospective technology service or product providers for information concerning their recommended approach to solving the problem, whether formally or informally. The justification for such an approach may be based on: perceived time constraints; the assumption that the business case (though not actually formulated in writing) is generally understood; a particular kind of "intuitive" management style; or upon trust in existing technology provider relationships. In my experience, technology transactions that rely on such ad hoc planning without the benefit of either a business case or even a well thought-out project plan are much more likely to suffer a higher incident rate of failure, false starts, project liabilities or delays.

Participant selection

1.4 The efficiency with which you select transaction participants is directly proportional to the amount of work that you have put into the preparation and planning for the transaction.

If you: (i) fully understand your transactional requirements; (ii) have a comprehensive business case and project plan; (iii) understand the relevant market, commercial or technological requirements or preconditions; (iv) have undertaken a reasonable due diligence process; and (v) have assembled the right team of internal and external experience and expertise, then you are likely to be in an excellent position to identify and select potential transaction participants.

Know the participant(s)

1.4.1 You should obtain as much information as possible about the project's other potential participants. Areas of enquiry may include the following matters.

Financial information

1.4.1.1 Information concerning the financial well-being of a prospective participant may not be discernable from the numbers alone. Such information may also be found in developing market trends for rising or falling demand in their services or products, information concerning their accounting practices (whether within or outside of GAAP), and in any changing circumstances in their financial reporting practices. Such information may be secured from the following sources.

(a) *Banking references*—often, the participant will authorise their bank to provide you with both a reference, empirical financial data (*e.g.* cash flow, assets, debts) and information concerning their knowledge of the person's creditworthiness.

(b) *Credit rating*—there are now many sources that provide a credit-rating assessment, and you may also want to get related information from the prospective participant's suppliers, credit card company and other sources of trade or finance credit.

(c) *Financial statements*—you may wish to secure copies of the participant's financial statements, preferably audited, that are dated as at the most recent date possible. Such historical information may help to identify trends or unusual circumstances. You may also wish to ask for permission to interview the accounting firm that prepared the participant's financial statements.

(d) *Financing information*—it may be helpful to understand how the prospective participant is financed, whether by debt, equity or cash flow. The structure of their financing can also provide you with a significant amount of valuable information that is related to who ultimately controls the participant, the related governance matters, the extent to which third-party consents are required to proceed with the proposed transaction and the participant's related commercial affiliations.

(e) *Independent analysis*—you may wish to consult independent third parties to provide you with advice concerning the participant's financial circumstances, such as market analysts, research consultants and related information services (*e.g.* Dunn & Bradstreet).

(f) *Dispute history*—a tremendous amount of information concerning the financial condition of a participant may be secured by researching whether or not the participant is involved in disputes, claims, litigation, proceedings or judgments. Even information concerning the emergence of contingent liabilities may provide you with important financial information—whether related to product liability, intellectual-property infringement, environmental liability, governmental investigations, bankruptcy petitions, statement of claims, registered security interests or otherwise.

(g) *Security searches*—there are a wide range of publicly accessible registries that can provide important information on the financial circumstances of a participant, including registered personal-property security interests, land-ownership registries, personal property or bank security and bankruptcy petitions.

Corporate information

1.4.1.2 (a) *Corporate filings*—Any incorporation, trade name or regulatory filings that are public (if the equity of the company is publicly traded, then more information is likely to be available. See, *e.g. www.companieshouse.com*); and

(b) *Public information*—Published information, including the company website, media reports, references in government or regulatory publications, articles and press releases.

Human resources

1.4.1.3 (a) *Participant growth*—If the participant has grown quickly, there may be several human-resource implications relevant to your due diligence enquiries. For example, fast-growing participants may be somewhat less diligent in checking the CVs and references of new employees, and they may be at more risk for having inadvertently misappropriated any knowledge assets, and perhaps confidential information, that new employees may have brought from a previous employer.

(b) *History of personnel attrition*—Obviously, circumstances of high personnel attrition rates may indicate other difficulties in an organisation. The circumstances of the attrition may also be important for you to know and understand.

(c) *Employee assistance programme*—Fidelity risk managers and information security professionals repeatedly stress that one of the most important knowledge-asset protection strategies that any organisation can implement is the existence of an employee assistance programme. When you consider that a relatively large percentage of knowledge-asset theft, sabotage, interference or destruction is actually caused by staff who have all the physical security codes and otherwise legitimate access to the knowledge assets, but that those incidents are heavily influenced by psychological stress associated with medical, family or money problems, or substance abuse, that they may be suffering, it is easy to understand how addressing these circumstances early on through employee assistance programmes can mitigate, if not avoid, many such unfortunate situations.

(d) *Personnel claims and other legal actions*—In the same vein as issues concerning personnel attrition, it is important for you to know the nature and severity of any claims, suits, proceedings or other legal actions that may have been undertaken by staff against the participant, whether as wrongful-dismissal claims or claims related to other matters, including sexual harassment, discrimination or compensation.

(e) *Labour relations*—Since technology transactions often depend upon knowledge workers, it may be very important to understand the labour-relations history of the participant, and whether or not their participation is dependent upon collective agreements. In that regard, you may also wish to secure information concerning the expiry of such collective agreements as well as the quality of the relationship between management and labour within the organisation.

(f) *Reliance on independent contractors*—In recent years, there has been a significant increase in the number of individuals who provide their services as independent contractors as opposed to full-time employees.

For reasons related to income tax liability, insurance coverage, employment contribution requirements, ownership of intellectual property rights and governance issues, it is very important to understand which individuals involved in the project are employees and which are independent contractors. Although in many circumstances, you may consider individuals who provide services to be "employees", as that term is commonly used in the non-legal sense, they may not legally qualify as such. This is a mistake that is very frequently made because there is a broad range of factual criteria that distinguish between an employee and an independent contractor. An enquiry should be undertaken, perhaps with the assistance of specialist employment lawyers, so that you have a clear understanding of the legal basis upon which staff will be governed, services provided and knowledge assets created and transferred.[6]

Customer relations

1.4.1.4 You should investigate the nature and quality of the participant's relations with its customers and clients. Although financial information is, by its nature, retrospective in focus, information concerning customer relations and client satisfaction can provide important insights into a participant's business. In that regard, you may wish to request the following information: (i) a key-customer list, even though it may be regarded as highly confidential and difficult to obtain without the protection of a confidentiality or non-disclosure agreement; (ii) history and current status of customer disputes, claims, suits, proceedings or other legal actions; (iii) what is their return policy and return (or complaint) incidence rate; (iv) the nature of any customer relationship management programme; (v) customer retention and repeat transactions; (vi) customer support records, activities and assistance information (whether by call centre support or otherwise); and (vii) customer testimonials, either by direct enquiries or self-report survey data.

Supplier information

1.4.1.5 Since the proposed transaction may indirectly involve both the participant's suppliers and all the third-party commercial relations that the participant will be expected to bring with it to the transaction, you may wish to request the following information: (i) list of suppliers, or at least key suppliers; (ii) supplier performance history, including supply delays, disruptions or embargos; (iii) any disputes concerning transfer of title, returns, product-quality disputes or acceptance disputes; (iv) the supplier's quality of control programmes; (v) product, service or financial (payment) disputes or litigation history; (vi) current financial standing and payment history; (vii) supplier relationship testimonial (see **1.5.6.1**); (viii) reliance upon electronic data interchange (EDI) or other automated inventory management or procurement systems; (ix) review of all relevant supply agreements that are either material to the participant generally, or to the transaction specifically; and (x) all relevant customer-to-supplier information, discussed at **1.4.1.4**.

---

[6] See **1.5.3.3** for discussions concerning when an employer will own what an employee creates, and the legal requirements to transfer intellectual property from independent contractors to those who hire them.

Ambit of operations

1.4.1.6 You might be surprised to know the number of times that one participant is more than halfway through the transaction process only to discover that the entire project will be much more complicated than first anticipated because one of the participants did not disclose that they carried on business in more than one (sometimes, many) jurisdiction and across many business locations.

Therefore, as early as possible in the process of getting to know the participants, you may wish to request the following information: (i) jurisdiction(s) where the participants carry on business, and all jurisdictions where they expect the transaction to be engaged in; (ii) locations where the participants have offices (including headquarters), warehouses, resident personnel, manufacturing facilities, holding companies, management entities and all other related management commercial location information; (iii) any use of offshore companies or other financial or management entities; (iv) any inter-company arrangements that may in any way affect the proposed transaction (*e.g.* personnel secondments, management services agreements, inter-company intellectual property or technology licensing, etc.); (v) information technology and related issues of electronic record maintenance, back-up, disaster recovery, technology operations and disruption history, technology vendor/service providers; (vi) any parts of the participant's operations that will be excluded from the project generally or transaction specifically; (vii) intellectual property protection and related asset management, including production systems, processes and methodologies; and (viii) reliance on any third party and unrelated or non-affiliated service providers, such as outsourcing, facilities management, technology goods or service suppliers or special-purpose trusts.

Governance and management

1.4.1.7 There are several reasons why a participant's governance and management infrastructure is important. First, this information may disclose how experienced and skilled the project's decision-makers are. Secondly, it could offer important information concerning the business and administrative culture of the participant—whether they are entrepreneurial, bureaucratic, hierarchical, quick-moving—or any other aspect of corporate culture that you may feel is important to know for the sake of the project. Thirdly, you will need to understand how the participant makes business and commercial decisions, and who the appropriate individuals are for you to work with, including due diligence co-operation, negotiation and the ongoing management of the project.

In that regard, you may wish to secure the following information: (i) board of directors composition, board committee membership and how often they meet; (ii) are there any executive, board, advisory committees who are the members, and when do they meet? (iii) executive management organisational chart; (iv) how often groups of executive management meet and in what groups or teams; (v) is the

General Counsel and/or the Chief Information Officers members of the executive management committee, or do they report to members of that committee, *e.g.* to the Chief Financial Officer (CFO) or to an Executive Vice President (V.P.) of Operations; (vi) management authority delegation, financial approval limits and subject-matter restrictions; and (vii) recent examples of management team composition for other commercial or technology transactions recently engaged in by the participant.

General market intelligence

1.4.1.8 In addition to the due diligence enquiries that are discussed at **1.5** of this book, there are a few sources of information that, as a preliminary step, may assist you in getting to know the participants. The following are only a few examples of additional information sources that you may wish to consider: (i) competitor assessment; (ii) investment analyst reports or financial market publications; (iii) review of media literature, industry newspapers, magazines, online publications, trade journals or industry association publications[7]; (iv) published government or public sector regulatory reports; (v) access to information government applications and searches; (vi) general litigation and dispute history or activities; and (vii) other information sources concerning goodwill, reputation, brand value, such as consumer reports, industry or trade associations and consumer-ratings agencies.

The selection process

1.4.2 There are many ways to select a participant in a technology transaction, and there are many papers and books on that topic. However, it is very important to identify some of the most important high-risk issues and considerations that may arise in selecting a transaction participant—and especially considerations that are often neglected in day-to-day practice.

Multi-source selection

1.4.2.1 In situations in which you are in the early stages of planning the proposed transaction and you are gathering information concerning the possible technological, commercial or other issues that participants may assist you with, you may wish to use open tender strategies that are designed to engage many possible participants. (a) *Request for Information ("RFI")*—The RFI process may narrow the scope of

---

[7] There are numerous media research services that you may wish to consider, including Westlaw (*www.westlaw.co.uk*); LexisNexis™ (*www.lexisnexis.co.uk*); DowJones Infoglobe, rebranded as Factiva (*www.globeinteractive.com*); Newscan (*www.newscan.com*); Bloomberg (*www.bloomberg.com*); Dialog (*www.dialog.com*).

potential participants based upon the relevance of the information that is provided to the business case or the project plan. Perhaps three of the most important advantages of beginning the transaction process by issuing an RFI involves: (i) your ability to take a broader approach to how potential participants might involve themselves in the overall project, thus taking the broadest approach possible in terms of technology transaction options; (ii) your ability to learn about potential participants in an efficient and direct manner; and (iii) your solicitation of information and recommendations on the formulation of a project plan and possible strategic options for the plan.

You should ensure that the RFI: (i) does not promise any potential participants that they will participate at the Request for Proposals stage (known as the avoidance of the "implied tendering contract" in public-sector contracting circles)[8]; (ii) allows you to rely on the information provided and permits you to use such information for the project; (iii) does not require respondents to overly qualify, or otherwise make conditional, the information so that it is practically meaningless; and (iv) includes a follow-up and response process that will create a fair and open method for you to seek clarifications of, and additions to, the information that is submitted.

Usually, all information contained in an RFI response will be the proprietary, and strictly confidential, information of the person submitting that response. If you believe that your organisation should own any particular aspect of the RFI which is particularly beneficial or important to your organisation, then you are well advised to confirm that requirement in the RFI. Although it may be very tempting to rely on any possible ambiguities or incomplete statements in the RFI to your benefit, it is important to avoid any risk of subsequent misunderstandings or disputes concerning such matters by clearly addressing those issues in the RFI.

One mechanism sometimes employed to speed up this process and to flush out issues at an early stage is to include with the RFI a draft contract. The logic behind this is that the sooner the contractual issues are being discussed, the sooner the buyer can assess whether his potential providers are indeed serious, able to deliver on acceptable terms and indeed are an organisation with whom the buyer will be able to reach agreement of a contract. More often, however, it will be more appropriate to issue the draft contract with the RFP, and this is discussed below.

(b) *Request for Proposals*—Where you have a more developed idea of the project's requirements, specifications and commercial objectives, and perhaps even the transaction's proposed structure, you may wish to issue a Request for Proposals ("RFP") to potential participants that you have already identified and preliminarily vetted. Although the level of specificity in an RFP will vary from project to project, it is easier to select participants if there is a significant degree of detail and specificity that will be required in any resulting bids. RFPs tend to be well organised and contain very clear operational and functional requirements which all bidders will be

---

[8] In the case of *Blackpool and Fylde Aero Club Ltd v Blackpool Borough Council* [1990] 3 All E.R. 25, the contracting authority was held to have agreed that if the tenderer submitted a conforming tender, it would be considered along with all other conforming tenders.

required to address. RFPs often also include a draft contract that participants are required to execute and deliver in the event that the bid is successful. However, because each bid proposal differs and you will likely have some flexibility in the arrangements that you are proposing, most RFP draft contracts are to some extent subsequently negotiated between the participants. Any commercial or legal matters that have not been addressed in the RFP, or any other ambiguities concerning an RFP, are usually addressed in the course of a "Bidders Conference", in which all potential bidders have their questions answered, with all such answers copied to all other bidders.

A key aspect of selecting participants in this manner is to ensure that no one participant is favoured or unequally treated in the course of the process, whether through the provision of information or in their evaluation. In that regard, it is extremely important to treat all bidders, and thus potential participants, fairly and equally through this phase of the transaction process. An important mistake that an issuer of an RFP can make is to be unreasonably inflexible concerning the response that a bidder submits. The RFP process is, to a great extent, interactive and reciprocal. Very often, the commercial, financial and management assumptions that existed at the time at which the RFP was issued, and the bidder's understanding of what was being requested, will have changed somewhat by the time the participants wish to formalise their commercial arrangements. Therefore, some contractual flexibility and room for reasonably accommodating a revised understanding of the proposed project should (in most circumstances) prevail right up to the point of executing the governing contract.

In my experience, too rigid and myopic a regard for simply restating the provisions of an RFP bid into the transaction's contractual arrangements unrealistically disregards the discursive nature of the RFP-bid process, and will often create a fertile environment for misunderstanding, disputes and subsequent transactional risk.

(c) *Bid review and assessment*—The RFP should, from the outset, specify the general grounds and preliminary basis upon which successful participants will be selected. Subject to the discursive process of the bid's clarification and evaluation, the RFP should stipulate the qualitative and quantitative criteria upon which the bid will be considered and evaluated. Although the selection of successful participants will not have to be made based upon any one criterion alone (*e.g.* the lowest price), all selection criteria should be applied fairly and equally across all potential participants. The issuer of the RFP should be in a position to provide reasons for non-selection to unsuccessful participants that are consistent with the bid process that you have engaged in. In that regard, it may be prudent to involve legal advisors throughout the whole RFP and bid-evaluation process, to ensure that your conduct will not give rise to any claims of misconduct, any cause of action or any ground for liability. The outcome of the selection process may be contentious and you will want to ensure that you have treated all potential participants fairly and equally.

As a protective measure, you should document the entire bid process and keep accurate, complete and reliable records of your participant-selection deliberations.

Such records may include: (i) all formal RFP and bid documents; (ii) RFP and bid questions and answers; (iii) proceedings of bidder conferences; (iv) minutes of evaluation meetings and related memoranda; (v) all correspondence with potential participants; and (vi) all internal emails and written reports, bid notations, meeting minutes and deliberations within your organisation. If you discover that any such information does not accurately reflect your organisation's conduct throughout the RFP and bid process or in any way misrepresents your activities in that regard, you should move quickly and comprehensively to set the record straight and ensure that all such records are reliable, accurate and complete.

Sole-source selection

1.4.2.2　(a) *Market research*—If you wish to select a participant on a "sole-source" basis and not within a competitive-bidding process, much of the information upon which you will base your decision will comprise market research, such as publicly available information, information that the participant provides to you or information that you gather concerning the proposed participant from others (see **1.4**). However, depending upon the veracity and reliability of such information, you may wish to: (i) independently corroborate all such information with at least two other sources; (ii) discount any information that may be provided in bad faith or where either a conflict of interest exists or where ulterior motives may cause you to question the information's reliability; and (iii) verify whatever information you can with the proposed participant directly.

(b) *Existing participants*—If you are selecting a participant to work with other project participants, you may wish to: (i) involve the other participants in the selection process (*e.g.* to help you to assess team compatibility); (ii) ensure that the selection criteria are dovetailed with and practically relevant to the needs of both the transaction and the other participants; (iii) consider the extent to which each of the participants should share in the risk of their related performance obligations (*e.g.* with joint liability); (iv) investigate any complications or controversies that otherwise exist among the proposed participants (*e.g.* competitive relationship, disputes, common suppliers, common customers, technology compatibility or interoperability, etc.); and (v) how the additional participant will affect (whether positively or negatively) the team culture of the overall project. Participant co-ordination and alignment are essential. Many technology projects fail because participants were not integrated, balanced and co-ordinated into the project as a consolidated and united team. A frequent example of project management that interferes with participant alignment occurs where prime contractors keep all of the project's participants (customers, subcontractors and consultants) very separate from each other, based upon the often misguided belief that such disconnection of participants will provide a prime contractor with greater control over, and ability to manipulate, all the other participants. Instead, the resulting lack of inter-participant alignment, failure to communicate among all participants, lack of team co-ordination, and lack of relationship-dovetailing often directly results in incomplete risk management, delays and project failures owing to the proverbial right hand not knowing what the left hand was doing.

Technology requirements

1.4.3 In assessing whether a prospective participant's technology is either adequate for the project or compatible (including interoperable and workable) with your technology infrastructure, there are important pitfalls to avoid. First, you should ensure that any technology comparisons are based upon as much detailed information as possible. Rather than simply relying upon a particular technology's promotional or marketing materials, you should undertake a detailed review and analysis of the operational and technical specifications for all such technology.

Secondly, you can expect to discover compatibility gaps among the technology of the participants. However, many transaction managers make the mistake of simply trusting the ability of the participants to overcome those potential impediments, rather than formulating a specific strategy as to how (and when) those potentially detrimental commercial and technology discrepancies will be overcome. Therefore, in addition to your technology due diligence activities, a technology compatibility and implementation plan should be prepared that sets out what will be done to ensure that each participant's technology will contribute to the project in the manner and timetable required by the project.

Thirdly, the technology requirements, including any obligations to overcome and address any compatibility deficiencies, should be documented and described in the functional and technical specifications section of the technology agreements. Once you have undertaken that comparative analysis for the purposes of selecting a participant, you can document the results of that analysis for use in any future commercial arrangements between those participants.

Operational/business requirements

1.4.4 There may be aspects of the transaction that will require certain business disciplines, whether as business processes, information-management systems, customer-management methodologies or even project-management systems. In such situations, you should ensure that all prospective participants are able to work within the framework of the operational requirements, and that all participants will work within that framework. One of the simplest ways both to confirm the compatibility of required business processes and to ensure that you have documented this commercial understanding is simply to describe the business processes in graphic form, whether as a flowchart or as a diagram of project relationships. All prospective participants will thus be able to understand their specific role in the overall transaction process, and each participant's expectations concerning the role of others can be summarily described to minimise misunderstandings and misconceptions. No two enterprises will administratively or operationally carry on business in the same manner. Therefore, the challenge at this stage of the transaction process is to evaluate a prospective participant both in terms of commercial compatibility and in terms of their ability to adapt flexibly and adjust their ordinary business processes to the proposed project.

Financial impact

1.4.5 It is very important to understand the financial impact that the technology transaction will have on the participants. Although the transaction will be designed to benefit all the project's participants, the transaction may be structured in such a way that a particular participant may not legally or commercially tolerate. For example, the transaction may require a significant amount of capital investment, it may have a detrimental impact on short-term cash flow, or it could require significant personnel expenditure. Therefore, in addition to all of the other evaluation criteria concerning a prospective participant's engagement, you should also clearly understanding what the financial impact of the project will be on participants and how each participant plans to cope with such circumstances.

Human-resource impact

1.4.6 Certain transactions may have a dramatic impact on a participant's human resources. That impact may simply be a requirement to hire additional personnel, or it may require participants to acquire and manage certain skills for which it has no experience. Drastic changes in personnel may also have a direct impact on how an enterprise is managed, and even directly affect its culture and method of operation. A significant technology transaction may be very labour-intensive, and a particular enterprise may be very excited at the prospect of hiring a significant number of new personnel to perform the required services. However, any significant change to the culture and successful management style of the organisation may indeed have a detrimental impact on both the participant and the success of the project. Therefore, you should clearly understand how the human-resource requirements of the project will directly affect or change a prospective participant.

Industry norms and competitive analysis

1.4.7 As previously discussed in the context of gathering market information and industry intelligence concerning prospective participants, you may wish to undertake a more comprehensive and detailed analysis of each participant in the context of their own market. Such a competitive analysis of a prospective participant may provide you with information concerning their unique contribution to the project which their competitors cannot deliver. Unfortunately, such detailed investigations and analyses require a significant amount of information about both the prospective participant and each participant's competitors. In order for you to undertake a comparative "benchmarking" of what alternatives are available in the participant's market, you will have to identify: (i) all of the comparative criteria that is particularly relevant to the proposed transaction; (ii) develop a common basis of comparison for certain attributes that are not otherwise common; and (iii) develop a scoring system or other empirical evaluation system in order to assess objectively the attributes of the participant in the context of their market. Obviously, such a benchmarking analysis will only be relevant in large or particularly complicated transactions, and it may only be relevant to one (or very few) of the prospective participants. However, even when such an analysis is reasonably required for a particular transaction, they are frequently not undertaken—often at great project risk. Therefore, it is important to exercise judgment and prudence when determining whether comparative benchmarking is appropriate to evaluate a prospective participant, and whether the associated reduction of risk is worth expending the resources to achieve it.

Solution alternatives

1.4.8   Although you will select a participant based on their suitability for a particular project, you should also consider whether that participant would be able to adapt if, during the transaction, the project itself was amended and the participant's involvement changed. For example, you may consider choosing a participant who is technologically "non-denominational" and not tied to any particular technology solution or product. In the same vein, you may wish to choose a participant who is "technology open" so that they are not encumbered by a proprietary, or otherwise exclusionary, technology infrastructure that cannot be flexibly adapted to changes in the proposed project. Therefore, you may wish to include in your selection criteria information concerning the ability of prospective participants to: (i) successfully perform the project's current requirements; and (ii) the extent to which they are able to adapt flexibly and manage change during the transaction process.

Business-case relevance

1.4.9   The selection of a participant illustrates why you should keep the project's business case clearly before you during all stages of the transaction process. The selection criteria for proposed participants should be a direct result of the business case, and you should tie all the selection criteria to the demands of the business case. Since the business case and the resulting plan of strategic implementation will specify the project's objectives and requirements, the selection of participants to achieve the business plan must be based on their ability to contribute whatever products or services will be required, regardless of any other attributes a participant may have.

Transaction due diligence

1.5   There are many circumstances that may either affect your ability to engage in a particular technology transaction, or that may at least have a direct influence on the nature and structure of how you achieve the business case through the proposed transaction. Due diligence activities should be divided into two aspects: internal due diligence and external due diligence.

Internal due diligence may be thought of as getting your own house in order, but these activities must not be underestimated. A failure to identify any governance, contractual, regulatory or other legal impediment to the proposed transaction may cost you and your organisation far more than a failed transaction. External due diligence may be thought of as gathering whatever information about others that is necessary and relevant to planning, structuring and implementing a transaction that reasonably balances risk allocation and project rewards.

This section of the book sets out a checklist of the due diligence considerations that you will want assurance about before too many of your organisation's resources are committed to the proposed transaction. It is important to remember that the principal role of any due diligence investigation is to ensure that each participant is capable of doing what they have promised to do—either in the course of sales presentations, in the ultimate contract, or otherwise. Therefore, a due diligence work plan and associated checklists (the "due diligence plan") should be developed in co-operation with your legal, technology and business advisors to ensure that it will adequately address all due diligence issues that are commercially and legally important, and that will not include investigations that are unnecessary or economically unjustifiable in the context of the particular transaction. Due diligence plans must balance the cost of the due diligence process against the benefits that will result from it. Factors such as: (i) the financial capacities of the participants; (ii) the nature of the relationship (*e.g.* whether the transaction is an isolated, single transaction or part of a continuing course of dealing); and (iii) the representations and warranties that participants will rely upon, together with reliance upon other risk-management strategies discussed later in this book, will all influence the scope and thoroughness of the due diligence enquiries that are reasonably and proportionately required for your particular transaction.

Whilst it is impossible to prescribe a single form of due diligence plan that can be used for all types of technology transaction, this book presents and discusses the issues that may be relevant and appropriate for your transaction.

Perhaps the first mandate that your transaction team should be assigned is the task of formulating the due diligence plan that will uniquely fit the specific needs of the proposed transaction, and that will identify both the internal and external resources that will be assigned to each due diligence task and the proposed timetable for completion of those enquiries. Unless you have done your homework and know that there are no serious impediments to the proposed transaction, or unless you have a strategy to address any potential impediments, even the best business case and project plan may not be an assurance of project success.

Governance

1.5.1

Corporate authority

1.5.1.1 Does the participant have the corporate authority to participate in the transaction? The incorporation and other "constitutional" powers of the participant should not include any impediments to the transaction, and you should ensure that the transaction is within the powers of the participant. Also, the statutory rules concerning the authority may also be relevant, and each jurisdiction's approach to these issues may vary. If a participant proceeds with a transaction on the basis of assumed authority to do so, your entire transaction may subsequently unravel if it turns out that the participant did not have the fundamental power to engage in or perform the transaction.

Corporate approvals

1.5.1.2 There are three levels of governance that may require transaction approval, whether as a function of corporate authority, statutory requirement, participant policy or otherwise. Depending upon the circumstances of the proposed transaction, governance approvals may be required by either the shareholders, the board of directors or by executive management. Therefore, you should secure a complete and accurate understanding of all external and internal requirements for the transaction's governance approval, and then ensure that all governance levels have provided their required approvals.

Management authority

1.5.1.3 You should ensure that the level of the participant's management with whom you are dealing have been either granted or delegated the authority to conduct the transaction, or has existing authority to do so on the basis of their seniority and normal executive responsibilities. Such enquiries will often lead you to assess whether the person with whom you are working truly represents and can obligate the participant. Not only is this aspect of governance essential to avoid the risk of commitment challenges later in the transaction process, but you will also want to know which individuals have the authority to make decisions during the negotiation of the technology agreement and other stages in the transaction process. Unnecessary transaction delays often arise because the participants have embarked on the transaction with individuals who, despite their project-management activities, do not have any decision-making authority. You will want to avoid or at least

31

control the situation where the person leading the transaction for a participant constantly requires others to make or approve decisions throughout the transaction process.

Third-party obligations

1.5.2 Many commercial circumstances, documents and business arrangements can provide a person who will not be a party to the transaction the right to prevent, interfere with, delay or otherwise detrimentally affect the proposed transaction. Therefore, your due diligence enquiries should determine as much as possible whether there are any such rights lurking and waiting to pounce. Obviously, the mission is either to ensure that no such rights exist or to identify any such rights accurately, and to formulate both a transaction risk assessment of them or a strategy to deal with them in some way that will not detrimentally affect the proposed transaction.

Shareholder agreements

1.5.2.1 When individuals invest in a business, they frequently enter into shareholder agreements that restrict the ability of the business enterprise to operate in specified ways without shareholder reviews and approvals. The matters requiring shareholder approval may extend to the types of business that will be engaged in, the monetary value or materiality of transactions or other governance and management responsibilities that the shareholders do not wish to surrender by delegation to the board of directors. Therefore, it is important to enquire as to whether any such shareholder arrangements are in any way applicable to the proposed transaction.

Financial documents

1.5.2.2 There may be a broad range of conditions that apply to an investment in a business, regardless of whether or not the investment has taken the form of debt or equity, that could provide third parties with the right to approve the participant's engagement in the project. For example, the terms of investment agreement, a guarantee, a loan agreement, debenture or other financial instruments and related obligations may stipulate certain conditions regarding the conduct of the business enterprise, the scope of its operations, its governance and even transaction approval requirements.

Commercial arrangements

1.5.2.3   There are many types of commercial arrangements that may contain some form of restriction, limitation or operational requirements that may have a direct impact on the proposed transaction. Although such restrictions may take the form of approval requirements, a participant's ongoing commercial arrangements may also interfere or overlap with the commercial intentions of the proposed transaction. You should enquire whether or not participants are subject to: (i) any third-party restrictive covenants; (ii) whether the participant is required to seek the approval or consent of any other person to the transaction; (iii) whether the participant is required to tell anyone about the proposed transaction; (iv) whether any person has the right (as a matter of discretion) to require their consent or approval to the transaction; (v) any market or competitive restrictions; (vi) any limitations concerning their ability to exploit any particular product or service commercially; (vii) whether or not they are subject to any territorial restrictions or limitations; (viii) whether or not any other individuals have an option or right of first refusal in any connection with the subject matter of the proposed transaction; (ix) whether or not there are any time restrictions or limitations that may be imposed by third parties; and (x) whether or not any of the participants have commercial obligations that would conflict with or otherwise interfere with the proposed transaction.

Such enquiries should be backed up by a proactive plan to seek the necessary consents at an early stage so that the requirement for consent at a later stage does not become a hurdle barring the way to your deal. Assessment of the transferability of existing contract from the incumbent service provider to a new provider (in an outsourcing arrangement) will be key. Obtaining confirmation by letter from existing suppliers that they will continue to supply you or your new service provider in the event that your planned transaction goes ahead will prevent delays at a later stage if done early in the project.

Confidentiality obligations

1.5.2.4   One of the most frequent difficulties that arise in due diligence investigations, or in the early preparation for a technology transaction, concerns a participant's inability to disclose or share information because they are subject to confidentiality obligations. If you hit that particular hurdle in the process of your transaction, you should also appreciate that these obligations may arise not only as a matter of contract but also as a matter of equitable obligation or at common law due to the particular nature of the relationship between the participant and third party. Obligations of confidentiality may arise in several commercial situations, including trust arrangements and perhaps in the context of principal–agent relationships. There is extensive case law that stipulates the factual criteria upon which confidentiality obligations may arise in the course of commercial dealings. In any event, it is extremely important for you to canvass these issues in the course of your due diligence enquiries, and that you ensure that you do not participate in the wrongful disclosure of confidential information, whether by inducing a participant to breach their confidentiality obligations or otherwise. In order to avoid any liability in connection with such situations, you should gain as much knowledge as you can about these circumstances and do all you can to respect both the rights of such third parties and the related duties of participants.

Miscellaneous obligations

1.5.2.5 As you might expect, it is extremely difficult to structure due diligence investigations based upon all of the possible categories of obligations that may restrict, delay or otherwise interfere with the proposed transaction. However, there are so many potential statutory, common-law, equitable or contractual bases for such obligations that you should pursue a very broad and open enquiry concerning any obligations that may otherwise be difficult to specifically identify, consider and address in connection with the transaction.

Intellectual property rights

1.5.3

Identifying the intellectual property

1.5.3.1 As noted in **1.2**, an early step in the transaction process requires the identification of the knowledge assets and intellectual property that will be the subject of the proposed transaction. If you understand what the most valuable and commercially relevant knowledge assets to the transaction are, you are likely to be in a position to undertake relevant due diligence enquiries concerning chain of title, ownership or whether or not the use of those knowledge assets will interfere with any third party's rights and proprietary interests. The most relevant knowledge assets to a technology transaction will include: (i) trade marks; (ii) copyright interests in documents, manuals, charts, business plans, diagrams and computer programs; (iii) hardware patents; (iv) process (system or methodology) patents; and (v) "competitive advantage know-how", which has as many manifestations as it has inherent values to a business enterprise.

Three Key Issues

1.5.3.2 (a) *Chain of title or rights*—Track all contractual conveyances/licences from the source of creation to the point of the transaction; verify intellectual property chain of title/rights.
(b) *Potential infringement of third-party rights*—Intellectual property, equitable, contractual, moral, confidentiality, privacy or statutory.
(c) *No outstanding claims*—Demands, judgments, encumbrances, contractual restrictions, litigation, security interests.

Intellectual property creation and ownership

1.5.3.3 (a) *How was intellectual property developed and created?*—What was the process and methodology that created the knowledge asset? How was that process supervised, by whom, whose equipment, where, research notes? Periodic development reports, etc.? A great deal of information concerning the true ownership of knowledge assets can be ascertained by simply asking for details concerning how the knowledge assets were created, and how the creation was documented during the process of conception and invention.
(b) *Who developed and created it?*—Who participated in the creation of the knowledge asset and what did each person contribute? You will need to ascertain the identity of the individuals who participated in creating the knowledge assets, so that you can determine whether or not any collaborative efforts, joint ownership or multiple moral rights will exist in the work. Details concerning each participant's respective contribution, and the role that each person played in the creation of the knowledge assets, will help you to determine what waivers, consents or written assignments will be needed for your use of the knowledge asset for the transaction.
(c) *Identify the idea "spark"*—What was the point of conception? How did the idea arise? What was the trigger for the innovation/work? If there is any concern of infringement or breach of any person's confidentiality rights in connection with the creation of the knowledge assets, information concerning the creative "spark" of the knowledge asset can be very helpful in documenting the creation of the knowledge asset to its source.
(d) *How long did the research and development take?*—The length of time that it took the inventor to create the knowledge assets may be an indication of whether or not the inventor either acted alone or misappropriated time-saving information to assist in the creativity process. I have experienced numerous situations where both medium and large enterprises announced a radical technology breakthrough and which they were about to exploit commercially, only to be forced to reconsider its ownership of the knowledge assets when it came to light that the breakthrough was far in advance of what their competitors had been working on for many years. Quite often, such assessments may lead participants to discover that one of their team of creators had in fact been recruited from the team of a competitor who had been working on the

35

same technology innovation for a significant period of time. Therefore, any unreasonably fast breakthroughs in technology innovation may be indications of undisclosed circumstances.

(e) *Where did they create it?*—The location of knowledge-assets creation is very important for several reasons, including what law will govern the determination of who owns the knowledge assets, whose equipment or tools were used in the creation of the knowledge assets, whether any export restrictions will apply to the knowledge assets and whether or not any international tax issues may arise. The location where the knowledge assets were created may also pertain to the question of whether or not the knowledge assets were created in the ordinary course of the inventor's employment, which is discussed in para. (f) below.

(f) *Was it created in the ordinary course of "employment"?*—It is important to understand whether or not the person who created the knowledge asset was, in fact and in law, either an employee or an independent contractor. For example, with respect to the creation of knowledge assets that are governed by the Copyright, Designs and Patents Act 1988, subs. 11(1) of that Act states the general rule that "The author of a work is the first owner of the copyright in it". However, subs. 11(2) of that Act creates an employment exception by stating that, "where a . . . work . . . is made by an employee in the course of his employment, his employer is the first owner of any copyright in the work subject to any agreement to the contrary". Therefore, where such knowledge assets are not made by employees in the ordinary course of their employment, the employer will not own the knowledge asset which that individual has created. Many businesses expect that the knowledge assets created by their full-time staff or by specifically trained independent contractors—who are often regarded as employees—will be owned by the business. They are often extremely surprised to learn that they do not own the knowledge asset, and that the independent contractor exclusively owns all right, title and interest to the knowledge asset. Unless the knowledge asset has been assigned or transferred (in writing) to the business by the independent contractor, the independent contractor will retain all such ownership by virtue of being "the author" and the "first creator of the work". Obviously, the very common commercial practice of "employing" independent contractors may create significant knowledge-asset chain-of-title problems that you will want to investigate and address.

(g) *What resources were used to create the work?*—If, for example, the inventor created the intellectual property at home, during non-work hours, and with his or her own resources (as opposed to those of his employer), then those facts may support the argument that the intellectual property was not created in the course of employment and therefore that the work is owned by the inventor and not by the inventor's employer.

(h) *Did the creator work on the project prior to joining the company?*—For how long, and in what capacity/context, was it created? In this regard, you may wish to speak to the company's human-resource managers to determine the extent to which such competitive issues are identified and addressed when a prospective employee is recruited and hired.

(i) *Any previous work/research and development done by any other person?*—Obviously, you will want to ascertain what rights, title and interest such other individuals have conveyed and assigned to the participant in writing.

(j) *Is there any contributing technology, and the identity of its source/creator?*—Who assisted in creating the work? Were they employees or independent contractors? Are they available to interview or obtain transfer of title documents from?

(k) *Any company policies on employee ownership of knowledge assets?*—Since the ownership provisions of the Copyright, Designs and Patents Act can be contractually amended, you should have a detailed understanding of the terms, conditions and policies within the organisation concerning knowledge-asset creation, development and ownership. Often, such employment conditions and policies will also stipulate obligations of invention disclosure, documentation, joint-ownership arrangements and which party has the right to register and protect any associated statutory ownership rights.

(l) *Identify all previous owners*—Who are all individuals and business entities that have at any time owned all or any aspect of the intellectual property rights to the intellectual property? The following issues should be particularly examined: (i) employee/consultant creation; (ii) corporate successors, amalgamations or acquisitions; (iii) documentary chain of technology transfer; and (iv) insolvency of any member of that chain of title.

(m) *Review curriculum vitae of creator*—What is the inventor's previous research/academic/employment record? Verify employment records and independently contact competitors concerning creator's employment history; check references, and whether or not there is any history of knowledge-asset or confidentiality disputes. What contact has the inventor had with competitors? Do any of the inventor's relatives work there? Is he/she a shareholder/investor in a competitor?

(n) *Creator under contract of employment or independent contractor?*—You should obtain and undertake a detailed review of employment or independent contractor arrangements with respect to whether or not the knowledge asset has been transferred in writing, whether or not the arrangements include written waivers of moral rights, whether or not there are any representations and warranties of independent and original creation, whether or not any use restrictions are specified, whether or not there is a "further assurance" obligation,[9] and whether or not any reversionary or conditional proprietary interests have been maintained by the creator of the intellectual property.

(o) *Any government or private sponsorship or research funding?*—Was funding given directly to the inventor or via any commercial entity? Carefully review any research support, funding, grants, endowments or other contribution agreements, as they often contain knowledge-assets ownership or rights-restriction provisions. Check whether the knowledge assets have ever been associated with a public-sector transaction, and were the assets properly reserved and exempted from any relevant freedom-of-information access and disclosure?

(p) *Security interests?*—Conduct financing searches, bank security, creditor/judgment searches: all to ensure that technology is unencumbered and free of all claims and demands. Follow all standard commercial due diligence procedures.

---

[9] See **3.16.1**.

(q) *Who else knows about the knowledge asset/research?*—Was the knowledge asset created in an open/unsecured environment? Any security or access breaches? Any claims concerning misappropriation or confidentiality protection? Has it been disclosed publicly, through publishing government filings or otherwise?

(r) *Do any confidentiality agreements exist?*—Have any documents been executed by the inventor concerning trade secrets/proprietary rights? You should undertake a detailed review of any such confidentiality agreements to determine their scope, to ensure that they have been complied with and that the proposed transaction will not in any way contravene any duties, rights or restrictions set out in those arrangements.

(s) *What are the confidentiality policies, security procedures, access/use records where the knowledge assets were created?*—How well was the creation of the invention documented and recorded? Are the creation notes, files and records complete and reliable?

Ownership—registration searches

1.5.3.4 (a) *Literature survey*—It may be appropriate to undertake a general search/review of publicly available information, *e.g.* literature/publications such as industry marketing, academic, technology or news periodicals.

(b) *Jurisdictions*—In what jurisdictions should searches be conducted, *e.g.* Canada/US/Europe?

(c) *Are there any judgments/order of courts and administrative tribunals?*

(d) *Are there any pending litigation searches?*

(e) *Commercial security searches*—It may be appropriate to undertake investigations concerning any knowledge asset: personal property security; banking security; collateral registration; creditor interests; or encumbrances.

(f) *Patent and/or industrial design*—You may need written consent to access and inspect those files: name searches; copy of files and registration documents; assignments (include security documents); and registered users.

(g) *Trademark*—Issues concerning trade-mark due diligence will be particularly important where the proposed transaction will involve any brand association among participants (see **3.14**). In that regard, the following are perhaps the most important enquiries that you can make in connection with requisite trade-mark rights: (i) registered trade marks owned by the vendor and registered user entries against such trade marks; (ii) pending trade marks owned by the vendor and applications for registered users against such trade marks; (iii) the strength of important trade marks (registered or unregistered) can be examined by conducting searches in the Trade Mark Registry at the Patent Office for potentially confusing trade marks or trade names; (iv) unregistered trade marks used by the vendor, which may sometimes be found on branded products, in marketing materials, trade directories, telephone directories, letterhead and promotional literature obtained from the participant claiming ownership; (v) additional searches should be conducted in the jurisdictions where the technology transaction will be carried on; (vi) manual commercial searches for public use, *e.g.* business cards, office signs, listings in telephone directories, marketing materials, computer-assisted key-word search in publications/periodicals and trade shows; and (vii) identify all trade names, logos and marks that are used in association with the business, product, service, goodwill, *e.g.* marketing, packaging, labelling and advertising.

When considering the participant's use of, or reliance upon, a particular brand (especially in connection with the issues identified in **1.5.3.4**(g), above), you should ask the following questions: (i) What are the relevant logos and trade marks? (ii) Whose name is associated with the goodwill? (iii) Are any intellectual property rights referred to? (iv) Are the marks being properly used (letterhead, business cards, telephone directory, labels, advertisements, promotional/marketing materials, signs/ billboards, etc.)? (v) Are there any telephone listings with similar names/logos (especially Yellow Pages or other advertising features)? (vi) Do the trade/business names include the logo/trade marks? and (vii) Is there a distinctive vessel design, packaging or shape of wares ("distinguishing guise") associated with the product's goodwill or brand identification?

(h) *Copyright*—It may be appropriate to: (i) review all copyright notices and verify any name/date references; (ii) identify any history of prior infringement, claims, demands known to the participants; and (iii) consider whether there are any independent or internal files/records concerning the creation of the technology (hard copy of software, flow charts, operational specifications, formulae, research notes, memoranda, progress reports, etc.)?

Intellectual property commercial rights

1.5.3.5 One of the most fertile sources of transaction delay and disruption, if not failure, is related to whether or not any of the participants have previously engaged in commercial transactions that in some way limit or restrict their ability to provide the goods or perform the services that will be required in the transaction. Therefore, you should undertake a thorough review and examination of the commercial activities of each prospective participant and determine whether or not (or the extent to which) any of those commercial activities, or third-party commitments, may interfere with their participation in the transaction. The following is a brief delineation of some of the most important enquiries you should make concerning the possible circumstances:

(a) identify all commercial arrangements and documents that pertain to the knowledge assets, whether concerning the creation, the acquisition or granting of rights, or the commercial exploitation of the knowledge assets; consider whether or not the arrangements are oral or in writing;

(b) the arrangements may take the documentary form of: license, assignment, arrangements for commercial exploitation, moral rights waiver, option, right of first refusal, or conveyance; review documentation with a view to ascertaining impact or the chain of title;

(c) any prohibitions or limitations on the right to use; any restrictions on use; conveyance qualifications/"carve outs";

(d) ability to create, and ownership of, derivative works, additions, new versions or releases, enhancements, customisations, modifications, innovations, improvements; who owns those changes or derivative works? Are there any cross-licence/licence back rights?

(e) length of use term (renewal options/termination rights); renewal subject to conditions precedent;

(f) any preconditions to continued use—performance requirements: event milestones, financial targets/hurdles or acceptance testing;

(g) how have the intellectual property rights been carved up, whether exclusively or non-exclusively, to date (e.g. by vertical market, by stipulated use or purpose, by territory, by association with another product or service, or by any other aspect or quality of the intellectual property) and what are the applicable restrictions, limitations or prohibitions for intellectual property use in the proposed transaction?

(h) does intended or current use conform to granted rights and related restrictions? Do the proposed project, technology transaction and intended use contravene, breach, infringe or exceed the rights or the nature of the participant's proprietary interest that are required for the proposed transaction?

(i) any reversionary rights; are any use or ownership rights subject to fundamental conditions precedent which if not satisfied cause the use rights to change or terminate? Options to require "conveyance back"; are there any remedial provisions requiring re-assignment of the knowledge assets back?

(j) use restrictions—personal to assignee; time restrictions; site/location/jurisdiction; to run on a stipulated network or hardware; industry applications; personnel access restrictions; use limited to a defined purpose; limited to named users, etc.;

(k) assignment provisions/restrictions; any limit on ability to assign or convey knowledge asset interests or rights to others;

(l) change of control restrictions; or on the sale of all, or substantially all, of the assets of the knowledge-assets owner/licensee;

(m) have the knowledge assets been previously commercially exploited? Are the knowledge assets referred to in any transaction documents or contracts whatsoever?

(n) how have the knowledge assets been commercially exploited previously? Carefully examine all commercial arrangements and contracts, and evaluate the impact/implications of such arrangements on the proposed transaction.

Regulatory issues

1.5.4

Industry regulation

1.5.4.1 (a) *Government consent*—Is ministerial or other governmental review or approval required?
(b) *Administrative body review*—Is review, consent or authorisation required from any administrative body, tribunal or commission, *e.g.* the Financial Services Authority (FSA) for a significant outsource of a regulated company, the Department of Trade and Industry, Customs and Excise, the Inland Revenue, the Information Commissioner, Companies House or the London Stock Exchange?
(c) *Governmental licence*—Are there specific statutory regulations or requirements that require compliance or licensing, *e.g.* health-care industry, telecommunications, banking, insurance, transportation or charitable activities?
(d) *Capital market regulations*—Are there any requirements of financial markets regulations, such as securities commissions or stock exchanges?

Many regulatory agencies and industry regulations have a broad range of requirements that will directly affect the transaction. Some of the most common requirements and regulations that pertain to technology transactions include: the electronic records must be maintained; processing information or maintaining all records in the jurisdiction of the regulating entity or body; privacy protection standards; standards of consumer confidentiality; record retention and content requirements, including regulatory inspection and audit; and the extent to which regulated participants may allow non-regulated participants to provide any services or perform the operational functions of the regulated participants. With regard to the latter example, the Financial Services Authority Guidance (CP 142) states that outsourcing may have a significant impact on operational risk because it involves change and reduced control. It obliges regulated firms to notify the FSA when it undertakes a material outsourcing.

Capital market regulation

1.5.4.2 (a) *Equity markets*—Equity (or securities) markets are regulated for two essential reasons: (i) investor protection; and (ii) to promote the integrity and efficiency of capital markets.[10] One way in which equity markets are regulated to achieve those objectives is by requiring the public disclosure of certain information, *e.g.* in the prospectus upon the issuance of security, financial statements, proxy circulars, insider-trading reports and material-change reports. Therefore, you should

[10] Mark R. Gillen, *Securities Regulation in Canada* (Carswell, Toronto, 1992).

ensure that the proposed transaction will be fully reported at each stage at which it is required. Equity markets also ensure the integrity of capital markets by regulating what information and records must be maintained.[11]

(b) *All other information management and record-keeping regulations*[12]—There are a broad range of regulatory requirements for information management and record maintenance that are likely to impact on most technology transactions. These include the information and record-maintenance requirements of most equity market regulations (discussed above), as well as: (i) employment and work-place records; (ii) income-tax records; (iii) sales-tax records; (iv) evidence-admissibility criteria; (v) insolvency records; (vi) customs records; (vii) information-privacy and personal-information records; (viii) health-care records; and (ix) the maintenance of financial records.

(c) *Competition regulation*—The purpose of competition (anti-trust) laws and regulations is to promote market conditions that are generally favourable to competition. Therefore, you will want to ensure that no aspect of the proposed transaction will be anti-competitive or otherwise offend the provisions of the Competition Act.[13] Aspects of the proposed transaction that may come within the purview of competition law and regulation include: (i) agreements in restraint of trade; (ii) bid-rigging; (iii) commercial pricing practices (*e.g.* price discrimination, predatory pricing or price maintenance); (iv) misleading or deceptive advertising; (v) refusal to deal or supply; (vi) market restrictions; (vii) abuse of a dominant position in the market; (viii) specialisation agreements; (ix) the formation of buying groups (as in B2B Exchanges); and (x) mergers and market concentration.

Commercial regulation

1.5.4.3 There is a broad range of commercial regulations that may affect the proposed transaction that are not specific to any particular industry segment or market activity. However, each of those areas of commercial regulation may have a direct impact on a technology transaction. The following are certain areas of commercial regulation that frequently arise in the context of technology transactions. Industry-specific data-protection laws may also apply to the proposed transaction. For example, there is an extensive network of data-protection legislation that introduces an additional level of regulation for medical data. Therefore, any technology trans-

---

[11] See Victor P. Alboini, *Securities Law and Practice, Part 7*, entitled, "Record-Keeping and Compliance Reviews" (Carswell, Toronto, 2002, Rel.1).

[12] See, *e.g.* Graham J. Smith, *"Keeping and Proving Electronic Records"*, SCL Computer Law Course, October 15, 1997; Kirsten Birkett, "Andersen: Reviewing Document Management" *PLC Magazine*, July 2002; Jonathan Kelly "Document Retention and Disposal: Reviewing Company Policy", *PLC Magazine*, May 2000.

[13] See the Competition Act 1998 and Art.81 and Art.82 of the EC Treaty. (For Canada, see R.S.C. 1985, c.C-34, as amended. See D.S. Affleck and K.W. McCracken, *Canadian Competition Law* (Carswell, Toronto), ed. 2002.)

actions pertaining to the health-care industry may indeed have significant data-protection implications.

(a) *Data-protection laws*—There are laws that exist to protect the privacy of an individual's personal information. Many technology transactions, including e-business projects, will involve the collection, management and commercial use of personal information for marketing and customer-management purposes. You should consider whether or not, or the extent to which, the proposed transaction will involve any data or information that is regulated by the Data Protection Act (*i.e.* protection of personal information). A series of books has recently been published on this topic and it is impossible to address all the fundamental privacy issues that you must consider in the course of your due diligence investigations. However, for the purposes of this book, it is important that you appreciate the enquiries necessary concerning whether or not your use of any data or information that will be required for, or that will be the subject-matter of, the proposed transaction, fully complies with all laws and regulations concerning the protection of personal information.[14]

(b) *Export-control restrictions*—It often surprises business managers to learn that a proposed technology transaction may be subject to domestic and international laws concerning the proliferation of advanced military weapons technology. However, there are many aspects of technology transactions that are indeed governed by such international laws and regulations, and you should ensure that they have all been complied with as the transaction proceeds. Such laws and regulations exist as a matter of national defence and their contravention may carry serious criminal sanctions. Therefore, if your technology transaction will involve the export of any sophisticated technology from the United Kingdom, such as advanced computing technology or software encryption, you should ascertain whether or not such exportation is regulated as an important part of your due diligence enquiries.[15]

(c) *Consumer protection*—There is a broad range of consumer protection laws and regulations that may have implications for certain types of technology transaction. For example, the Consumer Protection (Distance Selling) Regulations 2000 and the Electronic Commerce (EC Directive) Regulations 2002 have implications for the terms of online contracts. The Office of Fair Trading (OFT) provides guidance (in Reports and regular Bulletins) on certain standard terms in consumer contracts which it considers to be potentially unfair under the Unfair Terms in

---

[14] See the Data Protection Act 1998 and *www.informationcommissioner.gov.uk*. For a comprehensive listing of all such legislative and regulatory requirements in Canada, visit *www.privcom.gc.ca/legislation/index_ e.asp*. Note that federal privacy laws are comprised of two statutes, the Privacy Act (effective July 1, 1983) and the Personal Information Protection and Electronic Documents Act (effective January 1, 2001). Provincial privacy laws, together with health information protection laws, may also have a direct impact on a transaction in Canada.

[15] The Export Control Act 2002, coming into force on May 1, 2004, sets out a new legislative framework for the control of strategic goods and technology (see **3.7.9**).

Consumer Contracts Regulations 1999. Therefore, if the proposed project will involve the sale of products or services directly to consumers, then you should ensure that all aspects of the transaction are vetted by legal counsel who is experienced in consumer protection, product standards and consumer-dispute resolution laws and regulations.[16]

(d) *Criminal law*—Although a technology transaction's possible contravention of criminal law may appear to be somewhat remote, issues of potential criminal conduct arise fairly frequently. In addition to the possible criminal offence of exporting technology that requires an export permit (under the Export Controls Act 2002), there are several elements of criminal law that you will want to be aware of, such as: (i) the gaming and gambling provisions that may pertain to many emerging e-business projects[17]; and (ii) the invasion of privacy and interception of communication provisions.[18]

(e) *Money laundering*—The Money Laundering Regulations 2003 (effective March 1, 2004) are designed to prevent or restrict, as far as possible, the use of the proceeds of criminal activities into the United Kingdom's financial system. Therefore, if the proposed transaction will involve the cross-border transfer of funds, or any other cross-border financial activities, you should ensure that: (i) none of the international participants is engaged in any activity associated with money laundering; (ii) that you know the proposed participants very well and that you have complied with all client-identification requirements; and (iii) that your financial-activities records are secure, reliable, complete, accurate and current, and otherwise comply with the requirements of those Regulations.

(f) *Document management*—There are numerous statutory and regulatory requirements to process data, maintain records and protect electronically stored information that will directly affect the technology transaction. Your record-keeping investigations should include the following issues: (i) have they created, stored and reproduced their records in a reliable manner and in compliance with all common-law and statutory requirements concerning the admissibility of those records as evidence?[19] (ii) the record maintenance requirements of tax and customs laws[20]; (iii) the compliance of all records with GAAP control guidelines[21]; (iv) do the record maintenance security measures satisfy the requirements of the Data Protection Act 1998?[22] (v) are the

---

[16] Also see J.S. Ziegel and A.J. Duggen, *Commercial and Consumer Sales Transactions* (Emond Montgomery Pub., Toronto, 2002); Young and Fraser, *Canadian Advertising of Marketing Law* (ed. Release 4, Carswell, Toronto, 2001).

[17] See the Lotteries and Amusements Act 1976 and the Draft Gambling Bill (February 2004 consolidation).

[18] See the Regulation of Investigatory Powers Act 2000.

[19] See Art. 9 of the UNCITRAL Model Law on Electronic Commerce 1996 and s.5 of the Civil Evidence Act 1968. See **3.10.1.4** and Alan Gahtan, *Electronic Evidence* (Carswell, Toronto, 1999).

[20] See, *e.g.* the Tax Act 1988, Sch. 18, para. 21 (see **1.5.5.6**; ibid.)

[21] See **3.10.1.5**; above, n.19.

[22] See **1.5.4.3**(a); above, n.19.

electronic records maintained in accordance with the applicable electronic-transactions statutory requirements?[23] and (vi) do the records of the participant comply with all applicable industry requirements, including the record-retention, protection and maintenance requirements of data-protection legislation relating to medical records, securities and public-company regulations, financial-institution regulations, export-control legislation and anti-money-laundering legislation? If any of the foregoing requirements have not been complied with, then you should understand the nature and extent of those deficiencies. The success of technology transactions, and the entire project, may be at great risk if these requirements have not been complied with, *e.g.* if the accounting and tax records are deficient, if the participants cannot defend themselves in litigation due to unreliable and inadmissible records, if a regulatory authority takes action to delay or prevent the project due to an inability to audit and review the transaction, or any other liability is assumed by the participants for such failings and legal contravention.

Trade associations

1.5.4.4   The regulation of your industry, or of the proposed transaction, may not also be subject to the rules and policies of trade organisations and associations that stipulate membership obligations. For example, the Office of Government Commerce issues best-practice guidance for conducting a procurement and suggests contracting terms. Similarly, the Society of IT Managers promulgates advice and best practice in many areas relevant to the IT industry, including e-government, system security and key performance indicators (KPIs). Although such requirements, policies or membership obligations may not carry the same repercussions as a failure to comply with the nation's laws and regulations, there are important business, brand-management and legal issues associated with complying with relevant industry association guidelines and policies. Perhaps the best example of non-governmental transaction requirements that may have direct legal and liability implications occurs when a trade or professional organisation publishes standards, procedures or guidelines that a court may interpret as describing reasonable industry standards concerning such matters.[23a] For example the Law Society of England and Wales provides regulations for professional conduct which include the retention and maintenance of electronic records.

Technology standards and performance

1.5.5   You will probably not engage in a particular technology transaction solely because your competitors have engaged in similar transactions. However, organisa-

---

[23] See **3.10.1.4**, and see Lisa K. Abe, *Internet and E-Commerce Agreements Drafting and Negotiating Tips* (Butterworths Canada Ltd., 2001).

[23a] See *www.lawsociety.org.uk/professional/ conduct/guideonline.*

tions often consider what technology their competitors are relying upon, without blindly following them towards that particular technology solution. However, there are also some technology managers who, perhaps too blindly, rely upon the reputation and "brand persuasion" of multinational technology providers. As an important matter of risk management, it is extremely important to do more than take a superficial look at the participant contributions that you otherwise trust, regardless of any participant's reputation or brand credibility.

Operational/technical specifications

1.5.5.1 Will the technology adhere to and comply with specifically stipulated operational, functional and technical specifications? Have those specifications been published, or are they otherwise available for your review and scrutiny? Do those specifications provide you with adequate detail to avoid future misunderstandings? Are there any independent studies or performance-evaluation reports concerning the ability of the technology to perform in accordance with those specifications (*e.g.* a university technology evaluation lab)? Are the published specifications complete, and are they current? Do the specifications address all your operational and functional requirements, and have any uncertainties or ambiguities in that regard been addressed by your other due diligence investigations?

New or proven technology

1.5.5.2 New or innovative technology that has not been widely commercialised or proven over time will carry different risk-management considerations than technology that is, or that has been for some time, widely used and relied upon. There will always be risks associated with early adoption of technology, and your due diligence investigations and project-management strategies must address those risks on an ongoing basis; you will want to be "leading edge" but not "bleeding edge". However, it is important for you to thoroughly understand the extent to which the proposed technology has not been commercially implemented, or the limited environments or applications in which the technology has been deployed.

Performance record

1.5.5.3 Where the technology has been widely adopted for industry use, and has been commercialised for some time, you should secure information concerning its performance record, the extent to which it has had to have been "debugged", or required any other operational fixes, revisions or experienced implementation difficulties. Of course, this issue is closely related to the references you may seek when selecting transaction participants, but you may also wish to contact other users of the technology to discuss any difficulties that they have had.

Business environment demonstrations

1.5.5.4 Very frequently, technology demonstrations occur at the technology provider's place of business, and in an environment that may not reflect the commercial circumstances and operational environment of the project. Therefore, you should have the proposed technology demonstrated to you in an active operational environment where the technological and business circumstances will be reasonably comparable to the proposed project. Such demonstrations may occur in an existing "install base", or perhaps there is a way to demonstrate the technology in your current environment on a trial or observation basis.

Standards compliance

1.5.5.5 To what extent does the technology comply with standards that are stipulated by independent trade or technology associations or service bureaus? In that regard, how is the technology rated and compared to other technologies in the field, and are there any particular standard compliance certifications that have been issued concerning the technology? It may also be fruitful for you to contact the responsible organisations concerning the technology's standard certification. Notwithstanding any such certification, additional reports and evaluations may exist that indicate the extent to which the technology complies with a particular standards criteria or specific level of required functionality.

Tax/customs[24]

1.5.5.6 Does the technology comply with taxation and customs requirements for the maintenance of electronic records and data processing? The maintenance of commercial records for tax purposes in the United Kingdom is governed by a variety of statutes. The VAT Regulations 1996 (SI 1995/2518) oblige organisations to keep business and accounting records and all tax invoices issues together with documents relating to imports and exports for six years. The Inland Revenue Code of Practice (no. 3) states that organisations should keep records of wages, tax credits or payments to employees and sub-contractors together with records relating to expenses payments for three tax years from the current tax year. The Tax Act 1988

---

[24] Consider also whether computer software, especially financial applications, developed and designed outside the UK will comply with GAAP, tax and customs requirements for data processing and electronic records.

(Sch. 18, para. 21) states that organisations must keep records to substantiate the figures in a tax return for at least six years from the end of the relevant accounting period.

Electronic records and evidential weight

1.5.5.7 The UK Government's "modernising agenda" has meant a gradual move towards the ability to interact with government in all relevant ways, electronically. This includes the submission of tax returns for example. However, the digitising of data brings with it the ability to tamper with that data. This means that there is a greater risk that the data stored may not accurately reflect the data entered. In an increasingly paperless society, evidence to support a contention that tax has been paid correctly, or to make a claim will be in digital form. The Civil Evidence Act 1995, which came into force on January 31, 1997, removed the old rule against hearsay evidence in civil cases. The implications of that change in IT transactions and cases where evidence is digital is that the rules are now greatly relaxed and it is now far easier to bring digital data before the courts. The fact remains however, that for that evidence to be weighty, one must be able to show that the relevant storage regulations have been complied with and can be shown to have been complied with. As such, therefore, evidence to show that the systems have been working correctly at all relevant times and to show who has, and has not been allowed access to the digital records in question will be vital.

Participant references

1.5.6 Participant references are invaluable. My preference is to avoid problems wherever possible, rather than having to face managing those risks or suffering through disputes that drain significant resources. Although it is not always possible to avoid transaction risks entirely, one of the most important due diligence tasks that you can undertake is to gain as much information about the participants as you possibly can: their business reputation, their management culture, the extent to which others want to work with them and trust them, their business successes and failures, their financial and commercial health, any history of commercial disputes or litigation, and their relevant experience. One of the most efficient ways to achieve this perspective is by pursuing participant references. Assuming that the subject participant waives any associated confidentiality restrictions, references can provide essential information concerning possible problems and risks that may arise, as well as proposing strategies to deal with these problems.

Supplier references

1.5.6.1 If the participant's relationship with its suppliers is important to the transaction, then there is probably a wealth of information to gain from supplier references. In addition to information concerning the timely payment of their accounts, you may also make enquiries concerning the participant's attitude towards dispute resolution and relationship management. If the proposed transaction will in any way depend upon a particular supplier for a required good or service, then your due diligence enquiries may also extend to the "health and well-being" of the supplier and the continued involvement of the supplier, through the participant, in the project.

Financial references

1.5.6.2 One of the most important references that you secure will be from financial institutions that deal with the subject participant. Not only do these institutions possess direct and comprehensive information concerning the participant's financial circumstances, but, also, the references are often produced by well respected and sophisticated institutions. It is important for you to enquire about the precise nature of the participant's relationship with its financial institution, how the financial institution gathers its information, and whether or not the financial institution has undertaken any recent and independent enquiries concerning that information (as opposed to merely relying upon the self-reporting of the participant). Information that might particularly interest you may include: (i) the participant's credit rating, revolving line of credit uses and repayment cycles; (ii) does the participant seek advice from the financial institution? (iii) the quality of the information that the participant discloses to the financial institution and how regularly; and (iv) at what level of management seniority is the participant known within the financial institution.

Customer references

1.5.6.3 Although the participant's other customers may be your competitors, it may be important for you to understand fully the nature and quality of the participant's relationships with its other customers. Depending upon whether or not the participant's customers have engaged in transactions that are similar to the project, those customers could provide a wealth of information that could save you due diligence time and trouble, provide you with important negotiation insight and strategies, and provide you with advanced insight concerning the participant's commercial interests and negotiating positions. You should also enquire about the cultural aspects of such customer relationships, and the general attitude and sense of co-operation that the participant generally brings to commercial transactions.

There are many occasions where proposed participants appear to be outstanding on paper, but may be very difficult to work with on a day-to-day basis. Although a proposed participant may have all the right credentials, including the perfect product or service specifications, you should also consider their candidacy in terms of your ability to live with them on a day-to-day basis.

Strategic alliance references

1.5.6.4 Unlike participant–customer relationships that may be biased due to their inherent master–servant quality, it may be extremely helpful to seek references from the proposed participant's strategic alliance partners. Since those enterprises work with the proposed participant on a commercial, and perhaps more equal, footing, they may be in a good position to provide valuable insights into whether or not the proposed participant works well with others. The range of the participant's commercial relationships that you should consider for the purpose of such references include: (i) strategic alliances; (ii) principals or agents; (iii) marketing representatives; (iv) joint-venture partners or co-investors; (v) distribution channels; (vi) any persons that have either co-bid with the proposed participant on a procurement transaction, including any prime contractor or subcontractor relationships; and (vii) joint developers of technology (pursuant to collaboration or research and development arrangements).

Competitive references

1.5.6.5 (a) *Market competitors*—Although you will have to take into account the competitive context in which such references may be provided, you may wish to discuss the proposed participant with their competitors. Because competitors tend to keep close tabs on each other, competitors can be an excellent source of strategic information that may pertain directly to the participant's suitability for the proposed transaction. Obviously, your interest in such references will be limited to facts that are disclosed in good faith without any intention to harm or injure the reputation of the proposed participant. In that regard, you should ensure that you do not participate (whether through subsequent correspondence, record maintenance or otherwise) in any activities that may be defamatory. You can only benefit from factually accurate and complete information concerning the proposed participant.

(b) *Public sector*—You should consider whether or not there are any government agencies or public-sector departments that have any information concerning the proposed participant, and whether or not any of that information is relevant to the project. Such information can often be acquired very informally from government sources. Many branches of government may have developed very clear views of certain enterprises or organisations over many years of commercial dealings with them. To the extent that their views can be shared with you, the public sector may provide you with an important source of perspective and judgment when selecting a participant for the proposed transaction. Another way to secure information about the proposed participant's public-sector activities is through "access request" pursuant to the Freedom of Information Act 2000. The lion's share of this Act will apply from January 1, 2005.[25] However, those statutes also stipulate the range of information concerning participants and their public-sector transactions that the governing public authority can refuse to disclose, including information which is protected by legal privilege or which achieves the relevant threshold of commerciality.[25a]

Dispute history

1.5.7 An important selection criterion concerns the ability of the proposed participant to work well with others. That information may relate to the participant as either the defendant or plaintiff to disputes, and may include: (i) complaints, claims, demands, proceedings, disputes, litigation; court searches; trade services or associations; (ii) consumer-protection agencies; (iii) judgment searches; (iv) opinions from participant's counsel or auditors; (v) alternative dispute resolution (ADR) activities, including arbitration or mediation; and (vi) labour disputes, next renewal date for collective agreements.

Labour disputes

1.5.7.1 Labour and employment disputes are particularly important for technology transactions. Since the project's most important assets are its managers and highly specialised knowledge workers, it is extremely important to know whether the participants are engaged in any labour or employment disputes. A participant's ability to manage its employees on an ongoing basis will be information that is relevant to your due diligence enquiries. Such labour or employment disputes may be related to: (i) any collective agreements that may exist; (ii) the quality of the participant's relationship with any unions who represent employees; (iii) a history of any strikes, lockouts, work stoppages, or dispute-related delays or protests; (iv) wrongful-dismissal claims; and (v) any claims or actions that the proposed participant may have taken against its workers, whether concerning a breach of employees' duties, termination for cause, breach of confidentiality, or otherwise. The following information concerning the participant's human-resource affairs may also be helpful: (i) human-rights complaints, proceedings or tribunal judgments; (ii) policies concerning sexual harassment and related administrative processes; (iii) history of sexual-

[25] See the Freedom of Information Act 2000 (Commencement No.4) Order 2004. Though, as at November 1, 2004, the Commencement Order bringing the right to make an access request has not been published.
[25a] See s.42 and s.43 of the Freedom of Information Act 2000 respectively. It should be noted, however, that both of these exemptions are qualified by a public interest test.

harassment claims or legal action; (iv) work-environment or work-place safety complaints; (v) workers' compensation claims and insurance matters; and (vi) information concerning the criminal conduct of employees, such as employee fidelity, corporate espionage, technology sabotage or financial crimes.

Commercial alternative dispute resolution

1.5.7.2 You should secure information concerning how the proposed participant has carried on business with all of its suppliers, customers and strategic allies. Because the nature of such relationships are generally private, you should enquire as to whether or not the proposed participant has engaged in any ADR activities concerning its commercial dealings or transactions. For example, a proposed participant may have engaged in mediation, conciliation or arbitration activities, all of which are usually confidential activities that occur outside of the public forum of courts or tribunals. Therefore, detailed information concerning such disputes and the history of such dispute-resolution activities may provide you with information that is directly relevant to the proposed transaction.

Claims and demands

1.5.7.3 Until a commercial dispute has matured to the level of an exchange of pleadings in the courts, the matter will remain private. If a proposed participant is currently engaged in disputed claims or demands which have not matured to a level of public domain, you should determine the nature and extent of those disputes and whether or not they will pertain to or affect the proposed transaction. Depending upon the professional assessment of any such claims and demands, those disputes may constitute a contingent liability of the subject participant. You should remember that at such an early stage of a potential dispute's evolution, there are always two sides to every story, and you should obtain as complete an understanding as possible of the facts and circumstances surrounding that dispute and its related allegations before you make any judgments concerning how any such disputes or allegations may affect the proposed participant's role in the transaction.

Litigation

1.5.7.4 In addition to simply asking the proposed participant to disclose any court proceedings, actions or litigation in which it has been involved, whether as a party to such litigation or otherwise, you may also wish to search the court records in the relevant jurisdiction(s) in which the proposed participant carries on business. These enquiries and record searches can be carried on in each level of court, as well as with respect to any dispute investigation or resolution tribunal, such as the Human Rights Commission or a Securities Commission.

Judgments and orders

1.5.7.5 Generally, judgments and orders of the courts are public records. You can search the records of each level of court in your jurisdiction to determine whether or not the proposed participant has any judgments or orders issued against it. Those searches may include: orders and judgments; process writs and garnishments; trial dates; and all related process filings.

Chapter 2

The Preliminary Steps of Engagement

2.0 Checklist II: Beginning the transaction

2.1 Collecting the promises
- [ ] Sales materials
- [ ] Meetings and presentations
- [ ] RFP and RFI responses
- [ ] Commercial intelligence

2.2 Relationship management
- [ ] Relationship strategies
  - ○ Teaming
  - ○ Seminars
  - ○ Relationship investment
- [ ] Cross-culture awareness
- [ ] Good cop–bad cop

2.3 Negotiation conditions
- [ ] Standstill arrangements
- [ ] Exclusivity
- [ ] Restrictive covenants
- [ ] Non-solicitation of employees
- [ ] Remedies
- [ ] Dispute resolution
- [ ] Good faith
- [ ] Miscellaneous provisions
  - ○ Accuracy of information
  - ○ Return of information
  - ○ Press releases
  - ○ Confidential information

2.4 Confidentiality protection
- [ ] Definition of confidential information
- [ ] Information-quality warranty or disclaimer

- [ ] Non-disclosure standard of care
- [ ] Protection of confidential information
- [ ] Exceptions to confidentiality obligations
  - ○ Permitted disclosure
  - ○ Disclosure compelled by law
- [ ] Duration of protection
- [ ] Rights of controlled disclosure

2.5 Remedial considerations
- [ ] Duty to disclose breach
- [ ] Co-operation
- [ ] Rights to injunction
- [ ] Return or destruction of information
- [ ] Venue and choice of law
- [ ] Third-party guarantees
- [ ] No reliance

2.6 The step approach to engagement
- [ ] Participant proposal
- [ ] Performance statement
- [ ] Letter of Intent
- [ ] Memorandum of Understanding
- [ ] Drafting the contract
  - ○ Standard-form agreement
  - ○ Drafting control
  - ○ Revision process

2.7 Decision-making authority
- [ ] Business decision process

- ☐ Who will participate?
- ☐ Participation by professional advisors

2.8 Meetings and communications process
- ☐ In person
- ☐ By video conference
- ☐ By telephone
- ☐ Meeting location
- ☐ Discursive process

2.9 Public-sector participants
- ☐ Commercial v public interest
- ☐ Regulatory and political context
- ☐ Joint transaction structures
- ☐ Pro forma contracts
- ☐ Balance rewards and risks
- ☐ Public-sector procurement routemap

At this stage, all of your planning, organisation and preparation are completed and you are now ready to begin the process of structuring, commercially formulating, negotiating and contractually documenting the proposed technology transaction. To the extent that your preparation activities have been relevant and suited to the transaction, you have:

1. assembled the right team of personnel experience, expertise and management authority;

2. finalised the transaction's business case, and you may have created a project plan that describes how you will achieve the business case;

3. all the information you require concerning the project's participants;

4. fully defined and described what your requirements and expectations are for the performance obligations of all the transaction's participants, including the technology's or service's operational, functional and technical specifications; and

5. you have completed your due diligence enquiries and investigations into the most important and fundamental issues of the proposed transaction, including the unrestricted ability of the participants to perform their obligations, any possible regulatory requirements or constraints that may exist, and any other commercial or legal issues concerning the rights and abilities of the other participants to engage in the proposed transaction.

After those fundamental planning considerations have been addressed, there is a necessary intermediary stage in the transaction process before the participants become fully engaged. Between the completion of the transaction's planning phase and the commencement of thorough and detailed transaction negotiations lies an intermediary phase of engagement that the participants should recognise and use. That phase of the transaction is, in many ways, as commercially sensitive as it is important to the smooth flow of the project because it contributes so greatly to the foundation of the ongoing relationship among the transaction's participants. That intermediary step presents an outstanding opportunity to create a transactional environment that is conducive to the expedited resolution of transactional issues, commercial trust and alignment towards achieving the transactional objective. That phase of a technology transaction may be regarded as the cornerstone for all other subsequent phases in the transaction's evolution. The success of that intermediary will depend upon the success of your transaction planning.

How you begin the process of the transaction can, if managed correctly, minimise the complications that may arise in the event that transaction negotiations between the participants break down. Addressing those issues will also allow the participants to extricate themselves efficiently from the negotiating process if it becomes apparent that there will not be a meeting of minds concerning the proposed transaction. Phasing in the project through the following intermediary steps will assist the participants in preserving as many alternative options as possible while moving the proposed project ahead—whether by restructuring the proposed transaction, seeking other or additional participants, or even by allowing the participants to reassess the assumptions and requirements of the business case.

One of the most serious, and perhaps ironic, mistakes that a project manager can make at this stage of the transaction process is failing to regard the following resolution of the issues as a pre-condition to the otherwise free commercial engagement among the participants. That mistake is too often made because of the incorrect assumption that skipping those issues will save time and expedite the transaction. In fact, the opposite is true. Serious commercial and project difficulties and delays often arise in the early phases of the transaction directly because participants have ignored the following intermediary issues, and fully engaged the other participants without getting the proposed commercial relationship on the right footing. A headstrong approach that does not respect preparatory "rules of engagement" at the outset of the transaction often precipitates the very delays that the participants thought they were avoiding. It has been my experience that the measured and proportional implementation of the issues discussed in this chapter may actually expedite the transaction and improve the chances of avoiding (or mitigating) unwanted delays in the subsequent negotiation and contractual documentation phases of the transaction. That is not to say that any of the issues identified below will always require an inordinate amount of time or resources to undertake and complete. Many of those activities may be undertaken at the same time, and expeditiously. Once again, the key here is balance, and exercising reasonable judgment concerning what preliminary steps are necessary or prudent to begin the next phase of the transaction process. That judgment will lead to different results in every technology transaction.

Collecting the promises

2.1 One of the most important and yet frequently overlooked strategies at the beginning of any technology transaction involves the collection, organisation and perhaps documentation of all of the promises, commitments, guarantees and general representations ("promises") that the other participants have made in the course of your dealings with them. As those promises are made through the various preliminary steps in the transaction process, those promises may easily be pushed down to a subliminal level of understanding among the participants, and very often excluded from formal description and articulation, both during the transaction negotiations and in the contractual documentation. Although the performance commitments of any transaction may easily be regarded as the most fundamental aspect of the entire project, when the participants come to articulate those commitments in a formal way, much of the sales pitches, the presentations, meeting discussions and marketing and promotional materials may not, in part or in whole, be included in the participants' performance obligations. Therefore, you should ensure that you keep track of all of the promises that you have relied upon, and that they are properly documented and not forgotten in the course of formally documenting the transaction.

Sales materials

2.1.1 It is very common for participants in a transaction to generally describe their services, capabilities, products and core competencies in a wide range of marketing and promotional materials that are distributed in the course of preparatory discussions. Such sales materials may take many forms, including published reports, booklets, brochures, technology specifications, operational and functional descriptions, website content and technical manuals. You should ensure that copies of all sales materials that have been provided to you and all materials that the participants have published (whether on their website or otherwise) are collected for the purpose of making sure that all of the promises that are contained in those materials, and upon which you will rely for the purpose of your transaction decisions, will be contractually enshrined. Remember, of course, that you should also ensure that your requirements are transposed into the final contract. This will help the contract to portray a full picture of both what it is that you want your supplier to provide, and how the supplier intends to provide its solution. One final point, remember to deal with the supremacy of the two elements of the contract, *i.e.* in the event of a dispute at some later stage, which part should take precedence—what you asked for, or how the supplier promised to provide? When acting for the customer/buyer in an IT transaction, the normal position is to ensure (by express wording to this effect) that the "what" takes precedence over the "how" in the event of a dispute. If, on the other hand, you are the supplier to the transaction, and there seems no way to overcome this hierarchical position, you will need to ensure that your solution meets every aspect of your client's requirements, on a line-by-line basis.

Those marketing and promotional materials may take three common forms. The first includes all published and publicly available information concerning how the participant has described, represented or otherwise "held out" its goods or services. The second involves a participant's standard documentation that, although not published per se, is often provided to prospective customers or transaction participants where the circumstances warrant. Those materials may be in hardcopy "tangible" form, or they may have been in electronic form, whether by CD-ROM, on the participant's website or otherwise. Thirdly, some sales materials may have been specifically created for you, based upon your unique technology and commercial circumstances, and provided to you in the form of a report, recommendations, needs analysis, strategic options proposal, technology plan or other promotional document that may have been tailor-made for you for the purpose of the particular transaction.

Meetings and presentations

2.1.2 The promises that have been made to you in writing are extremely important, and they can be reproduced as a clear record of those promises. Another fertile ground for participants to create performance expectations without ever formalising those promises into transaction obligations is in the course of live meetings and presentations. Perhaps the most common reason for that occurrence concerns the very natural motivation that a prospective participant has to impress someone else with their products or abilities. The problem, of course, arises where those promises, which are made in the course of those meetings, do not reflect what the participant is actually capable of performing, and thus create a false expectation on the part of others that may wrongly induce them to proceed with the transaction. You should determine which of those promises and commitments are, in fact, important to you in connection with the transaction, and remember that such representations are often made quite innocently, and perhaps without adequate reflection and consideration by the party advancing them. In my experience, it is very rare for one participant to a transaction intentionally to mislead or fraudulently entice another participant into a transaction with promises and commitments which it knows it cannot satisfy. The vast majority of misleading circumstances can, and should, be classified in the much more innocent category of unintentional misunderstandings, miscommunications and failures to understand the implications that such representations may have in promoting the proposed transaction. It is for that reason that all participants to the transaction are well advised to keep track of all promises that are made in the course of such meetings and presentations, and to ensure that the expectations and requirements of all participants can, indeed, be satisfied as they have been represented. The more completely and accurately that all such representations are documented, the easier it will be for the participants to identify any misunderstandings, mistakes and miscommunications that may have arisen, very early in the transaction process.

The strategies for documenting the discussions between participants during meetings and presentations varies widely. For example, you may wish to: (i) have an independent third party take minutes of those meetings; (ii) have each participant assign a person to attend those meetings and presentations for the sole purpose of making notes; (iii) require each person participating in those meetings to create and keep written notes; (iv) keep a copy of all materials, slides and documents that were provided to you in those meetings and presentations; and, (v) record those meetings either in audio or audio–visual format. If the latter option is chosen, you may wish to advise the other participants of your intention to record the meeting and you should provide them with a copy of those recorded materials so that they will have a reasonable and fair opportunity to review those materials and to correct any falsely created expectations, incorrect information, misunderstandings or mistakes that may have been advanced in the course of those meetings or presentations. Some jurisdictions may require the prior consent of the individuals whom you propose to record.

Not only may those materials and information be very helpful in the course of negotiating and contractually documenting the transaction, but they may also help the participants to avoid misunderstandings and subsequent disputes concerning their respective performance obligations. In the event that such a dispute arises, those materials may also prove to be valuable evidence, in certain circumstances, where the intention of the participants concerning those matters is subsequently challenged.

RFP and RFI responses

2.1.3 A common strategy in both preparing for a technology transaction or in beginning the process of defining what the commercial arrangements will be among transaction participants, is to engage in a bid-response process where you have issued an RFP or an RFI (see also **1.4.2.1**). Typically, an RFP will set out the general parameters for the proposed technology transaction, thus inviting bidders either to provide you with the information you require to further the planning process or to advance a commercial proposal for your consideration. As you might expect, the resulting proposals will inherently contain a wide range of "promises" and offerings that will have a pronounced marketing flavour to them. Obviously, no provider of technology goods or services wants to exaggerate their capabilities or to mislead a potential customer concerning the nature or quality of their proposed goods or service. However, such proposals may contain ambiguities, or describe their proposed obligations in vague terms that require clarification. You should ensure that such proposals do not create any unintended expectations. Subject to those very reasonable concerns, you should carefully document all of the proposal's performance promises, and ensure that you do not lose track of those proposed obligations in the course of the transaction process. An alternative method for capturing all of the information provided by the bidder is to make it clear that all the totality of the response will be incorporated into the contract.

Commercial intelligence

2.1.4 Although not specifically related to the collection of promises that participants have made to you directly, you may wish to gather information concerning what commercial obligations the other participants in the transaction have or have not committed to other individuals in the course of similar transactions. Obviously, you should not collect any information that breaches anyone's confidentiality obligations, but there may be a great deal of publicly available information concerning a particular participant's willingness or ability to commit to performance obligations that are important to the proposed transaction. Just as with promises that have been made to you in the course of preliminary dealings with proposed participants, your knowledge of the participant's past commercial conduct may assist you in structuring, negotiating, implementing and managing the transaction agreement. It may be difficult for a participant to avoid a particular performance obligation or commercial commitment that it has widely made available to other individuals in comparable transactions.[25b]

Relationship management

2.2 It is often said that transaction negotiations go much more smoothly when the participants get off to the right start. There is a tremendous amount of merit in that adage, and participants to a technology transaction who underestimate the importance of relationship building early in the transaction process do so at their peril. Emphasising the need to establish a solid working relationship among participants to the transaction early in the process does not suggest that it is necessary to create friendships in order for the technology transaction to proceed. However, it is very beneficial if the participants begin the transaction process by establishing trust, especially as a foundation for communication during the good times of the transaction process, which will provide them with a greater chance of project success. There are numerous ways in which to accomplish that objective, including a well executed due diligence process. However, there are a few relationship-management issues that project managers should be particularly cognisant of in the early stages of the transaction process.

Relationship strategies

2.2.1

Teaming

2.2.1.1 One valuable relationship-building exercise involves the matching and grouping of team participants by their common interests in the transaction. If your team comprises executive managers, operational personnel, technical experts and professional advisors, you may wish to consider organising meetings among the participants that allow those common-interest groups to meet separately to get to know each other. Such meetings are often not devoted only to business matters, and they may involve a social component, such as dinner or even a round of golf. Note, however that the latter method will rarely be appropriate in the public sector pro-

---

[25b] See **1.5.6.5** regarding Freedom of Information Act "access requests" relating to public sector information.

curement arena and may not be helpful in a purely private sector transaction as it may give rise to conflicts of interest, and distort the need for impartiality in a competitive scenario. Indeed in public sector contracting in the UK it is normal to include a clause dealing expressly with "corrupt gifts" in both the final contract and the preliminary procurement documentation such that any gift or inducement will give rise to a right to terminate (once the contract has been entered into), or a right to exclude a bidder from the remainder of the competitive procurement (in a pre-contract situation).[25c]

Seminars

2.2.1.2 Another successful relationship-building technique involves bringing together the participants for an inaugural meeting to discuss each other's companies and business philosophies, and to share information about each other's corporate culture or approach to doing business. Perhaps undertaken over breakfast or lunch, such seminars or presentations can be very helpful in breaking the ice as the process begins. Of course, the extent of those relationship-building strategies will be directly proportional to the time and resources that will be devoted to bringing the transaction to fruition.

Relationship investment

2.2.1.3 You should keep in mind that many transactions take much longer and involve more resources than the participants anticipate during the early stages of the transaction process. Subsequent problems may arise if the participants underestimate the time and resources that are required to forge a lasting commercial relationship. Where participants decide not to invest the time and energy necessary to build a strong relationship foundation in the early stages, it may be more difficult to establish open lines of communication when they are particularly needed. In my experience, it is far better to err on the side of caution and invest in relationship-building early in the technology process, if only as insurance against subsequent circumstances which may complicate or prolong the transaction in ways that are not foreseen in its early stages.

Cross-culture awareness

2.2.2 In our globally integrated economy and multinational approach to business, it appears obvious to observe that different cultures approach the process of technology transactions very differently. Notwithstanding that obvious truth, it is difficult to underestimate the number of times that technology transactions have either

---

[25c] See also the Prevention of Corruption Acts 1889–1916.

failed or been extraordinarily delayed as a direct result of the failure of transaction managers to inform themselves about the different cultural norms that will affect the proposed project. Issues concerning the cultural protocol of an IT transaction are not restricted to international or cross-border transactions. On the contrary, those issues may also arise in uni-jurisdictional transactions where the participants are culturally diverse. Many of us can recall a transaction where the person leading the transaction process got themselves and the project into serious trouble because they had devoted very little, if any, time to understand those complexities before the negotiations commenced.

Since ignoring this issue may have profoundly detrimental consequences for the success of the transaction, transaction managers will want to invest a reasonable amount of time and energy to understand the cultural dimensions of the relationship among the participants. There are many ways, and research tools, available for you to investigate and inform yourself about the cultural dimensions that may exist concerning the proposed transaction. A common research approach may include: (i) retaining experienced consultants; (ii) working with professional advisors within the cultural jurisdictions of other participants; (iii) working with your country's diplomatic service (which has a wealth of information concerning the cultural aspects of international commercial transactions); and (iv) even having one of your staff undertake preliminary research to identify what (if any) cultural issues may exist for the project.

Good cop–bad cop

2.2.3 The proverbial "good cop–bad cop" negotiation strategy is generally relied upon to advance positions that will be negatively received, while preserving the relationship with the participant. However, many negotiators feel that there is a dishonest dimension to that strategy of relationship-building, and that it is an inefficient way to reach consensus among participants. Therefore, far from recommending it as a particular relationship strategy, you should know that good cop–bad cop situations often develop naturally rather than by design. In that context, participants in technology transactions often look to their outside advisors to advance the issues that are the most contentious and adversarial. By preserving the "good faith" aspects of the relationship between the client and the other participants to the transaction, the professional advisor is often advanced (a.k.a. sacrificed) as the more adversarial "bad cop" for the sake of relationship presentation. It is expected that as the transaction closes, and the professional advisors go their separate ways, that strategy will leave the relationship of the business partners relatively intact. However, if any negotiator is taking an approach that is aggressive to the point at which that style of interaction and communication is threatening the very fabric of the commercial relationship among the participants, then there may be other problems concerning the transaction that require attention, and which the "good cop–bad cop" strategy is obscuring. If discussions between the participants reach that point, then it may be preferable to avoid continuing such methods or styles of communication and to re-examine the fundamental issues that have created such controversy and disagreement. In my experience, negotiations are almost always best conducted in a non-adversarial, calm and co-operative manner where the participants firmly express their interests, while striving to understand the other side's interests to creatively find common ground.[26]

Negotiation conditions

2.3 There may be various commercial circumstances in which the participants may seek to control the transaction process in order to minimise commercial or competitive distractions, and to ensure that the negotiation process will be conducted fairly and ethically. It is not uncommon for those issues to be addressed in a form of preliminary agreement between the participants that sets out the pre-conditions for their discussions, and perhaps negotiations—all of which are intended to foster an environment of fair dealing, open expression of interests and reasonable treatment during the earliest stages of the transaction process. The following are some of the most important negotiation pre-conditions that you should consider as you select participants with whom you wish to negotiate the terms and conditions of a technology transaction.

Standstill arrangements

2.3.1 In order for the participants to devote the time necessary to consider and negotiate a technology transaction, they may require a period of time in which the participants will not be distracted by other potential commercial opportunities. Those arrangements are commonly referred to as "standstill periods". Standstill agreements include terms and conditions that prevent either participant from doing the following for a stipulated period of time: (i) participate in any commercial arrangements concerning the subject-matter of the proposed transaction; (ii) to solicit any offers from other individuals concerning the subject-matter of the proposed transaction; (iii) involve themselves with any other person concerning the subject-matter of the proposed transaction; or (iv) enter into any agreement with any other person concerning the subject-matter of the proposed transaction. In addition, standstill agreements may include the participants' representation and warranty that they are not currently involved in any such activities and that they are not a party to any arrangements that would conflict with their ability to commit themselves to the stipulated conditions of negotiation.

---

[26] A recent ICN Conference on the topic of high-technology procurement in the US, Orlando July 1–3, 2002, offered negotiating seminars that it promoted under the tag line "Are You Begging or Negotiating" and "Don't Beg! Manage Your Acquisition Process" (see *www.caucusnet.com*).

Exclusivity

2.3.2   Another way to create a standstill period is for the participants to agree that their transaction discussions will be exclusive between them, and that neither party will carry on similar discussions or negotiations with any other participants without the prior written consent of either participant. Such provisions may also state that the participants' commercial interests are being protected by such exclusivity, and that any breach of that exclusivity obligation will cause immediate and irreparable harm to the injured party for which monetary damages alone cannot adequately compensate the injured participant. Any such exclusivity right should be subject to a time limitation, and should clearly state the ambit and subject matter of exclusive discussions or negotiations.

Restrictive covenants

2.3.3   In addition to preventing other participants from engaging in collateral discussions and negotiations concerning the subject-matter of the proposed transaction, the participants may wish to restrict and restrain each other from particular activities that may be regarded as contrary to the ultimate objectives of the transaction. For example, if the proposed transaction will be among individuals in a particular industry who are combining their research, development and intellectual property to achieve a particular technology solution in a particular market, then it may be a reasonable pre-condition for the negotiations for the participants not to launch competitive solutions in that market. Such commercial restrictions may also be stipulated in a myriad of ways, including commercial restraints by such variables as territory, particular customer or markets, or particular activities or engagements. The intention of the participants in that circumstance is to ensure that the discussions and negotiations towards the proposed transaction are not detrimentally affected or compromised by the competitive activities of the participants.

There are several legal issues that are associated with such restrictive covenants, concerning which you should seek legal advice, including: (i) the enforceability of such provisions, on the basis that they are reasonable in the commercial circumstances of the transaction; (ii) that their scope and effect is reasonably consistent with the commercial interests that are protected by the restrictive covenant; (iii) that the restrictions do not offend competition and antitrust laws; and (iv) that such restrictions do not offend any regulatory restrictions that may apply to the participants.

Non-solicitation of employees

2.3.4   It is extremely important for participants in a transaction to preserve the integrity of their most important knowledge assets—their employees. This concern is compounded by the fact that the negotiation process provides each participant with a great deal of information concerning the experience, skills and expertise of each other's respective employees. Therefore, it is very common for transaction negotiations to be conditional upon each participant's agreement that it shall not solicit anyone who is employed by any other participant. Such non-solicitation restrictions will often continue beyond the period of time of the mere standstill period, and may be continued in the proposed transaction's governing contract. In some cases, concerns may be raised concerning competitive restrictions that prevent personnel from leaving the employment of one participant and independently applying for employment with another participant. In such cases, the restrictions should be strictly limited to the non-solicitation of employees, and allowance made for unsolicited applications by another participant's employee.

Remedies

2.3.5 Since participants intend that the conditions for discussion and negotiation be respected throughout the entire standstill period, they often consider stipulating remedies that may both motivate the participants to live up to their respective obligations, and which would fairly compensate the participants in the event that those obligations are breached. Such remedies may include: (i) financial compensation for amounts invested in the negotiation process up to the date of termination, including expenses related to professional advisor and legal fees; (ii) perhaps liquidated damages constituted as a "breakaway" fee (see **4.7.5**); and (iii) injunctive (and other equitable) relief to enforce important restrictive covenants (see **4.7.7**). Although the latter relief may only be awarded in the discretion of the court, and where certain criteria concerning the circumstances where the relief is sought are satisfied, covenants concerning the right to secure equitable relief may include provisions where the participants acknowledge that a breach of any particular obligation will result in immediate and irreparable harm, that monetary damages alone cannot compensate the injured party, and that such relief is fair and reasonable in the commercial circumstances of the transaction.

Dispute resolution

2.3.6 If the participants want the negotiations to be strictly confidential, and if they want disputes to be immediately resolved by individuals with particular expertise in the subject-matter of the proposed transaction, they should stipulate that disputes during this preliminary phase of the transaction are either mediated or arbitrated, which will allow them quickly and confidentially to resolve the dispute with the assistance of someone with the relevant expertise in the subject-matter of the dispute.

Good faith

2.3.7   It may surprise many business managers to know that there is no legal obligation for participants to a technology transaction to use good faith in negotiating the terms and conditions on which the project will proceed and be contractually governed.[27] Often described as a duty to act fairly and not contrary to the interests of the other participants,[28] the law has generally pointed away from a duty to negotiate in good faith (especially among arm's-length parties of comparable commercial power) and to consider the interests of the person on the other side of a commercial negotiating table.[29]

Even where parties have put in place Memoranda of Understanding, Letters of Intent or Heads of Terms, legal commentators have described such documents as having "moral" rather than "legal" effect. The test, irrespective of the name given to the document in question, seems to be one of detail—the less detail the less likely to create legal relations, the more detailed the more likely to constitute a contract.[29a]

Therefore, it may be important for you to consider whether or not it is in your interests to secure the contractual obligations of the participants to conduct all such negotiations in accordance with community standards of honesty, reasonableness or fairness, *i.e.* in good faith. A good-faith obligation may also restrict the ability of the participants from negotiating strictly in their own interests, and require the participants to consider the interests of the other participants.[30] Such

[27] With reference specifically to Canada, the British Columbia Supreme Court determined that the law ". . . has generally never recognized a duty to bargain in good faith in normal commercial transactions between parties acting at arm's length", in *Westcom TV Group Ltd. v Can West Global Broadcasting Inc.* (1996), 26 B.C.L.R. (3d) 311 (B.C.S.C.) at para.13. See also *Martel Building Ltd. v Canada* [2000] 2 S.C.R. 860, where the Supreme Court of Canada held that, ". . . a duty to bargain in good faith has not been recognized to date in Canadian law.", at para.73.

[28] Again, with reference to Canada, one of leading cases in Canada on "good faith" obligations is *Gateway Realty v Arton Holdings Ltd. and LaHave Developments Ltd. (No.3)* (1991) 106 N.S.R. (2d) 180, see para.38, aff'd (1991) 112 N.S.R. (2d) 180 (App. Div.). The approach in that case to the issue of good faith was followed in *Cougs Investments (Pickering) Ltd. v Forbes* (1996) 1 O.T.C. 279, and in *Garrett v Ayr Ventures Inc.*, 21 O.R. (3d) 407 (Gen. Div.).

[29] See Steven F. Rosenhek, "The Duty of Good Faith", Troublesome Business Torts Conference, Ontario Bar Association, Toronto, April 15, 2002, section title "A Duty of Good Faith in Pre-Contractual Negotiations", pp.23–28.

[29a] See *e.g.* Scrutton L.J. in *Rose and Frank Co. v J R Crompton Bros* (1925) A.C. 445 describing the relationship as one based on "honour". See also M. Lau , "Letters of Comfort and Heads of Terms" February 2004 (*www.out-law.com*).

[30] See *978011 Ontario Ltd. v Cornell Engineering Co.* (2001), 53 O.R. (3d) 783, CA, wherein the Ontario Court of Appeal noted that individuals negotiating a contract expect each other

an obligation may prove to be particularly relevant in any transactions where you will be entering into commercial arrangements with current or potential competitors. Many transactions are structured as so-called "co-opetition" transactions, where individuals who are competitors combine certain personnel, investment, intellectual property or other resources for the particular purpose of a narrowly-defined commercial project.

Miscellaneous provisions

2.3.8 In addition to the preceding terms and conditions, which are often considered at the beginning of formal discussions and negotiations in the transaction process, there are additional provisions that you should also consider.

Accuracy of information

2.3.8.1 At this stage of the transaction process, you may have two opposing concerns regarding the nature and quality of the information that is provided either to, or by, other participants. First, you may wish to stipulate that all information provided to you will be complete, current and accurate, and of a quality that you may rely upon in connection with the proposed transaction. Secondly, you may wish to deny any representation or covenant concerning the nature and quality of information, and exculpate yourself from any participant's dependence or reliance on that information. With regard to the latter, you may wish to specify that: (i) the information is provided on an "as is" basis; (ii) you are not making any representations or warranties with respect to its currency, completeness or accuracy; (iii) you have not undertaken an independent verification concerning any aspect of the information that you have provided; and (iv) you will not be responsible or liable for any reliance that is placed on such information.

Obviously, each of those two approaches is diametrically opposed to the other, but either may be commercially appropriate in the circumstances of any particular transaction. Even where you agree to provide information in the expectation that participants will rely on that information for the purposes of the transaction, you should both specify the very narrow purpose for which the information is provided and disclaim any responsibility whatsoever in connection with any other person's reliance on that information.

Footnote 30 *continued*

to act in their respective "own interests" (at para.32), and that in the absence of a special relationship, the common law in Canada does not ". . . recognize that in the negotiation of a contract, there is a duty to have regard for the other person's interests", *i.e.* to act in good faith (at para.32); above, n.42.

Return of information

2.3.8.2 If the transaction does not proceed, the participants should promptly return all copies of information that have been provided to them in the course of your discussions. Often, audit or inspection rights may also be requested to ensure that all such information has been returned, and that all electronic manifestations of that information have been entirely deleted and are no longer in the participant's possession.

Press releases

2.3.8.3 Participants often address the issue of public relations and the requirement for each participant to consent to the specific wording of any press releases that may be issued concerning the proposed transaction. Occasionally, participants may mutually retain a public-relations consultant, who will represent all of the participants to manage all media communications concerning the proposed transaction. Equally, in some transactions the parties may take the view that a blanket ban on all publicity is the most appropriate route, subject to the ability to publicise in the event that one party has secured the prior written consent of the other.

Confidential information

2.3.8.4 There are many aspects of the proposed transaction that you may wish to keep confidential, including: (i) participant identities; (ii) the nature or objective of the proposed transaction; and (iii) the commercial arrangements that will be negotiated. Therefore, you should ensure that all individuals who have knowledge of any of such information will be subject to the terms and conditions of a "non-disclosure agreement". Such obligations may be included in the agreement of engagement that you may wish all of the participants to enter into to commence the transaction process, or you may feel that such confidentiality issues are important enough to be reflected in a separate contract. (For discussion on the commercial and legal aspects of such agreements, see **2.4**).

However, you should remember that the most efficient way to protect the confidentiality of your information is . . . not to disclose it. As trite as that sounds, you should take a very restrictive view of precisely what information you are required to disclose, and be sure that you do not provide any more information than is strictly necessary in the early stages of the transaction. It may be prudent to err on the side of caution by generally refraining from information disclosure where possible, and to regard a "confidentiality agreement" or a "non-disclosure agreement" merely as a safety net for that information which, after careful consideration, must necessarily be disclosed.

Confidentiality protection

2.4 In the early stages of the transaction process, you should be careful about the confidentiality of information that you disclose to other participants. Confidentiality concerns are crucial where the participants will be required to disclose extremely intimate and valuable information about their business and operations in the course of determining whether or not the transaction will proceed. Of course, once the commercial arrangements of the proposed transaction have been settled, the associated contracts will probably contain thoroughly considered confidentiality restrictions and protections. However, until those commercial arrangements have been finalised, you should require interim contractual protections concerning such matters. Although those provisions may be included in the contract that sets out the "standstill" arrangements (as noted above), technology transactions are particularly sensitive to confidential information concerning intellectual property, technology developments, business strategies and customer information. Indeed, the law of confidence can be a rather useful tool to mop up the shortcomings of intellectual property rights protection, providing protection for less tangible or protectable ideas and concepts. Therefore, participants to technology transactions increasingly insist that the confidentiality arrangements concerning their preliminary discussions be set out in a separate confidentiality agreement or non-disclosure agreement.

Definition of confidential information

2.4.1 The definition of what information will be considered to be confidential is crucial. First, the participants should consider whether or not they will take a very broad and inclusive view of what information is confidential, or whether or not confidential information will be very narrowly and specifically defined. For example, confidential information may refer to: (i) specific categories of information; (ii) specific documents or other materials; or (iii) information that is specifically labelled or otherwise identified as confidential by the person disclosing that information. The practical concern regarding the latter alternative is that managers may not, in the ordinary course of their day-to-day administration of a project, have the infrastructure or discipline to examine, consider and identify particular information or categories of information as confidential.

To be protected by the law of confidence, the information concerned must have a quality of confidence about it.[31] Human nature being what it is, any

---

[31] For explanation of this concept and a useful exposition of the principles of confidence, see *Coco v AN Clark (Engineers) Ltd* (1969) R.P.C. 41, and *Seager Limited v Copydex Limited* [1967] 2 All E.R. 415, *per* Lord Denning, M.R. The effect of the latter case is that it makes clear the principle that if you receive something in confidence, whether or not the information is protected by an agreement, you ought not to be able to take unfair advantage of that information.

requirement that information that flows between participants is to be kept confidential may not be practical or realistic in the circumstances of many transactions.

Secondly, the issue of whether or not information is confidential is a very separate one from whether or not the participants should, in particular circumstances, be excused from their obligations of confidentiality. For example, even though a participant may be legally compelled to produce the source code of another participant as evidence in a legal proceeding, the existence of that circumstance should not mean that the source code is no longer the confidential information of the disclosing participant. An assumption permitting disclosure should only mean that the person who is permitted to disclose the source code should not be held in breach of the confidentiality agreement in the specified circumstances. As a result, you should be careful to approach the exceptions discussed in **2.4.5** below as exceptions to the confidentiality obligations, and not as exclusions from the definition of confidential information.

Information-quality warranty or disclaimer

2.4.2 You should consider whether any confidential information that is disclosed is to be either warranted as accurate, current and complete, or whether there should be an express disclaimer of any risk or liability associated with any reliance that recipients may place on such confidential information. The appropriateness of either approach depends entirely on the context of the proposed transaction, and the willingness of the participants to assume the risk for any harm or damage that the other participants may suffer for their reliance on any inaccurate, incomplete or out-of-date information.

Non-disclosure standard of care

2.4.3 The risks and potential liabilities that participants may assume to protect the confidentiality of information may vary greatly, depending upon the stipulated standard of care. For example, the participants may simply agree that "the confidential information shall not be disclosed . . .", in which case any disclosure may constitute a breach of contract. Alternatively, the participants may wish to qualify that obligation by specifying that they will use either their "best efforts" or "reasonable efforts" to prevent disclosure. In many cases, the former duty of care may be extremely onerous and inadvisable, depending upon the circumstances of the proposed transaction. However, the qualification of "reasonable efforts" is likely to create a standard of care that individuals in similar commercial circumstances could easily employ to prevent disclosure.

Lastly, the nature of the relationship among the participants may also have a bearing on the appropriate duty of care. For example, if a fiduciary relationship exists,[32] then the participants may be subject to an onerous equitable standard of care and protection.

Protection of confidential information

2.4.4 One of the most important, yet frequently forgotten, aspects of any confidentiality arrangement is the obligation to protect confidential information from a broad range of circumstances that could either damage the confidential information or lead to its release into the public domain. In that regard, you should consider whether or not your confidentiality arrangements should include obligations to protect confidential information from unauthorised access, alteration, or use, theft, harm, destruction, loss, unauthorised transmission or communication, sabotage, interference and unauthorised reproduction. You may also wish to address how and where the recipient of confidential information will store it in order to ensure its safety; such provisions will include such requirements as physical security standards and who will have access to that confidential information. With regard to the former, you may wish to stipulate what physical security methods will be maintained, such as vault storage, access-code security, personal security clearance and controlled premises access. With regard to the latter, sometimes it is appropriate to specify contractually which individuals will have sole and exclusive access to the confidential information, and to ensure that they are the only individuals who will have the necessary access authorisation. Obviously, not all such measures will be appropriate and practical in every circumstance. However, protection

---

[32] There are many circumstances in which fiduciary obligations may arise in the context of a technology transaction. In situations of a principal–agent, trustee–beneficiary or other commercial circumstances where equitable duties may arise, you should understand the impact that such onerous obligations may have for all of the participants, and the proposed transaction. For more information concerning this potential issue, see John Glover, *Commercial Equity: Fiduciary Relationships* (Butterworths, Syndey, Australia, c1995, 1954); M.H. Ogilvie, "Fiduciary Obligations in Canada: From Concept to Principle", J.B.L. at pp.638–649, November 1995; Lionel D. Smith, "Fiduciary Relationships—Arising in Commercial Contexts—Investment Advisors: *Hodgkinson v Simms*", 74 Can. B.R., n.4 at pp.714–732, December 1995; S.M. Waddams, "Fiduciary Duties and Equitable Compensation", 28 *Canadian Business Law Journal*, n.3 at pp.466–472, November 1996; John D. McCamus, "Prometheus Unbound: Fiduciary Obligation in the Supreme Court of Canada", *Canadian Business Law Journal*, n.1 at pp.107–140, February 1997; Lionel D. Smith, "Constructive Trust for Breach of Fiduciary Obligation",[114] L.Q.R. at pp.14–17, January 1998; Robert Flannigan, "Commercial Fiduciary Obligation", 36 *Alberta Law Review*, i.4 at pp.905–922, December 1998; Jeff Berryman, "Equitable Compensation for Breach by Fact-based Fiduciaries: Tentative Thoughts on Clarifying Remedial Goals" (Symposium on Restitution) 37 *Alberta Law Review*, i.1 at pp.95–113, May 1999; Steven White, "Commercial Relationships and the Burgeoning Fiduciary Principle", 9 *Griffith Law Review*, i.1 at pp.98–111, June 2000; and Mark Vincent Ellis, *Fiduciary Duties in Canada* (Don Mills, Ontario: Richard De Boo, c1998).

measures and secured-access obligations should be considered separately from the recipient's non-disclosure obligations.

Exceptions to confidentiality obligations

2.4.5 It is customary for confidentiality agreements to include several important exceptions to the participants' confidentiality obligations.

Permitted disclosure

2.4.5.1 A recipient of confidential information will normally be permitted to disclose relevant aspects of a disclosing party's confidential information to its officers, directors, employees, professional advisors and agents to the extent that such disclosure is necessary for the performance of its duties and obligations or the exercise of any rights or privileges granted under the agreement. This disclosure is usually made conditional on the receiving party, prior to any such disclosure, informing such individuals of the confidential nature of the information. The receiving party will also usually be responsible for ensuring that such individuals comply with the confidentiality obligations contained in the governing agreement.

A receiving party will also usually be given the right to disclose confidential information that:

(a) is independently developed by the receiving party, without use of any confidential information of the disclosing party;

(b) becomes part of the public domain (other than as a result of unauthorised disclosure by the receiving party);

(c) was in the possession of the receiving party prior to its disclosure to the receiving party by or on behalf of the disclosing party, provided that:

(i) such prior disclosure to the receiving party was not made in contravention of the agreement; and

(ii) was not made by any other person in contravention of a confidentiality obligation to the disclosing party or any other party that is known or reasonably ought to be known by the receiving party; or

(d) becomes available to the receiving party on a non-confidential basis from a source other than the disclosing party, provided that such prior disclosure to the receiving party was not made in:

(i) contravention of either the confidentiality agreement; or

(ii) in contravention of any other obligation of confidentiality that is known, or reasonably ought to be known, by the receiving party.

Disclosure compelled by law

2.4.5.2 Confidentiality restrictions should exempt any disclosure pursuant to any applicable law or an order of any court of competent jurisdiction or government agency, provided that the disclosing party provides the non-disclosing party with prompt prior written notice of its disclosure obligation. Such a notice obligation means that the non-disclosing party may have an opportunity to seek a protective order or other appropriate remedy concerning the disclosure of its confidential information and/or waive compliance with the confidentiality provisions. In addition, the disclosing party should use its reasonable efforts to remove from any confidential information which is to be disclosed any parts or aspects that are not required to be disclosed; another way to express this is to require the disclosing party to use reasonable efforts to disclose as little of the confidential information as possible. Unauthorised disclosure may also be justified as being in the public interest (the so-called "public interest" defence). Recent case law in the UK has sought to establish what constitutes genuine public interest as opposed to voyeurism. This area of law is active in the UK and Europe given recent legislation and attempts to harmonise the concept of privacy within member states.[32a]

Duration of protection

2.4.6 If the parties do not specify a specific time period during which the confidential information will be protected, then the law generally recognises that the confidentiality of the information will be protected for a reasonable period of time, taking into account the nature of the confidential information, the commercial interests of the participants, the market sensitivity of the confidential information, and what is generally regarded as the confidential information's "shelf life" of value, relevance and currency. Perhaps the most important issue to consider when determining the duration of confidentiality protection is to fairly and reasonably consider the interests of the participants that are being protected, and to ensure that the period of protection does not unrealistically extend far beyond a period during which there will be practical implications arising from that information's disclosure. Too often, participants considering this issue simply guess at a reasonable "sounding" period of time without seriously considering and substantiating (and preferably documenting) the commercial interests that are being protected by the stipulated period of confidentiality protection. When dovetailed with the provisions concerning permitted disclosures (referred to in **2.4.5.1**), the duration of confidentiality protection should be regarded as reasonable and practically relevant by all of the participants.

[32a] See *Naomi Campbell v Mirror Group Newspapers plc* (2002) EWCA Civ 1373—where disclosure was stated to be to put the record straight. Contrast *Douglas v Hello! Ltd* (2003) EWHC 786 (Ch D) where the Court upheld the Douglas's claim and rejected the public interest defence.

Rights of controlled disclosure

2.4.7   The parties should also consider whether or not recipients should have specified rights to disclose confidential information to others, and what the conditions should be for permitting this. If the parties agree that such disclosure is permissible, they should restrict it: (i) to individuals approved by the owner of the confidential information; (ii) to individuals who need, or are required, to know that information for the purposes of the transaction; or (iii) to individuals who are under the direct control of the recipient, such as an agent, independent contractor, subsidiary company or subcontractor.

Furthermore, such disclosure may also be restricted by, and subject to, the following conditions: (i) the receiving party remains fully and absolutely liable for the conduct of the individuals to whom it discloses confidential information; (ii) the receiving party guarantees such individuals' compliance with all of the terms and conditions of confidentiality that you have required of the receiving party; (iii) the designated individuals are contractually required by the receiving party to protect and maintain the confidentiality of the information to the same extent, and in the same manner, as the receiving party is so required; (iv) the designated individuals are required to execute and deliver a confidentiality agreement with the owner of the confidential information in order to create a direct contractual connection with that person concerning the confidentiality of the information; and (v) the rights of those individuals to use and possess your confidential information are coterminous with your confidentiality agreement with the receiving party. Finally, the receiving party should be required to report to you, in writing and on a regular basis, concerning the identity of and conduct of all third parties who are in possession of your confidential information.

Remedial considerations

2.5

Duty to disclose breach

2.5.1   The first place to start with the commercial consideration of what your rights and remedies should be in the event a participant breaches their confidentiality obligations is to require the participants to monitor their own compliance and to report any breaches of those obligations with accurate completeness. Often, participants who have disclosed confidential information will not know if or when the confidentiality of that information has been compromised. Therefore, recipients of confidential information should be required to notify you of any breaches of confidentiality so that you can take immediate steps to mitigate any resulting harm.

Co-operation

2.5.2 In order to mitigate the harm caused to you by wrongful disclosure of your confidential information to others, you may want to take legal action against those other individuals to either retrieve that confidential information or to otherwise prevent the unauthorised use of the confidential information. Therefore, the confidentiality agreement should include a provision that requires the recipient to assist and co-operate with you in any remedial action that you may take against those individuals, including: (i) the recipient's obligations to provide you with accurate and relevant information concerning the identity and activities of the unauthorised recipient; (ii) assisting you with, or participating in, court proceedings or applications for arbitral relief; and (iii) taking immediate and comprehensive steps to prevent any further confidentiality breaches.

Rights to injunction

2.5.3 Provisions concerning a participant's rights to secure an injunction to prevent a breach of confidentiality, or to cause another person to engage in certain activities to protect the confidentiality of information, must be drafted very carefully. Such provisions are often drafted as simple covenants, where they agree that they are entitled, as a contractual right, to such relief in the event of a confidentiality breach. However, the ability to grant such equitable relief is in the sole and absolute discretion of a court, and it is arguably not possible for participants contractually to entitle themselves to secure such relief. However, because such relief may be granted upon the facts and circumstances of each particular case before a court, the parties may wish to acknowledge contractually, and agree to, relevant facts and circumstances that may facilitate the granting of such relief by a court.

For example, if relevant to the proposed transaction, you may wish to stipulate that: (i) a breach of confidentiality will cause irreparable harm to the participants; (ii) a breach of confidentiality cannot be remedied by monetary damages alone; (iii) the participants will not object to, or otherwise defend against, an application by another participant for such injunctive relief; (iv) the confidential information is of a particularly valuable and sensitive nature; (v) that granting of such equitable relief is convenient, reasonable and fair (or just) in the commercial circumstances of the transaction; and (vi) that the participants' agreements and acknowledgments with respect to such relief have been inducement for the participants to enter into the transaction and that the participants have relied upon those agreements and acknowledgments accordingly. Although no one can predict how a court may exercise its discretion in any particular situation, the foregoing agreements and acknowledgments may be put to the court in support of circumstances that are, to some extent, conducive to granting such relief.

Return or destruction of information

2.5.4 Obviously, in the event of a confidentiality breach or upon the termination of the confidentiality agreement, you should require the recipients to either return or destroy any confidential information that is in their possession, as such mirroring the normal court order sought in such situations: that of injunction and delivery-up. This requirement should extend to any copies of the confidential information that have been made, as well as to the deletion of any confidential information that has been electronically stored in an IT system. You should also require the recipients to disclose, in writing, all the individuals to whom they have disclosed any confidential information, and you should require the recipients to ensure that all such individuals have also either returned or destroyed all such confidential information. Sometimes, it is appropriate also to require participants to execute and deliver an officer's certificate attesting to the fact that all confidential information has either been returned or destroyed, and that their respective organisations no longer have any confidential information under their control or possession. Although such officer's certificates, depending on how they are structured, may provide you with a cause of action for any errors or misrepresentations, the most important practical use that they serve is to require the senior executives of a recipient to undertake the necessary investigations and enquiries to ensure that all confidential information has been returned or destroyed.

Venue and choice of law

2.5.5 Although issues related to the technology transaction's governing law, and the choice of venue for potential disputes, are discussed in **3.16.5**, there are several aspects of this issue that are particularly important to the protection of confidential information.

First, it is important to appreciate that each jurisdiction's confidentiality laws are different. For example, the protection of confidential information in the European Union has some very important differences from the confidentiality laws of the US, or the confidentiality laws of Canada and in each of the provinces. Although it is not possible to delineate all of those differences in this book, the important planning and management issue for you to consider is the extent to which the laws of the governing jurisdiction will adequately protect your confidential information.

Secondly, you should consider what remedies are available in the governing jurisdiction. The rules of procedure, the remedies available, the ability reciprocally to enforce court judgments, etc. may all vary from jurisdiction to jurisdiction.

Thirdly, you should consider whether or not, and to what extent, the courts of the jurisdiction in which you are protecting the confidentiality of information are favourably disposed to protecting knowledge assets and related confidential information as an important and invaluable commercial asset. For example, courts that regularly try cases in jurisdictions that are particularly known for their technology industries and knowledge-based economy may be more familiar with all of the issues associated with protecting confidential information, including economic value and appropriate remedial action. Conversely, courts in jurisdictions that are not familiar with the commercial and economic interests of a knowledge-based economy may not be as experienced or knowledgeable concerning such matters. You may also wish to consider whether or not the relevant jurisdiction would try commercial issues of fact related to the protection of confidential information by jury, or by a judge alone.

The jury is truly out as to the relative benefits of trial with, or without a jury for complex IT transactional disputes. Some US trial attorneys prefer a jury because they are able to rely upon their advocacy skills to ensure that the members of the jury agree with their client's case. By comparison UK lawyers may shudder at the idea that complex technologically-laden cases could be decided by non-experts.

Third-party guarantees

2.5.6   Although Chapter 4 of this book addresses risk-management strategies, it is worth noting that third-party guarantees can play an important role in protecting information confidentiality. For example, it is not unusual for confidential information to be used by individuals with whom participants must work on an ongoing basis. Therefore, if participants have the right to provide confidential information to those individuals, then you will want to ensure that the disclosing participant guarantees the conduct, and confidentiality obligations, of those individuals. This can be done relatively simply by including a confidentiality declaration as a schedule to your main agreement with your supplier, and imposing an obligation upon that supplier to ensure that all his employees or subcontractors who will be involved in providing services to you sign the declaration in your favour, so as to create a direct contractual link between you and those individuals in addition to the contractual link that you will have with the employer. In situations where it will not be possible for you to secure the written confidentiality obligations of all individuals who will have access to and knowledge of your confidential information, you should make those participants who disclose your confidential information responsible for ensuring that the confidentiality of the information will be protected through normal drafting (covenant and indemnity).

No reliance

2.5.7   In order to mitigate, if not avoid, any liability that may be associated with another person's reliance upon confidential information that has been disclosed to them, you may wish to ensure that the risk-management and remedial provisions of your confidentiality agreement clearly exempt and exculpate you from any liability, damage, harm or responsibility with respect to any person's use of, or reliance upon, the confidential information that you have provided. In that regard, you may wish to stipulate that all confidential information has been provided on an "as is" basis, and that the other participants acknowledge and confirm both your disclaimer of liability in that regard, and the fact that you have not undertaken any investigations or enquiries to ascertain or verify that such confidential information is true, current, accurate, complete or otherwise reliable. You may further wish to restrict the recipient from allowing any other individuals who are not a party to the confidentiality arrangement from similarly relying upon any confidential information that may be disclosed to, or used by, them. Therefore, you should consider the purposes for which the confidential information will be used, and what your risks and possible liabilities may be in those circumstances. Remember that for a disclaimer to have a chance of being effective, it should be brought to the attention of the reader and as such there will be little point in burying a disclaimer in the small print if you hope to rely on it in the future.

The step approach to engagement

2.6　One of the most awkwardly handled steps during this phase of the transaction process involves the decisions concerning how to begin the full commercial engagement of the participants in the transaction. There is a wide range of ways to start the project, and there are definite advantages and disadvantages to each alternative, depending upon the nature of your transaction. For example, off-the-shelf software-procurement transactions may be reasonably commenced with the technology provider's standard form boilerplate agreement that is rarely, if ever, negotiated before execution. However, that approach would probably be ill-received in the context of the formulation and structuring of a unique strategic alliance to develop very similar software for a unique vertical market. Similarly, uncomplicated transactions that do not have mission-critical implications for your organisation may require fewer steps to begin the commercial engagement, whereas large and sophisticated technology transactions that are not mission-critical to the enterprise, and which require unique and creative commercial arrangements, may require a significant effort in communicating the project's requirements, building relationships and participant trust, and in designing the appropriate commercial structure for the transaction. Therefore, you should consider each of the following alternatives in the specific context of the transaction, but always with a view to considering which of those alternatives will best serve the needs of all of the business case and the participants over the entire life of the project. The stronger the foundation of the building is, the more sturdy and durable the building will be.

From my experience, there is often an unquantifiable advantage in being the author of the contract in question, or working on your client's standard terms. Sometimes referred to as the "10 per cent rule" (as some would say that authorship confers a 10 per cent negotiation advantage), being more familiar with the contractual terms than the other negotiating party can certainly mean that you and your client will have an advantage during negotiation, if only because you will be more familiar with the structure of your contract and be able to move around that document more easily.

Participant proposal

2.6.1 A frequently used method of expressing the concept of a proposed transaction is simply to document that description, and possible commercial terms, either in correspondence or as a memorandum for the other participants to review and consider. Such an informal way of initiating the commercial discussions can be extremely efficient and direct. Because such correspondence and memoranda are considered to be very preliminary in their nature, and business-oriented in their approach, the participants may feel freer to express their ideas, concepts and commercial proposals without fear that any deficiencies in the presentation (whether legal or otherwise) will have a detrimental impact on the progress of the transaction. A beneficial way to use the technique of commencing discussions between the participants is to ask the participants to describe their understanding of their ongoing discussions and commercial expectations in writing. Although the parties may believe that consensus is being built in the house of their informal discussions, attempts to confirm such understanding in writing will often identify misunderstandings early enough in the transaction process for the issues to be easily addressed and resolved.

Performance statement

2.6.2 In a manner similar to commencing transaction discussions by way of correspondence or memoranda, participants also frequently begin the discussion process through the exchange of informal documents that provide a significant amount of detail concerning performance obligations and specifications, pricing and fee structures, and other proposed aspects of the commercial relationship and transaction for the participants to consider. Whether or not those documents are advanced as sales proposals, published product or service specifications, or are prepared in response to specifically described requirements, such documentation can ensure that the expectations of all participants are consistent, and that there is adequate consensus concerning the very nature of the proposed transaction. Often, such detailed performance descriptions may reappear in the transaction process as schedules (or parts of schedules) to the transaction agreement.

The particular benefit of this approach, either on its own or in tandem with the other approaches discussed in this chapter, is that such documentation focuses project managers on extremely important transaction information as early as possible. For example, detailed information that is exchanged early in the discussion process will help the participants to consider what their respective interests and positions are concerning performance obligations, project management, dispute resolution and change-management strategies, possible restrictive covenants, financial arrangements, intellectual property issues and related risk-management strategies.

Letter of Intent

2.6.3 The term "Letter of Intent" in this book means the written (and somewhat informal) description of the most important commercial aspects of the proposed transaction. The preparation of a Letter of Intent requires the parties to carefully consider those commercial issues so that they can sign it to indicate and confirm their mutual understanding concerning fundamental commercial intentions. However, in the interest of flexibility and ensuring that the participants have a subsequent opportunity more finely to describe and articulate the matters discussed in the Letter of Intent, they may not wish the Letter of Intent to be legally binding, or to create any contractual obligations. A non-binding Letter of Intent may provide the participants with a valuable opportunity to describe their commercial intentions for further consideration without fear that such an early and preliminary expression of the proposed transaction will legally obligate them and prevent their extrication from further discussions. Obviously, if the participants wish to create binding obligations of confidentiality or any other commercial arrangements (*e.g.* standstill arrangements) at this stage of their discussions, they should ensure that those obligations are contained in a separate contractual document and are not included in a non-binding Letter of Intent. As obvious as that suggestion may sound, many Letters of Intent that contain both obligatory standstill and confidentiality arrangements routinely include provisions that state, "This Letter of Intent is intended only to express the general understanding of the parties concerning a proposed transaction, and is not intended to create (nor shall it create) any legally binding obligations between the parties, whether contractual or otherwise", and to avoid the situation where an implied tendering contract is deemed to arise in public sector procurements (see Chapter 1), it is useful to continue as follows: "nor shall this letter be construed as constituting an agreement, offer or representation that an agreement shall be entered into between (x and y) or at all."

Memorandum of Understanding

2.6.4 The term "Memorandum of Understanding" in this book means a legally binding document that expresses only the most fundamental and essential terms and conditions of a proposed transaction, and that is executed and delivered between the participants to indicate their agreement concerning such provisions. In most situations, participants will rely on a Memorandum of Understanding in situations where they want to formally articulate the most material commercial obligations of the proposed transaction, and where they want to ensure the contractual commitment of the participants at an early stage in the transaction process. Although Memoranda of Understanding may contain varying degrees of specificity concerning the transaction's commercial arrangements, they are most often used as an intermediary contractual tool to frame and structure the technology transaction, while allowing the participants the time to negotiate and settle all of the remaining terms and conditions in the form of a comprehensive transactional agreement that will contain terms and conditions that are reasonably consistent and commensurate with industry practice for similar transactions. In order to find a balance between contractually formalising the most important commercial aspects of the proposed transaction, and still permitting the flexibility of the participants to give further consideration to all the remaining and extremely important aspects of the proposed transaction, Memoranda of Understanding are often limited in duration and will expire within a specified period of time unless the participants are able to negotiate, settle and execute the more detailed and comprehensive transaction agreement.

The decision concerning whether or not to proceed with a Memorandum of Understanding in any commercial circumstance is always subject to many considerations, including: (i) whether or not it will ultimately take as much time to negotiate the Memorandum of Understanding as it will to negotiate the comprehensive agreement, *i.e.* if you are not careful, you could actually double the negotiation time; (ii) whether or not business circumstances and market conditions require pre-emptive contractual action; (iii) the relative importance of the commercial arrangements addressed in the Memorandum of Understanding compared to all of the remaining issues that must be addressed; (iv) whether or not, and in what time frame, the participants will be able to negotiate, settle and execute a comprehensive and formal technology agreement; (v) are you far enough along in your commercial consideration of the transaction to use terminology in the Memorandum of Understanding that will not be vague, misleading or incomplete, avoiding financial terms that do not, on their own, have any recognised accounting or legal meaning (*e.g.* "gross margin" or "net profits"); and (vi) all of the circumstances that may be associated with the relationship between the participants and the level of trust that might motivate them to enter into a Memorandum of Understanding, as opposed to merely a Letter of Intent.

Drafting the contract

2.6.5 The administrative issues concerning the preparation of the transaction's governing agreement can be as strategically important to the successful outcome of the project as they can be an interrupting nuisance to the momentum of settling the commercial arrangements. However, understanding the significance of those administrative issues will help you to instruct your professional advisors to proceed in ways that are both efficient for the progression of a successful transaction and advantageous to your commercial interests.

Standard-form agreement

2.6.5.1 Many participants will introduce at the outset an off-the-shelf form of agreement which it proposes to be adapted and applied to the transaction. If the transaction is as normal and customary as the proposed form of agreement is standard and boilerplate, then the use of a standard form of agreement in those circumstances may make sense. The use of that standard form of agreement may also make sense, from the participant's perspective, because they wish to standardise technology transactions that are otherwise divergent into a form that is consistent across all of their customers, clients or commercial relationships within the jurisdictions. Standard form contracts (*i.e.* non-negotiated terms) have implications for the draftsman. Legislation in the UK restricts an organisation's ability to limit its liability if dealing with a consumer, or upon written standard terms of business, even if dealing business to business.[32b]

A transaction's governing contract should, at both its most simple and complex levels, unequivocally describe the business transaction and the commercial obligations and responsibilities of the participants. In drafting a commercial agreement, including a technology contract, the first priority and step in that process is the settlement of the business and commercial interests and issues. A written agreement should never be a document tail that wags the transactional dog. In fact, the entire perspective of this book is premised upon the fundamental principle and presupposition that a written agreement is nothing more than the precise and detailed articulation of the participants' business and commercial arrangements. Although standard-form agreements and precedent contracts from other transactions have their benefits, and may be used as efficient tools in the appropriate circumstances, you should be extremely careful never to let those mere reference tools corrupt the authentic and discursive process of building the business (preferably with the assistance of the entire transaction team, including legal advisors), and then reflecting the resulting business deal in a written contract in a manner that is as simple, clear, specifically designed for the unique commercial circumstances of the transaction, and that is unequivocal with regard to those arrangements. Unfortunately, very practical and reasonable time pressures often lead managers to the erroneous and misguided belief that allowing a boilerplate, standard-form contract to drive the business deal will expedite the transaction and save valuable time. The opposite is true, more often than not. When well intentioned systems for the efficient preparation of common terms and conditions become the entrenched and inflexible structure for all technology transactions, then the participants will very often run the risk of trying to ram a square transaction peg into a round contract hole.

Instead, as if it is just too tempting than to do otherwise, the participants must be careful not to force the specific transaction inflexibly and astringently in order to fit artificially into the one-size-fits-all structure of a standard-form precedent contract. In my experience, a mechanical, assembly-line approach to formulating, structuring, negotiating and articulating technology transactions can be a recipe for transaction delay, relationship decay and perhaps failure. Instead, you should con-

---

[32b] See the Unfair Contract Terms Act 1977, s.3, and the Unfair Terms in Consumer Contracts Regulations 1994, although note that the latter regulations only relate to consumer contracts, on standard terms and for the supply of goods and services.

sider the truest and simplest approach to documenting the transaction. Most often, the only authentic way to capture each transaction's unique attributes is to simply roll up your sleeves, define the commercial transaction and construct an agreement that unequivocally expresses those unique arrangements. If a standard-form contract or precedent can assist you without controlling the process, then you should take advantage of it. However, the differences between each technology transaction are subtle, and the nuances quite profound, so ensure that you drive the transaction with the business and commercial issues first, and then consider the best approach to articulating the unique commercial arrangements.

Drafting control

2.6.5.2 With the advent of email and the electronic transmission of documents, the issue of which participant maintains control over the drafting of documents and the governing agreements has become less relevant than it was just a few years ago. However, there are a few issues of drafting protocol that will likely expedite the document and contract-settlement process. First, as noted above, avoid allowing a standard-form precedent agreement, with irrelevant boilerplate provisions, to control the drafting process. The participants should have drafting control—not a mechanised document-management system. Secondly, there should be drafting continuity and consistency by virtue of maintaining a common drafting style and administrative approach. In that regard, it is extremely helpful if one of the participants takes drafting responsibility throughout the negotiation and settlement process. However, such drafting responsibility does not mean drafting "control", nor should it be interpreted as such. Proposed revisions to the documents should still be drafted and proposed by any of the participants; however, the required continuity and consistency is usually best achieved if one of the participants serves as the "administrative secretary" to ensure that the commercial arrangements are clearly and unequivocally interpreted and drafted into the documents. Lastly, some of the participants will be represented by legal counsel or other advisors who are less experienced and familiar with technology transactions than the legal counsel or advisors of other participants. In my experience, the transaction process can be greatly expedited, with increased efficiency, if the participant with the most experienced legal counsel and advisors takes the leadership role in both drafting the required documents and co-ordinating the submission and consideration of proposed revisions. In this way, all the participants will benefit from the most experienced legal counsel's knowledge of industry norms, terminology and general drafting standards that will assist the participants to structure and implement a technology transaction that is, in that way, generally consistent with industry practice and interpretation.

Revision process

2.6.5.3 Once the issues of drafting protocol are settled, it is also very helpful to settle the administrative process by which all of the participants will express their views and advance drafting proposals. There are probably as many ways to structure that process as there are different participants. However, the following issues may maximise drafting efficiency and expedite the process by which commercial agreements are contractually articulated.

(a) *Commerce first, contract second*—It is extremely important for the commercial deal to drive the drafting. Therefore, all contract-drafting activities should clearly express and articulate the business arrangements that are either being proposed or otherwise agreed to. In many cases, it is much more efficient to advance a commercial interest, for discussion as a business concept in order to create consensus, than it is to advance a particular position in the form of finalised legal language. Obviously, it will depend upon what stage the participants are at in the contract-negotiation process, but the participants should generally avoid advancing business proposals as "definitive" contract language when drafting and revising the required documents.

(b) *Explanation and provision*—Where the parties have advanced a business proposal, whether verbally at the table or in writing, it may be efficient to accompany such a business proposal with suggested provisions solely for the purpose of better communicating that particular participant's commercial interest. Presenting specific drafting proposals in the form of both a written explanation and specifically proposed contract revisions can be an effective way of communicating the particular participant's position on that issue.

(c) *Blacklining*—When revisions to any document are made, either in conjunction with a proposed business or as proposed contractual language to reflect consensus concerning a particular business issue, those revisions and additions should be highlighted in some way so that it will be clear to the other participants what exactly has been deleted, revised or added since the last draft of the document was circulated among the participants. Most often, those revisions are underlined, with indications of what provisions were deleted or otherwise amended. Some editing software will even display which provisions have been deleted since the last draft. In any event, a clear indication of revised or additional provisions will greatly expedite the drafting and consensus-building process in the transaction. There is nothing more frustrating for participants, and even injurious to the relationship-building aspects of the proposed transaction, than receiving a revised draft of a document that does not clearly and prominently indicate the changes that have been made to the document. Nonetheless, it does happen; whether by accident or design, and so it is sensible to run an automated document comparison against your last version whenever a new version is received.

(d) *Technical details*—Very subtle drafting changes, and both grammatical and diction nuances, can have an immense legal impact on the documents being drafted. However, few things will frustrate you more about the drafting process than fastidious bickering in situations where your legal advisors have not fully explained such important drafting nuances as they arise. Therefore, you should ensure that during the revision process, your legal advisor keeps you current and fully informed concerning all drafting issues that may not be readily apparent to non-lawyers, or that may not appear to be directly related to the commercial issues that the drafting is intended to address. Since the position of a comma or the choice between either a definite or indefinite article can mean the difference of an entire provision's interpretation and effect, the interests of the project are best served by ensuring that you are fully informed about such drafting issues, and that any such related discussions are consistent with your commercial objectives.

Decision-making authority

2.7 Participants very often have a difficult time making a governance decision about who should make transactional decisions. Partly because technology transactions are consortia projects that involve several management departments and divergent skill sets, participants often run the risk that the transaction will be significantly impeded by the failure to create a decision-making process and appoint transactional leadership. Technology transactions that are managed by committee are extremely vulnerable not only to delays and possible impediments, but such committees may also run the serious risk of making poor business decisions. Much like the wise adage that many cooks spoil the broth, technology transactions require an effective process of issue identification and escalation, and decisive leadership. If your transaction team is not properly led, it may run the serious risk of drifting away from the defined objectives of the business case and being consumed by irrelevant distractions that "committee management" so often succumbs to.

Most importantly, your project team will have to actually read and re-read the documents and all the relevant materials—probably many times—as well as all of the various drafts and incarnations of those documents and materials. Since the transaction team is responsible for the project's success, it must not delegate the most fundamental aspect of that responsibility to just anyone. Your team must own that ongoing job, regardless of whether or not you require others also to read and re-read the documents and materials. You must never assume that your professional advisors or legal counsel are the only people who have to read all the documents, materials and related minutiae. The deal is made or broken in the detail, and if you or your team do not have the time to read all of the transaction's required documents and materials thoroughly, then you and your team do not have time to undertake the transaction at all. There is no getting around the mandatory principle that the transaction documents and materials have to be thoroughly read by those with whom the buck stops.

Business decision process

2.7.1 Your transaction team should have a clear understanding of how transactional issues will be identified, escalated for appropriate management consideration, and decisively made in a timely manner. That leadership may come from a broad range of management options, including the enterprise's Chief Executive Officer, CFO, Chief Information Officer or perhaps the organisation's General Counsel. One effective strategy is to assign an experienced business leader, who is otherwise not connected with the project, to manage the transaction process. One benefit of that strategy is that the transaction will be managed by a somewhat impartial executive who will be able to rise above the micro aspects of the transaction to make decisions that are in the overall best interests of the organisation. In that regard, some participants prefer to have the transaction managed by someone who is not necessarily emotionally attached to the project and who will not hesitate to pull the plug on the project if that is the right thing to do.

Other project-leadership and governance strategies include: (i) assigning a member of the organisation's board of directors to oversee the transaction team; (ii) retaining experienced and specialised outside legal or business advisors to manage the day-to-day affairs of the transaction, and to report to an otherwise less involved senior executive officer; (iii) assigning technology transactions to senior procurement officers who will manage and co-ordinate the substantive areas of expertise within the organisation that are required for the project; and (iv) hiring an independent contractor on a consulting basis, who will lead and manage the project and the transaction process on a full-time basis.

Who will participate?

2.7.2 The issue of who among your organisation will directly participate in the transaction process can be politically difficult and complicated for several reasons. First, you want to ensure that any individual with a vested interest in the project has a role to play in the transaction process. As a general rule, the transaction process usually requires the hands-on expertise and management judgment of at least a technology, finance, business operations and legal advisor. There may be others in your organisation, depending upon the nature of the proposed transaction, whom you may also feel should directly participate in the transaction process; however, there is a limit to the number of people who should attend business-discussion and contract-negotiation meetings.

The second issue, therefore, becomes one of making the distinction between project team membership and direct participation in the business and legal meetings that will be required during the transaction process, and ensuring that there are clear reporting lines to all internal and external stakeholders. One common and effective strategy is to create break-out teams, or groups that have common specialised areas of interest who will meet separately to address the business (and perhaps legal) issues that are specifically and uniquely related to their respective areas of business concern. Therefore, finance and procurement managers will work together to discuss pricing and finance issues, while technology managers will meet with other technology managers to discuss the operational, functional and technical specifications of the required technology. Human-resources executives could all meet to discuss the project's personnel requirements, while those responsible for risk-management strategies could meet to discuss the issues related to Chapter 4 of this book. However, although such specialised meeting strategies may be of tremendous assistance in the early stages of discussions between the participants, as the transaction progresses, all of those issues will become more and more convergent, and will be consolidated under the decisive leadership of the person who will be responsible for concluding the transaction.

Lastly, there is always the related issue of whether or not (or to what extent) independent contractors, subcontractors or others who are directly involved in the performance of transactional obligations should be directly or indirectly involved in the decision-making process. Some of the factors that you will want to consider in addressing that issue include: (i) whether or not their involvement can be limited to only the specific issues that directly affect them; whether or not you require "downstream" agreement from those third parties before you can commit to performance of "upstream" obligations to other participants; (ii) whether or not those individuals have confidential or proprietary information that you require in order to address a particular transactional issue; and (iii) the extent to which increased participation at the negotiating table, or in the transaction process itself, will either improve or harm the relationship among participants.

Participation by professional advisors

2.7.3   The extent to which you may wish to involve professional advisors in your transaction process will depend upon many variables, including: the specialised and unique nature of the transaction; the degree of experience and specialist expertise your professional advisors can bring to the transaction; the extent to which your professional advisors will add business value to the transaction, in addition to the professional value that you should otherwise expect; the extent to which your professional advisors are familiar with the relevant technology industry, your business operations and the commercial objectives that you are striving to achieve through the proposed transaction; and their transactional experience and specialist skills in negotiating and settling a transaction in a manner that will, to the greatest extent possible, get the deal done.

There are certain technology transactions that organisations will only experience a few times over the course of any 10- or 20-year period, and where you are well advised to rely upon the transaction experience, judgment and specialised expertise of professionals who routinely engage in such transactions. On the other hand, you also want to ensure that your professional advisors do not hijack the business decision-making process, and that they do not permit irrelevant legal, financial or technical issues to corrupt the transaction process and objective. You should thoroughly discuss all of the participation options with your professional advisors, and ensure that you are entirely comfortable with whatever role they will play in moving the transaction towards a successful conclusion. As long as you are satisfied that your professional advisors will be team players and that they understand their role (with whatever level of responsibility you decide) in the transaction process, there will likely be a role for your professional advisors throughout the entire process.

Meetings and communications process

2.8 Until very recently, there were very few options concerning the communication methods and media that you could use to conduct the transaction process. However, today there are an increasing number of communication media that can be used to facilitate the transaction. Participants are now available 24 hours a day in any location in the world, including from their cars, by mobile phone, by wireless email, by pager and by video conferencing. Because business managers have only recently had the ability to participate in transactions and communicate through such a broad range of media, they are learning that there are particular pitfalls associated with some forms of communication, rather than others. Therefore, you should give serious consideration to the means by which you, and all the other participants, will communicate and negotiate your interests in the course of the transaction.

In person

2.8.1 In my view, there is still no better way to discuss your interests and advance your position than in person. Although the way in which any such face-to-face meetings are conducted may vary a great deal among various cultures, generally European and North American cultures regard face-to-face meetings as extremely conducive to honest and frank communication. The time and expense of travel to attend those meetings, and ensuring that all the members of the transaction team who have to be consulted are available, can be challenging considerations. You will have to weigh the cost of travelling to meetings against their benefits, including the ability to clarify misunderstandings, advocate particular interests or positions, relationship-building and developing trust among participants. In particular, face-to-face meetings can be extremely efficient in their ability to thoroughly consider and resolve transactional issues. Often, telephone conferences or video conferences require much more follow-up and confirmation than live meetings do, even though the same issues were discussed.

By video conference

2.8.2   If the participants cannot meet to discuss the transaction in person, perhaps the next best alternative is to meet via video conferencing. Since communication experts tell us that a significant part of meaning is communicated through the visual cues of body language, at least video conferencing allows some opportunity to observe visual cues that can be helpful in assessing the meaning and attitude of the participants. However, there is a broad range of opinion in this regard, and I know many very sophisticated negotiators who prefer not to conduct discussions through video conference, and instead would prefer to discuss the matter by telephone if the meeting could not be held in person. Perhaps as the quality of video technology improves, and related collaborative technologies over the internet improve, video-conference meetings will become much more lifelike and therefore of greater value to participants.

By telephone

2.8.3   The most frequently employed alternative to live meetings are telephone conferences because they are much more convenient and relatively cost-effective. Telephone conferencing also allows parties to simply mute their end of the conversation to hold private discussions, and they allow participants to communicate through alternative means while the conference is under way, including collateral discussions via email. However, there are obviously shortcomings to telephone conferences, such as possible poor sound quality, the inability to identify the speaker easily, the inability to see and interpret body language, and the general sense of distance that will to some extent affect the nature of the communication. You should not automatically default to a telephone meeting simply because it is the most convenient. You should give careful consideration to whether or not any particular meetings should be in person, and make sure that your long-term commercial interests are not compromised for the sake of short-term convenience.

Meeting location

2.8.4   The issue of where to meet, whether en masse or in break-out teams, will arise at various stages of the transaction process. You should consider whether there is any advantage in conducting meetings on your "home turf" or at the other participant's location. That assessment will vary from transaction to transaction, and will depend upon the relative security that the participants feel they have in connection with the proposed transaction. For example, participants that are relatively insecure in their ability to influence others may be more co-operative if they are made to feel more secure by hosting the meeting at their location. Conversely, those who have administrative responsibility for drafting the related documents may prefer to conduct meetings closer to their operational infrastructure—regardless of whether or not the participants are using mobile equipment (such as messaging devices or laptop computers) for that purpose. Alternatively, the participants may wish to simply locate meetings at a neutral place of convenience—perhaps one that is equidistant from their respective business operations. As a final matter, in deciding the location for your transaction meetings, you should avoid locations that are inconvenient for participants. All participants will want to carry on the transaction in an atmosphere that will be conducive to open and frank communication that will, in turn, expedite the transaction process.

Discursive process

2.8.5 It is difficult to leave the topic of communication without discussing an important aspect of transaction planning and preparation that frequently disrupts the ability of the participants to reach an understanding of the most important commercial and legal issues concerning the project. In my experience, particularly adversarial and confrontational approaches to presenting and communicating transactional interests and positions may do more to interfere with consensus-building than it does to achieve it. That is not to say that advocacy, even the aggressive presentation of interests and positions, is not an important aspect of the negotiation process, but negotiations that are entirely coloured by polarity and intransigence may actually do great harm to the transaction process. Since technology transactions tend to involve a consortia of interests and participants, and because they tend to reflect commercial arrangements that require performance over significant periods of time, an overly aggressive adversarial approach to transaction negotiations may cause irretrievable damage to your commercial relationship with the other participants, which in turn may create difficult administrative and management circumstances throughout the life of the project. As previously discussed at **2.2.3**, I believe that the best interests of all participants are, in most circumstances, achieved through a co-operative approach to the honest and reasonable presentation of interests, and by accommodating as many commercial interests as possible in a discursive process of balanced give and take. Although there will be many commercial and legal matters that various participants believe are deal breakers, the manner in which those fundamental interests are addressed can mean the difference when it comes to achieving the project's objectives. True advocacy is about results, not showmanship. Technology transactions are about concerns and relationship-building, not about an "us against them" mentality. Therefore, as a part of your preparation and planning for the proposed transaction, you should work closely with the members of your team and professional advisors to discuss the communication approach that you believe will be most conducive to achieving your commercial objectives.

Public-sector participants

2.9 In Europe, as in North America, any discussion concerning the business and legal aspects of technology transactions has to address the extremely important public-sector market, including all related technology procurement, research and development funding programmes, export assistance programmes, international trade assistance and all related aspects of the public sector's commercial participation in technology transactions. As you might expect, the public sector does not always approach their involvement in technology transactions in the way that private-sector participants would. Given the importance of public-sector participation in the technology sector of most national economies, it is equally important for the private sector to understand that the commercial considerations, expectations and methods that they are used to do not always apply to public-sector technology transactions. In recognition of that inescapable reality, the following discussion is intended to highlight the most frequently misunderstood aspects of the public sector's participation in technology transactions.

Commercial v public interest

2.9.1 As you begin to engage a public-sector participant in a technology transaction, you must keep in mind that public-sector participants will, first and foremost, regard the transaction as a matter of public interest to be engaged in for the benefit of their constituency, be it at local or national level. Therefore, on balance, public-sector representatives may take the view that the needs of the many will, if conflict arises, outweigh the needs of the few. There are occasions when public-sector participants may express the view that the interests that they represent (indeed their "cause") will have a relatively higher moral ground than those of a private-sector participant. For example, UK HM Treasury policy, as promulgated and replicated through central and local government, highlights the need to achieve and demonstrate "value for money", "best value" or other benchmarking mantras which combine both financial and other less quantifiable factors in order to establish that public money is being spent correctly. In such situations, the interests of private-sector participants may seem comparatively selfish and less worthy. Now, as a constituent of any such local or national representation, you may not be critical of such a perspective. In fact, my only point in that regard is that private-sector participants have to respect and take into account the legitimate public-interest perspective of government representatives in order to begin building a commercial consensus that will satisfy all the project's various participants.[33]

---

[33] See *e.g.* the Office of Government Commerce (OGC) at *www.ogc.gov.uk*. The OGC works with government to improve procurement and project/programme management and to make the government marketplace more efficient and attractive to business. For example, an excellent review of the public policy and public-interest foundation for the Federal Government of

Regulatory and political context

2.9.2   Before you engage a public-sector participant in the transaction, you should secure a complete understanding of both the regulatory and political context within which that particular branch of government must operate. Whether the public-sector entity with whom you are dealing is a government department or an entire ministry, there may be certain restrictions within which the public-sector entity must operate with regard to the proposed transaction. In Europe the Procurement Directives[34] transpose principles of competition law directly into UK law. As such, a public entity entering into a proposed procurement must act in accordance with the underlying principles of openness, transparency and proportionality to effect a level playing field as between potential bidders.[34a]

In my experience, the more you know about the regulatory political parameters within which the public-sector entity can operate, the better able you will be to plan for and accommodate the interests as you structure, negotiate and implement a public-sector transaction. In order to secure the information and to fully under-stand the regulatory and political perspective, you may require the services of public relations and governmental affairs advisors both to consult you on those matters and to plan a strategy to address those interests. For example, when bidding on a public-sector technology procurement RFP, information concerning the adminis-trative, regulatory and political circumstances in which the RFP was issued can prove to be invaluable. The greater the sensitivity to the particular circumstances within which a public-sector transaction must be conducted, the better prepared you will be to forge successful long-term relationships with public-sector participants.

Joint transaction structures

2.9.3   Increasingly, governmental departments are becoming interested in combin-ing resources with the private sector both to improve and expand their constituency

Footnote 33 *continued*

Canada's procurement services department, Public Works and Government Services Canada, *www.pwgsc.gc.ca* ("PWGSC") can be found in the *Report of the Royal Commission on the Bren Machine Gun Contract* (transcript of hearings held September 19, 1938 to November 24, 1938) The Commission, Ottawa (1938), which was the cornerstone for the creation of PWGSC.

[34] Shortly to be updated and consolidated by Directive 2004/18/EC of the European Parliament and of the Council on the co-ordination of procedures for the award of public works, supply and services contracts. The Directive was adopted by the EU's Council of Ministers and the European Parliament on February 3, 2004. The Directive must be imple-mented into UK national law as Regulations under s.2(2) of the European Communities Act 1972 within 21 months of its publication (see Art.80 of the Directive). This means that imple-mentation will need to be completed by January 31, 2006.

[34a] See Art. 28 of the EC Treaty.

services. Often, for reasons due to the public sector's interest in increased efficiencies and cost-effective ways to procure commercial expertise and experience, such joint ventures or "partnership" arrangements[34b] are very often technology-intensive. Therefore, if you are considering any corporate or commercial combinations with the public sector, you may wish to consider the range of corporate and commercial structures that are both suitable to the specific transaction contemplated and which are most conducive to the public-sector participant from administrative, regulatory and political perspectives. Such transactions frequently involve the creation of a separate corporate entity (to which each participant will contribute finances, employees and assets) and will provide the public sector with specialised services on a more efficient and cost-effective basis than the public sector was able to achieve on its own. Such creative outsourcing arrangements may often lead to significant cost savings for the government, improved constituent services and an opportunity for the newly created and highly specialised service company to leverage its competitive advantages commercially in the private sector—thus further decreasing the cost of delivery service by distributing the demands for a return on capital and investment across a much larger market. Such transactions require a range of specialised corporate and commercial services, including: corporate structures; public-sector regulatory issues; financing and investment; shareholder arrangements and corporate governance; human-resource and employee-transfer issues; technology transfer; and all of the commercial arrangements that will, in most cases, depend greatly on technology-driven business efficiencies.

Pro forma contracts

2.9.4 Public-sector technology transactions are particularly vulnerable to the potential problems associated with relying upon a standard-form "square peg" document being forced upon a "round hole" transaction. However, although such standard-form agreements and highly structured contract processes ostensibly exist to promote transactional efficiency, there are many situations in which the proposed boilerplate provisions will not apply to the particular transaction. You should identify all such inapplicable provisions and communicate them to the public-sector participant as early in the transaction process as possible. It will be extremely difficult to advance such concerns after the selection of a transaction participant has been made based upon the assumption that the boilerplate provisions were, indeed, appropriate for the proposed transaction. Therefore, any concerns that you may have concerning the applicability and appropriateness of standard-form agreements in public-sector technology transactions should be advanced early in the transaction process, whether at the bidding conference or otherwise, before the date upon which formal responses to the RFP are required. The next chapter at **3.15**, reviews some of the most distinctive and important com-

---

[34b] Note, not a partnership in the strict legal sense, but instead a partnering between public- and private-sector entities.

mercial ways in which public-sector technology transactions differ from those in the private sector.

Balance rewards and risks

2.9.5   As with any other technology transaction, you will have to consider the involvement of a public-sector participant in the overall context of the rewards of that participation and the risks that that participation may precipitate. Although public-sector participants want to approach transactions in a reasonable and co-operative manner, you may find yourself having to step outside the normal commercial practices of the private sector that you are used to for the sake of accommodating public interests. However, the extent to which you move away from commercial norms will depend upon your tolerance for risk and the practical likelihood of potential project failure. As participants consider their commercial options in the context of any particular transaction, they may either decide that the rewards are worth the possible risks or that they are better served by allowing their competitors to undertake the transaction.

Public-sector procurement routemap

2.9.6   Whilst public-sector procurements will differ, depending upon the technology required and the approach taken by a public-sector body, the rules for the procurement will be the same. The diagram below shows the typical steps from initial establishment of the need to the award of contract in the public-sector field. Procurement procedures in the United Kingdom are changing, particularly in the light of the new European procurement directive (Directive 2004/18/EC of the European Parliament and of the Council on the co-ordination of procedures for the award of public works, supply and services contracts).

New provisions have been added to take account of modern procurement methods and developments in best practice. These include explicit provisions on framework agreements, E-auctions and so-called Dynamic Purchasing Systems for the first time. There is also a provision on competitive dialogue—a new procedure for large, complex projects.

The new Directive is making explicit what is already considered to be permissible under the existing EC rules regarding the use of frameworks. As such, a public body does not have to await adoption or implementation of the new Directive before making use of a framework. If that public body decides to pursue a framework, then in the Official Journal of the European Union (OJEU) it should include the names of the contracting authorities entitled to call-off under the terms of the framework agreement. It should also state the length of the framework agreement (under the proposed new Directive, it will be a maximum of four years, unless there are justifiable exceptional circumstances).

Whether a public body decides to follow a framework path or normal path, it will also need to establish the extent to which it wishes to follow the OGC Gateway Process. The OGC Gateway Process meets the requirements of the *Gershon Report* on government procurement and the Cabinet Office report, *Successful IT: Modernising Government in Action.*

The following is a snapshot of activity involved in a procurement:

Procurement checklist

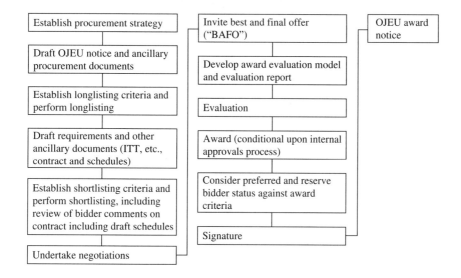

Chart provided courtesy of Bird & Bird.

Chapter 3

Strategies and negotiation of key business and legal issues

"The purpose of negotiating is to serve your interests. The chance of that happening increases when you communicate them. . . . Part of the task of impressing the other side with your interests lies in establishing the legitimacy of those interests."—Roger Fisher and William Ury, *Getting to Yes*[35]

3.0 Checklist III: The transaction's commercial and legal terms

3.1 Interpretation
- ☐ Recitals and statements of objectives
- ☐ Definitions
- ☐ Gender
- ☐ Plurality
- ☐ Statute references
- ☐ Division of agreement
- ☐ Language of contract
- ☐ Currency
- ☐ Sophisticated party
- ☐ Severability
- ☐ Calculation of days
- ☐ Avoid "loaded" relationship terms
- ☐ Incorporation of schedules
- ☐ Agreement structure

3.2 Performance obligations
- ☐ Description
- ☐ Deliverable v consultative

- ☐ Service levels
- ☐ Implementation issues
- ☐ Governance process
- ☐ Performance standards
- ☐ Quality control and continuous improvement measures
- ☐ Co-operation and assistance
- ☐ Good faith
- ☐ Performance benchmarking
- ☐ Performance milestones
- ☐ Customer obligations
- ☐ Time requirements
- ☐ Excusable delays
- ☐ Performance audits
- ☐ Participant-satisfaction reporting
- ☐ Collateral services
- ☐ Future goods and services
- ☐ Security obligations
- ☐ Change management

---

[35] Roger Fisher and William Ury, ed. Bruce Patton, *Getting to Yes* (2nd ed., Penguin Books, 1983), Chap. 3, "Focus on Interests, Not Positions", pp.50–51.

☐ Performance warranty
  ○ Risk allocation
  ○ Scope of warranty
  ○ Remedial rights
  ○ Financial benefit of warranty
☐ Business-continuity planning

3.3 Subcontractors
☐ Subcontractor approval
☐ Confidentiality
☐ Intellectual property transfer
☐ Dovetail obligations (a.k.a. "back-to-back arrangements")
☐ Replacement rights
☐ Multi-channel communications

3.4 License provisions
☐ Scope
☐ Restrictions
☐ Time
☐ Audit rights
☐ Right to copy
☐ Right to modify

3.5 Delivery
☐ Shipping and delivery
☐ Customs clearance
☐ Inspection
☐ Installation
☐ Configuration
☐ Title and risk
☐ Trade treaty compliance

3.6 Acceptance testing
☐ Test protocol
☐ Scope of test
☐ Participant co-operation
☐ Independent third party
☐ Compliance threshold
☐ Interim acceptance
☐ Non-compliance determination
☐ Reasonable time periods
☐ Repeated non-compliance implications

3.7 Restrictive covenants
☐ Exclusivity
☐ Transaction-specific
☐ Activity restrictions
☐ Scope of covenant

☐ Personnel non-solicitation
☐ No subcontractors
☐ No third-party benefit
☐ No-restriction clarification
☐ Export restrictions

3.8 Human resources
☐ Key individuals
☐ Team composition
☐ Turnover controls
☐ Qualifications
☐ Security clearance
☐ Confidentiality and intellectual property
☐ Rules of conduct

3.9 Financial arrangements
☐ Price discrimination
☐ Pricing and fees
☐ Price escalation
☐ Penalty/price rebates
☐ Bonuses/price premiums
☐ Payment terms
☐ Payment milestones
☐ Currency
☐ Tax
  ○ Transaction structure
  ○ Other direct tax issues
  ○ VAT
  ○ General
  ○ Inclusive/exclusive price
  ○ Tax audit
  ○ Records and retention
  ○ Performance audit
☐ Offshore arrangements
☐ "Favoured nation" pricing
☐ Fair market value benchmarking
☐ Volume discounts
☐ Right of set-off
☐ Benefit participation remuneration
☐ Payment security
☐ Financial metrics review

3.10 Documents and records
☐ Standards
  ○ Regulatory
  ○ Electronic transactions
  ○ Tax/customs

- ○ Evidence
- ○ GAAP requirements
- ☐ Audit access
- ☐ General record requirements

3.11 Term
- ☐ Length
- ☐ Renewal rights
- ☐ Termination
  - ○ Breach
  - ○ Remedial period
  - ○ Specified events
  - ○ For convenience
  - ○ Automatic v discretionary
  - ○ *Force majeure*
- ☐ Transition assistance

3.12 Intellectual property
- ☐ Background technology ownership
- ☐ New technology ownership
- ☐ Rights to use third-party intellectual property
- ☐ Joint ownership
  - ○ Tenants in common
  - ○ Joint tenants
- ☐ Written assignment
- ☐ Employee contributions
- ☐ License-back provisions
- ☐ Right to create derivative works
- ☐ Creation-reporting requirements
  - ○ Residual knowledge
  - ○ Assistance with intellectual property protection

3.13 Brand association
- ☐ Association benefits
- ☐ Brand-association continuum
- ☐ Brand licensing
- ☐ Brand management

3.14 Representations and warranties
- ☐ Authority to transact
  - ○ Corporate existence
  - ○ Authority
  - ○ Approval
- ☐ Regulatory and legal compliance
  - ○ Regulatory compliance
  - ○ Legal compliance
- ☐ Transaction not encumbered

- ○ Intellectual property asset ownership
- ○ Non-infringement
- ○ Third-party obligations
- ○ No document restriction
- ○ No asset encumbrance
- ○ No judicial interference
- ☐ Performance requirements
  - ○ Technology disclosure
  - ○ Necessary skills and qualifications
  - ○ Control
  - ○ Technology operations
  - ○ Key person/employee performance
  - ○ Environmental issues

3.15 Public-sector provisions
- ☐ Documents incorporated by reference
- ☐ Termination for convenience
- ☐ Intellectual property ownership
- ☐ Freedom-of-information requirements
- ☐ Regulatory requirements
- ☐ Risk-management approach

3.16 Miscellaneous provisions
- ☐ Further assurances
- ☐ Relationship of participants
- ☐ Waiver
- ☐ Amendments
- ☐ Governing law
  - ○ Other laws
  - ○ Avoid multiple choices
  - ○ Governing law exclusions
- ☐ Venue
- ☐ Publicity
- ☐ Gifts and gratuities
- ☐ Assignment restrictions
- ☐ Change of control
- ☐ Successors
- ☐ Compliance with laws
- ☐ Contract execution and delivery
- ☐ Notice
- ☐ Survival
- ☐ Entire agreement

I strongly believe that the best approach to structuring and settling a technology transaction is through interest-based negotiations, rather than by participants' inflexibly focusing upon myopic positions. At the root of any formulated position is an interest. Although there is only one position, there are usually many alternative ways to achieve and satisfy your interests. In my experience, it is through communicating and understanding each participant's interest that a fair and mutually beneficial transaction will be formulated and successfully performed throughout the project. Therefore, the commercial and legal issues discussed in this chapter should be regarded as a delineation of participant interests and not as a presentation of any particular position as to how to satisfy those interests.

All the interests discussed in this chapter, and in any particular position that the parties may mutually agree upon to satisfy those interests, can rarely be isolated as separate, stand-alone issues. Usually, the issues and interests are interdependent, and they are reciprocally and inextricably connected to all the other interests and issues that are relevant to the overall transaction. Discussions concerning one interest will, very likely, have a direct impact on how other interests and issues in the transaction will be resolved. For example: (i) the length of the term will often affect pricing; (ii) the inclusion of acceptance-testing requirements may limit the scope of remedies; (iii) time of the essence requirements may be dovetailed with specified remedies for performance delays; (iv) key person obligations may affect the right to use subcontractors; and, (v) particular aspects of the performance obligations may have a direct influence on what representations and warranties are required. As a matter of negotiation process, a flexible and interest-based approach to resolving transactional issues will often involve trading off some issues for others in order to create a fair and balanced deal among the participants.

As you review and consider the interests discussed in this chapter, you should keep in mind that they all reflect a proactive approach to identifying and addressing issues that are directly related to mitigating, if not avoiding, transactional risks. Each of the commercial and legal terms discussed in this chapter directly addresses transactional risks and potential difficulties that are common to most technology transactions.

You will have to determine which, if any, of the following commercial and legal terms are applicable and relevant to your particular transaction, and which are reasonably needed to accommodate your commercial interests. Balanced judgment and a strong sense of the practical will be required to undertake that assessment as you justify the legitimacy of your interests at the negotiation table.

Interpretation

3.1 The introductory provisions of a technology agreement are found in both the recitals and in the interpretive provisions that are contained at the outset of the technology agreement. Although those provisions may appear to be similar in all technology agreements, they may have important differences that carry serious implications in the event that ambiguous or equivocal provisions require interpretation and determination as to what the participants originally intended.

Recitals and statements of objectives

3.1.1 Although recitals are not usually presented in the text of a technology agreement in the same manner that commercial provisions are presented, they can have
profound implications for the interpretation of each participant's obligations. In the
event that the operative and substantive terms of the technology agreement are
unclear and ambiguous, a court may rely upon the plain meaning of the recitals to
explain ambiguous covenants.[36] If the recitals are drafted in such a way that they
intend to be followed by operative covenants to implement the recitals, but the covenants are not included in the technology agreement, the court may interpret the
recitals to have imported that covenant or promise into the technology agreement.[37]
Therefore, you should be extremely careful to ensure that the recitals to the technology agreement do not express an intention to achieve or accomplish more than the
covenants of the technology agreement otherwise require. If you do not intend the
recitals to be legally binding then you should state this fact expressly, *e.g.* if the recitals are merely intended to be a historical record of the paper trail to date. Although
it may appear reasonable for the recitals to express the technology transaction's
overall objectives and its desired commercial results, the generality and scope of
those stated expectations and desires may extend far beyond the narrower scope of
the performance obligations that the participants have specifically agreed to
perform. In order to avoid any unintentional expansion of the participants' obligations, you should restrict the recitals to the mere expression of the background dealings or to the commercial context in which the technology agreement has been
structured and negotiated.[38]

Many technology agreements include provisions entitled either "Scope of the
Relationship", "Statement of Objectives" or "Transaction Goals". Those provisions may be expressed as acknowledgments of fact, or they may be expressed as
binding covenants. Either way, their inclusion in the main body of the technology
agreement, rather than merely in the recitals, may have much more damaging impli-

---

[36] See *Re McKellar* [1972] 3 O.R. 16 at pp.26–27; affirmed [1973] 3 O.R. 178, CA; *Mahone
Oar & Block Works Ltd. v Rector* [1953] 3 D.L.R. 609 at p.614, NSSC; *Lavigne v Marcoux*
(1990) 33 Q.A.C. 104, CA (hiring clause implying that purchaser being employer; company
actually making purchase; promoter of company not liable); *Co-operative Trust Co. of
Canada v Receveur* (1985) 40 Sask.R. 315, CA; *British Columbia Hydro & Power Authority v.
Gregory Manufacturing Ltd.* (1978) 93 D.L.R. (3d) 503, BCSC; *White v Beeton* (1980) 24
B.C.L.R. 114, Co.Ct (recital indicating doubt about vendor's ability to give good title pre-
cluding assertion that encumbrances inconsequential).

[37] *Quart v Eager* (1908) 18 O.L.R. 181 at p.183, CA; *Majestic Mines Ltd. v Royal Trust Co.*
[1930] 2 D.L.R. 21 at pp.24–25; affirmed [1930] 3 D.L.R. 1010, Alta. CA; *Yarrows Ltd. v
France (Republic)* [1949] 4 D.L.R. 137 at pp.140–41, BCSC.

[38] Where the recitals to a contract describe the participants' background dealings or arrange
ments, very clear and satisfactory evidence will be required in order to contradict those recitals. See *Monklands Ltd. v Preston* (1923) 25 O.W.N. 163, HC.

cations if the intentions of the parties are overstated, or exceed the expressly stated performance obligations in the technology agreement. In my experience, such statements of objectives lead to far more misunderstandings, unintended liabilities and project delays than they are intended to avoid, for the following reasons: (i) the use of vague or subjective adjectives[39] in those provisions may greatly contribute to misunderstandings that arise when reconciling the stated objectives of the technology agreement with the agreement's definitively stated performance obligations; (ii) the statement of intentions, opportunities, objectives or expectations may easily be confused with performance obligations and create unintended obligations and duties; (iii) any statement of, or reliance upon, statements of transaction goals or objectives in a consultative or non-deliverable service agreement is a profound contradiction (see **3.2.2**); (iv) if the transaction requires "deliverables", then the only appropriate way to express desired results is in one comprehensive definition of that deliverable (see **3.2.2**); (v) those provisions contradict most technology agreements' customary exclusion of any other performance representations, warranties and covenants that are expressly stipulated, and the express denial that the obligations of the parties are designed, or otherwise fit, for any intended or particular purpose; and (vi) the participants should never summarily abdicate their responsibility of ensuring that the project, transaction and technology agreement have been structured and prepared in the manner and to the extent necessary to achieve each of their respective commercial objectives to a short form statement of catch-all "desires". These, invariably, are dangerously drafted in vague, nonverifiable and subjective terms that are generally inconsistent with the agreement's definitively (and, perhaps, narrowly) stated performance obligations. However well intentioned such provisions are, they present many more risk-management challenges and dangers to the transaction than project managers otherwise expect they will resolve.

Definitions

3.1.2 Since the words in any contract will generally be interpreted as having their ordinary meaning, or the meaning that is usually ascribed to them within a particular statutory, commercial or industry context, you should define any terminology that is ambiguous, or otherwise required for the purpose of drafting efficiency. You should be sure that your definitions: (i) do not conflict with any other definitions or terminology used in the agreement; (ii) are drafted clearly and unambiguously to express the intentions of the participants; (iii) are not circular in their reference to other definitions in the agreement[40]; (iv) you do not incorporate, by reference, any

[39] Such as "stable relationship", "mutually beneficial", "rapid achievement of cost savings", "improve the quality of the services", "enhance access to new technology", etc.

[40] All too often, terminology is defined in a circular manner, where "definition means definitions b and c", and where "definition c means definition a". The more that interdependent definitions are used in the agreement, the easier it will be to make this very common mistake.

other documents or materials that are not otherwise incorporated into or form a part of the agreement; and (v) the agreement is not overly zealous in its definition of terminology that does not reasonably require any definition above and beyond the ordinary meaning of that terminology, whether as a matter of normal trade usage or common dictionary meaning. As a final matter, make sure all team members review and agree with the agreement's definitions. A general business term may have an unintended tax or accounting meaning, and a common technology term may have an unintended legal meaning. Typically a defined term will then appear through the agreement with a capitalised first letter. It is important to police this usage and not to leave the definitions to the end of the process. All too often large transactions may involve the production of numerous documents by various authors and it is very easy for many people to mean the same thing but to define it in a different way.[40a]

Gender

3.1.3   When it comes to referring to individuals in gender neutral terms, the English language has some obvious limitations. Since English-language pronouns must take a gender form, most commercial agreements include a provision that directs the participants to interpret gender-specific terminology as gender-neutral. Some contract drafting styles eliminate the use of gender-specific pronouns entirely by relying upon specific definitions to refer to the participants.

Plurality

3.1.4   Without a covenant that makes it clear that singular terminology and plural terminology can be used interchangeably, legally significant drafting complications can arise that may have implications which the participants did not intend for the transaction. Therefore, it is extremely common to include a provision where words denoting the singular form shall include the plural form, and vice versa.

Statute references

3.1.5   Because the provisions of statutes change over time, you should ensure that any statutory references in the technology agreement will either include those future changes, or strictly refer to the statutory law as it existed on the effective date of the technology agreement—depending upon the intentions of the parties in any particular transaction. The issue is especially important to technology transactions because much of the digital economy relies upon industrial-based statutes that are

---

[40a] *e.g.* one person's "SLA" may be another's "Service Levels", one's "Contractor" may be another's "Provider", "Supplier" or "Company".

being constantly revised or replaced.[41] During the course of the technology trans-actions, there are many statutes that may directly affect the commercial arrange-ments between the participants, which may be revised or replaced. Provisions that state, "Any reference to a statute shall mean the statute in force as at the date hereof, together with all regulations promulgated hereunder, as the same may be amended, re-enacted, consolidated and or replaced from time to time, and any successor statute thereto" are extremely common provisions in technology agreements.

Division of agreement

3.1.6   In order to restrict the obligations of the participants to only those that are expressed in the technology agreement, you should ensure that the division of the agreement into separate articles, sections, subsections and schedules, or any other titles or headings in the text of the agreement is done only for the purpose for con-venient reference, and that such division or headings must not affect the construc-tion or interpretation of the agreement in any way.

Language of contract

3.1.7   There are several reasons why the participants may wish to stipulate the lan-guage in which the agreement will be drafted and interpreted. First, domestic laws of particular jurisdictions may require commercial transactions to be conducted in a particular language unless otherwise expressly agreed to by all the participants.[42] Secondly, international technology transactions may not have one language that is common to all of the participants. You should ensure that all participants have expressly agreed that their commercial arrangements may be expressed in, and gov-erned by, the English-language expression of their obligations. Lastly, the partici-pants to the transaction may subsequently request the transaction agreement, and its related documents, to be translated into additional languages. In those situations, it is important to stipulate what language will govern the commercial arrangements in order to avoid any potential conflict or inconsistency in the use of terminology, concepts or diction that is not common among language transactions.

Currency

3.1.8   As a matter of drafting efficiency, it is common for technology agreements to stipulate the general rule that all monies addressed in the agreement shall be of a

---

[41] See D. Card "Outmoded Laws Pose Dangers to International Electronic Commerce", *IP Worldwide*, June 1995, The New York Law Publishing Company, Premier Issue.
[42] For example, the Province of Quebec stipulates the use of the French language in commer-cial transactions, in certain circumstances, pursuant to the Charter of the French Language, R.S.Q. c.C-11.

particular currency, unless otherwise expressly stipulated in the technology agreement. For UK agreements, this will routinely be pounds sterling, and likewise, Euros for the EU. Increasingly, however, agreements entered into with US companies specify payments to be made in dollars. This may have interest-rate implications for your organisation. Similarly, considering that Canada is the largest technology trading partner of the US, and that there has been an extended period of significant currency value difference between Canadian and US currency, such a provision can be extremely important to most technology transactions (see also **3.9.8** concerning further important currency terms and conditions).

Sophisticated party

3.1.9   In technology transactions that occur among participants who may be much less sophisticated or commercially experienced than other participants, you should consider whether or not each participant has secured independent professional and legal advice in connection with the transaction's commercial and legal issues, and concerning the negotiation of the technology agreement.[43] The concern in such situations is that sophisticated parties to the transaction should not in any way take advantage of less sophisticated parties, and courts will often protect the interests of the less powerful participants in a commercial transaction. In considering the enforceability of the technology agreement, courts will take into account the extent to which unequal bargaining power and a lack of commercial sophistication was unfairly exploitive and did not lead to a true "meeting of the minds" when forming the agreement.[44]

Under English law inequality of bargaining power is not necessarily a reason for a court to re-write a contract or to declare a contract invalid. This marks a difference of approach between English and US law (the latter having enshrined the protection for the weaker party in its Uniform Commercial Code). Courts will however look at whether a contract may be rescinded on the basis of factors such as undue influence.

Severability

3.1.10   If any provision of the technology agreement is determined by a court to be unenforceable, or otherwise contrary to law, then the validity of the entire agreement may be at risk. Therefore, you should ensure that the remaining provisions of the technology agreement will continue in full force and effect, to the extent appropriate and reasonable in the circumstances of the intended commercial arrange-

---

[43] See *Eddy Mackay Building Co. v Nova Scotia (A.G.)* (1982) 52 N.S.R. (2d) 495; *Clements v Mair* (1980) 2. Sask.R. 1, QB.k

[44] See C.E.D., above, n.54, para. 722, Title 32, Contracts, where nn.9 and 11 therein cites an extensive line of cases supporting the proposition that financial naivety and shrewd opposite parties may involve unconscionable bargains or gross unfairness where the courts will grant relief.

ments. It is extremely common to include provisions that stipulate those arrangements, and to ensure that the in-valid or unenforceable provisions do not affect the ordinary continuation of the remaining provisions of the agreement. Those provisions may also request the participants to interpret and to perform the remaining provisions of the agreement in such a way that reasonably gives effect to the commercial intention of the participants and to an extent that will allow the participants to continue their commercial arrangements in an ordinary manner, except as otherwise affected by the obligations that are no longer enforceable between them. Those provisions may also require the participants to meet, and use their reasonable efforts to negotiate mutually acceptable replacement provisions that will be enforceable, and reflect the commercial intentions otherwise set out in the agreement.

Calculation of days

3.1.11 Most time periods in the technology agreement will be stipulated by the number of days, as opposed to hours or months. The technology agreement should stipulate: (i) that unless otherwise agreed to, the time periods stipulated shall include the day on which the period commences and exclude the day on which the period ends; and (ii) distinguish between calendar days and business days, which should exclude Saturday, Sunday or statutory holidays in the relevant jurisdictions.

Avoid "loaded" relationship terms

3.1.12 Two hundred years of mercantile law has led to the legal recognition that certain commercial relationships carry with them certain duties, responsibilities and obligations. As discussed in **3.16.2**, nomenclature of those relationships may not be consistent with common trade usage—and therein lies a minefield of unintended liabilities and risks that the participants neither expected nor intended. Some of those onerous relationships that can be inadvertently conjured include: (i) partnership; (ii) principal–agent; (iii) fiduciary duties, via power of attorney, or obligations of "trust"; or (iv) employer–employee. In that regard, terminology such as "strategic partners", "distribution partner", "principal authority", "represent with power of attorney", "manufacturer's agent", "authority to accept as an agent on our behalf" and "holding confidential information in trust" may create a level of onerous obligation, legal duty and potential risk that may neither be fully appreciated nor intended by the participants. Although a court will determine the nature and existence of those relationships based on the substance of the stipulated duties and obligations among the participants, the terminology used can be an important and sometimes persuasive indication of the participant's intention—at least, perhaps creating a presumption of a relationship that the participants may rebut. However, be very careful about relationship descriptions and nomenclature in the technology agreement, and ensure that such terminology is not in any way misleading or misrepresentative of the participants' true intentions.

Incorporation of schedules

3.1.13 Technology agreements are almost always drafted in a way that separates the substantive commercial and legal obligations of the parties from the more specific and detailed administrative and operational aspects of the proposed transaction. Whereas the former are usually contained in the main body of the technology agreement, the latter are contained in separate schedules (or appendices) that are separately identified and attached to the main body of the technology agreement. Therefore, the technology agreement should include a provision that both incorporates those schedules into, to form a part of, the technology agreement, and which gives some priority of interpretation between those schedules and the main body of the agreement should a conflict, contradiction or inconsistency exist among the provisions of those documents. Usually, in English contracts, those provisions stipulate interpretive priority to the legal obligations set out in the main terms, in priority over the technical detail of the schedules, unless stated otherwise (and, as discussed in the previous chapter, may state that the provisions of the customer's requirements take precedence over the supplier's solution). However, such a convention is merely due to the agreement of the parties concerned, and there is no legal rule that says that it must be this way. Therefore, you must ensure that very detailed provisions in all schedules accurately reflect the intentions of the participants and interrelate properly with the main body of the agreement. The principles of interpretation also apply to all other documents or materials that are being expressly incorporated, by reference, into the agreement. If you have not participated in the drafting or other preparation of such extraneous documents or materials that are being incorporated into the agreement, you should undertake an especially careful and diligent review of those documents and materials to ensure that they do not conflict with, contradict or are inconsistent with the intentions and obligations of the participants that are otherwise stipulated in the agreement.

Agreement structure

3.1.14 If the commercial arrangements require creative contractual structures, those structures should be stipulated at the outset of the technology agreement. For example, multi-jurisdictional transactions often require a governing "umbrella" agreement that stipulates the general commercial arrangements, while allowing for customised agreements in each jurisdiction through sub-agreements between each of the participant's local subsidiaries.

Performance obligations

3.2 One of the most frequent causes of litigation in technology transactions is due to the failure of the participants to accurately and completely describe their performance obligations. Those interests are so fundamental to the entire technology transaction that participants are strongly urged to discuss and settle all operational, functional and technical requirements and performance obligations fully prior to the execution and delivery of the transaction documents. If, as often happens, you do not yet know what your performance requirements are at this stage of the transaction process, you may not be ready to proceed with the transaction. The transaction, itself, may be premature. Until you have a clear understanding of exactly what your product or service needs and requirements are and what the performance obligations of the participants should be, you will incur the substantial risk of having to address such fundamental issues after the transaction has commenced and when the participants are no longer in a negotiating position. Time and time again, participants to technology transactions assume that those interests and issues can be resolved after the fact, without appreciating that such an approach creates the most fruitful grounds for disputes and litigation than any other aspect of a transaction.

If those performance requirements and obligation specifications are not yet known, then you should consider separating the transaction into two distinct phases: the first to define those specifications and requirements, and the second to provide or perform the described good or service. Very often, technology projects require those two distinct phases and transactions in order to avoid such serious risks. Arguably, since many of the other interests and issues discussed in this book are entirely dependent upon the nature and the scope of the specific performance obligations that will be agreed to, it will be extremely difficult for you to negotiate and settle all of those other dependent interests and issues until the product or service requirements are defined in reasonable detail. It is a bizarre truth that some technology managers will undertake extremely diligent planning and due diligence activities, only to fail to carry through on all of that planning by deciding to proceed with the transaction without clearly and definitively describing the participant's performance obligations.

Description

3.2.1   As noted above, you should describe the product or service requirements or performance obligations in the greatest detail and specificity possible; again, if you do not know what the requirements and specifications are, the performance phase of your project is probably premature and you should engage in the determination of the requirements and specifications, whether internally or as a separate, intermediate technology transaction.

The performance obligations may be described as operational or functional requirements, or they may be described in precise technical terms. They may also be described in schedules to be attached to the transaction agreement, or they may simply be incorporated by reference in other documents containing that description and specificity. Alternatively, many technology vendors publish performance specifications, or can refer you to operating manuals that may also describe your requisite functionality. You may have already stated your transaction requirements earlier in the transaction process (whether by RFP, or otherwise), and you should consider the extent to which those requirements should be continued and restated in the transaction agreement. Obviously, you should avoid the use of broadly descriptive terminology and subjective criteria that cannot be defined or quantified. All of the stated requirements and specifications should be objectively described in qualitative or quantitative terms that are verifiable, measurable and capable of empirical evaluation. Where the participants default to describing performance obligations in terms of "industry norms" or "customary trade practice", you should also: (i) consider the specific jurisdiction in which such norms or customs apply; (ii) try to ground those performance obligations in industry standards that have been described in writing by a relevant trade association; and (iii) perhaps consider examples of industry norms that, for greater certainty, reflect your mutual understanding.

Deliverable v consultative

3.2.2 Generally speaking, service obligations in technology transactions can be divided into two categories. First, services may be provided on a consultative and advisory basis, whereby no particular result, or "deliverable", is promised or guaranteed. Secondly, services may stipulate a particular occurrence or event, such as the requirement to deliver a particular good or to ensure that a particular end result of those services is achieved. While the former services are usually provided on a "time and materials" basis,[45] the latter services are often provided on a fixed-fee basis, where the participant assumes the financial risk of achieving the promised result or delivery obligation. It is extremely important that the two approaches are neither legally nor commercially confused, and that the participants are very clear as to in which of those two obligation categories they are to perform. Perhaps the most important implication of the difference is apparent in situations where customers' expectations concerning the desired result are not achieved. In the former case, the participant is not responsible for the outcome of the services, and therefore may only be liable to the extent that those services were not provided in a reasonably professional and diligent manner. On the other hand, service providers who are responsible for delivering a particular product or outcome of their services may be liable to the extent that that product or service outcome was not achieved. Therefore, the description of the performance obligations should make those distinctive responsibilities very clear and unambiguous, and the remuneration and risk-management provisions should also make that distinction abundantly clear.

---

[45] "Time and materials" contracts stipulate ongoing remuneration structures, like client expense obligations, since the lack of an end result or deliverable product or service generally makes it difficult to assess what the cost for the service will be.

Service levels

3.2.3 In addition to the detailed description of the participants' general performance obligations, there may be certain performance obligations that are especially important or even essential (so-called "mission critical") to the entire transaction and project. In those situations, it is common for participants to separately delineate those very important obligations as either "mission-critical services" or as "service levels". Carving out mission-critical service levels has several transactional implications. First, it allows the participants to practically focus on service or performance obligations that are especially important to the transaction. That way, the participants will devote the time and attention that are required to ensure that those obligations are adequately addressed in the technology agreement. Secondly, it allows the participants to design practical remedies that are uniquely suited to any failure to perform those obligations. Although those remedies are discussed in greater detail in Chapter 4, they may include separate: (i) repair time requirements; (ii) reporting obligations; and (iii) even financial incentives to motivate a prompt resolution of those performance deficiencies. Thirdly, a separate delineation of mission critical obligations will assist those who are operationally responsible for the project and its administration on a day-to-day basis. By highlighting those essential performance obligations, the project managers are thereby provided with separate guidance concerning the most important operational interests. Fourthly, it may also allow the participants to design an expedited dispute escalation and resolution mechanism to resolve any concerns involving such important performance obligations (perhaps by simply providing expedited time periods, as an exception to the technology agreement's other ADR provision, for such important matters).

The illustration on p.110 shows how service credits ("SCs") can compensate a party for relatively small breaches of an agreement without adversely affecting the continued life of the agreement. As the illustration shows, the parties should consider where to draw the line (represented by a "tolerance level") below which the aggrieved party might wish to seek to exercise its other rights and remedies. This tolerance level could also be exceeded if failures to achieve the necessary service levels occur once too often in a given time period.

Implementation issues

3.2.4 Many technology transactions require an intermediary step before all of the performance obligations of the participants may be fully performed. Often, those transition periods are referred to as the "implementation phase" of the project. Therefore, if there are any intermediary steps or undertakings that must occur prior to the participants being required to perform all of their obligations fully under the agreement, those implementation obligations should be clearly and completely stated. Such obligations are often also associated with or include: (i) the detailed

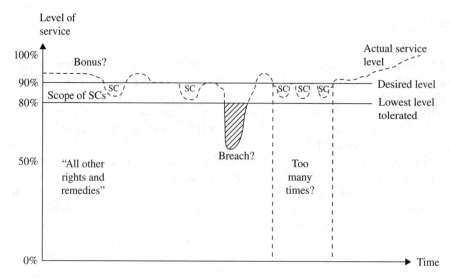

NOTE: The service levels are for demonstration purposes only and will vary depending on the facts and circumstances of each transaction.

Chart provided courtesy of Bird & Bird.

provisions of an implementation plan, which may be attached as a schedule to the technology agreement; (ii) strict timetables for "ramping up" the transaction; (iii) financial payment milestone obligations for each stage in the implementation process; (iv) the ability of participants to extricate themselves from the entire transaction should the implementation phase not proceed as stipulated; (v) obligations of closely managed governance and performance supervision, especially where the implementation phase represents a beta trial or a functionality verification; and (vi) less onerous performance and service-level obligations until the implementation phase is concluded.

In addition to preliminary services that are merely building up to a "go live" launch of the participant's performance obligations, the implementation phase may reflect the full performance of obligations that are cornerstones of the entire project, but which may not be included in the ongoing performance obligations required by the business case. For example, implementation obligations may include the obligation to implement or integrate technology infrastructure that will be required before the transaction can proceed, such as: (i) establishing a network; (ii) resolving technology issues related to connectivity and interoperability; (iii) establishing a telecommunications or internet infrastructure; or (iv) simply recruiting and hiring the personnel who are needed to move the transaction forward. In any event, each participant's interests concerning all such intermediary and transitional obligations should be fully addressed and clearly articulated in the technology agreement.

Governance process

3.2.5   There are many aspects of a technology transaction that may require either strategic or operational governance, and which the project's managers should address as contractual obligations. Such governance obligations may include: (i) regular reporting requirements; (ii) obligations to forecast performance changes; (iii) continuing quality improvement and performance criteria reassessment; (iv) management infrastructure, including chain of command, information flows and business-process management; (v) budget preparation and approvals; (vi) periodic operational reviews and assessments; (vii) ongoing consideration of marketplace and competitive changes, and related impact analysis; and (viii) management responsibility for the project's legal and regulatory compliance.

Performance standards

3.2.6   In addition to the specifically stated and detailed performance obligations that are stipulated in the technology agreement, you may also consider stipulating that the standards by which those obligations will be performed will be in accordance with generally accepted industry practice, trade custom or other generic standards. For example, you may also wish to tie the participants' performance obligations to expressly stated industry standards that have been promulgated by trade associations; public-sector standards services; or by independent standard bureaus, such as ISO 2000 Worldwide (see *www.iso2000.ws*) or technology-vendor associations that promulgate international standards for technology performance and operation. By adding a default standard of performance, you can create a mechanism to catch any performance obligations that are not otherwise specifically defined in the transaction agreement. However, to the greatest extent possible, you should have an understanding of what those generic standards are, and you should state the specific jurisdiction in which those practices and standards are performed.

Quality control and continuous improvement measures

3.2.7   Depending upon the circumstances of the particular transaction, you may also wish to stipulate the way in which certain obligations will be performed, whether in terms of performance method, specific business processes or in terms of quality-control measures. Such provisions are usually designed as "belt and braces" provisions, to provide you with greater comfort that the participant will, indeed, perform the obligations required. However, that additional level of performance requirement will create an additional level of liability for the participant, since its failure to adhere to those "control" obligations will constitute a breach of the technology agreement, even though that particular breach may not have resulted in any failure to perform the agreement in accordance with its service levels or as otherwise required. Therefore, you should consider, where appropriate, what the participant's liability should be for any such breaches that do not result in any failure to perform the obligations that are stipulated in the transaction agreement. Examples of frequently relied-upon quality-control measures include: (i) specific security measures for the maintenance of confidential information; (ii) stipulating periodic data and record accuracy and reliability tests; (iii) so-called "key person" provisions stipulating specific individuals that will be assigned to perform the actual service; (iv) stipulated performance methods or processes; (v) continuous improvement obligations (including technology-refresh obligations, best-of-breed benchmarking, implementing improved technologies, continuous training commitments, business-process re-engineering and systematic implementation of problem resolutions); and (vi) specific quality-control measures that must be performed by the participant as a matter of its internal business processes.

Co-operation and assistance

3.2.8 Unless otherwise expressly stipulated, the participants to a technology transaction will not have any obligation to either co-operate with or assist each other in the performance of their respective obligations, whether by providing each other with reasonable information or even by returning telephone calls. Therefore, if the particular technology transaction involves the interdependence or ongoing relationship among participants, then you should include a provision that requires them to use their reasonable efforts to assist and co-operate with the other participants for the purpose of performing the agreement. Those provisions often stipulate, for greater certainty, that the general obligations of assistance and co-operation include: (i) the provision of accurate, complete and current information that is necessary for each participant to perform their respective obligations; (ii) obligations of promptness and timeliness in communications; and (iii) activities related to their "further assurance" obligations, discussed in **3.16.1**. Such provisions may also stipulate that any cost or expense, perhaps subject to specific aggregate minimum expenditure, incurred by one participant to assist another participant will be borne by the participant benefiting from such assistance.

Good faith

3.2.9 Participants routinely stipulate that they will either perform their obligations or that they will otherwise exercise their discretion in "good faith" without understanding the possible implications of that duty. As previously discussed in **2.3.7**, you should carefully consider whether or not it is in your best interests to allow your discretion, and the way in which you perform your obligations, to take into account the interests of other participants.

Performance benchmarking

3.2.10 Depending on how you have stipulated or described the participant's performance obligations, you may wish to compare the actual performance quality to other standards, such as: (i) industry norms; (ii) your competitors; (iii) other ventures that are similar to the project; (iv) a particular organisation's performance of similar activities; or (v) standards that are empirically ascertainable (see **3.2.6**).

Those comparative and assessment activities are generally referred to as "benchmarking". Where you are unable to describe specific performance requirements, and have defaulted to performance standards and requirements that require comparative analysis, you will require benchmarking provisions that: (i) define the benchmarking process and activity phases[46]; (ii) describe the benchmark standard or source for the comparison; (iii) determine whether or not multiple benchmarking standards are required; (iv) stipulate the frequency with which that analysis will be undertaken; (v) whom, or how, such analysis is triggered; (vi) whether or not the participants or an independent third party conduct the analysis; (vii) determine at whose expense the analysis will be undertaken (*e.g.* it may be shared unless the performing participant is shown to be in default, in which case the defaulting participant assumes the cost); (viii) determine the nature and content of the comparison report; (ix) determine the ability of the participants to dispute or correct the findings; and (x) determine whether or not, or to what extent, the empirical standards ascertained should be translated into clearly stipulated and detailed performance obligations without further benchmarking requirements.

Performance milestones

3.2.11 The transaction process may involve many stages and developmental milestones. There are many reasons why participants may wish to designate particular milestones in the performance of the transaction, including: (i) to stipulate accomplishment-based remuneration obligations; (ii) to stipulate accomplishments that are required in order for the transaction to continue; (iii) to stipulate transaction stages of increased contribution, whether of investment, transfer of personnel, transfer of technology, or otherwise; or (iv) for the sake of providing specific and customised remedial rights to specific milestones that are not achieved.

Those milestones are often set out in the applicable technology agreement schedule that sets out the performance obligations, although it may also be included in the payment requirements schedule, if appropriate. Milestones may be event-

---

[46] See H.E. Fradkin and P.M. Sullivan's detailed analysis of benchmarking processes and their recommended four phases of preparation in "A Primer on Benchmarking a Licensing Operation: Preparation and Process", Two Parts, *Les Nouvelles*, September 2001, p.73, and March 2002, p.27, Vol. XXXVII, No.1.

specific, they may be date-specific, or they may even be discretionary—where one participant determines (usually, acting reasonably) that a particular circumstance, perhaps external to the project, exists that would allow the transaction to progress. If external events (*i.e.* occurrences that are outside of the project and beyond the participant's control or influence) are chosen for any of the milestones, you should have an objective and reliable way to substantiate that such an event has or has not occurred. Milestones may include: (i) executive or board approval; (ii) regulatory approval or consent; (iii) completion of government filings or notice; (iv) execution or delivery of technology agreement; (v) delivery; (vi) inspection; (vii) acceptance testing completion and acceptance; (viii) end-of-warranty period; (ix) specified performance levels or standards achieved; (x) specified service result achieved; performance "deliverable" achieved; (xi) confirmation of performance based on benchmarking report; (xii) an anniversary date of the technology agreement; or (xiii) as incentive events are accomplished, such as retaining employees past a specific date, or maintenance of confidentiality past a specified date.

Customer obligations

3.2.12   A frequent cause of transaction dispute and litigation arises due to the participant's claim that they were not able to perform an obligation, either directly or indirectly, because the other participant either did not contribute something that was required for that performance or otherwise "got in the way". The first thing that happens in any situation of alleged breach of a technology transaction is accusatory finger-pointing. To manage such a risk from the outset of the transaction, you should comprehensively stipulate what all of the contributing obligations are of all transaction participants, including customers and clients. Those obligations typically include: (i) provision of accurate and complete information that is necessary for the other participants to perform their obligations; (ii) access to the premises in a manner and to an extent required for the project; (iii) the use of specified resources, equipment and technology—and all licenses, lease or other required rights; (iv) general co-operation and assistance, including access to key individuals to ask questions and secure information; (v) management supervision, both for day-to-day performance issues and for dispute escalation; and (vi) all other specific contributions that are required for the purpose of the technology transaction. Be careful however (if you are the customer, or acting for the customer) not to allow the drafting to develop such that you (effectively) underwrite the provider's solution, *i.e.* avoid ". . . provided that the customer has satisfied obligations a, b and c, the provider will perform x, y, z . . ."

Time requirements

3.2.13   Most technology transactions are subject to very strict performance time requirements. There are several ways to stipulate those time requirements, each with different commercial and legal implications. First, you may simply state that all obligations shall be subject to a "time is of the essence" obligation, thus rendering any failure to perform in any time period stipulated to be an important breach of the technology agreement, giving the right to terminate.[47] Since such a general provision would apply to all timing obligations in the technology agreement, including notice provisions, report deliveries, acceptance testing determinations, etc., you should consider whether such serious implications of non-conformance should apply to all timing obligations; it is often too heavy-handed (and it cuts both ways, of course, and will bite upon your own obligations to pay). Secondly, you can simply state which timing obligations will constitute the fundamental and material obligations of the participants. Thirdly, you can dovetail certain timing obligations and performance milestones with the remunerative provisions of the agreement. A missed time requirement may then only constitute a minor breach of the technology agreement but it will have implications founded on financial motives for the participant who is late. Fourthly, for those timing obligations that are particularly important to the project, you can stipulate a broad range of specific rights and remedies that will fall out of performance failure, including: (i) the duty to report the timing failure; (ii) the duty to comply with a stipulated (now material) time period; (iii) the duty to devote additional resources for compliance; and (iv) liquidated damages to "motivate" compliance. Lastly, you can also stipulate which timing requirements shall be performance covenants, and which shall be subject merely to an obligation to use reasonable efforts to achieve such timing objectives. In any event, you should give important consideration to which timing obligations are commercially important to the success of the transaction, which timing obligations are preferable, and how you will structure those timing obligations to promote and motivate compliance throughout the transaction process. In my experience, simple "time is of the essence" covenants are rarely applicable to all timing interests and aspects of technology transactions, and participants are well advised to focus on practical and proactive approaches to the timing obligations that are most significant and practically relevant to the project's overall success.

Excusable delays

3.2.14 There are many circumstances that may arise in the course of the transaction process that would reasonably excuse participants from performing their obligations under the technology agreement. However, it is important to address those possible circumstances from the outset, and to fairly and reasonably describe those circumstances in the agreement for the benefit of all participants. Such *force majeure* provisions often stipulate that no participant shall be liable for any loss or damage for any delay or failure in their performance of their respective obligations

---

[47] Section 10 of the Sale of Goods Act 1979 provides that obligations regarding time of payment are not deemed of the essence in a contract for the sale of goods unless otherwise provided for by the terms of the contract.

by reason of any cause that is beyond its reasonable control, and which the participant could not reasonably anticipate and take action to either avoid or mitigate. For example, such circumstances usually include any acts of God, war, legislative or regulatory acts of government, utility failures, fires, floods, earthquakes, climatic circumstances, epidemics, quarantine restrictions, illegal strikes, illegal lock-outs or plant shutdowns, shortages in materials that are necessary to perform those obligations, embargos or any administrative or governmental acts or measures which substantially restrict the lawful performance of that participant's obligations. Furthermore, such provisions may require the participant affected by a *force majeure* event immediately to inform the other participants of those circumstances and to require the reinstatement of those obligations immediately upon the conclusion of those circumstances. However, the participants may also want to consider the time limitations associated with those circumstances and the point at which the inability of a participant to perform its obligations under the agreement may constitute the complete frustration and prohibition of their continued obligations. Depending upon the transaction, the participants may also require: (i) the assistance and co-operation of the non-performing party to find a replacement; (ii) participants to carry insurance coverage of those *force majeure* rights that are practically relevant to the project, and stipulate that the other participants be named as named insured, or co-loss payees, to the extent of their interests (see **4.9.3**); and (iii) the remaining participants to use their reasonable efforts to negotiate alternative commercial arrangements to achieve the project objectives without the non-performing participant.

Performance audits

3.2.15   One of the most proactive risk-management provisions that you can include in any medium- or long-term technology transaction is the requirement for the participants to undertake regular performance reviews, assessments and reports. Often referred to as performance audits, those provisions have several benefits, including: (i) the early identification of small problems or performance deficiencies, before they become large problems; (ii) they are excellent management and project-government tools which promote the gathering and dissemination of information that is relevant to the transaction progress; (iii) information acquired from those audits contribute to change-management proposals that allow the parties to actively consider commercial performance alternatives outside the context of litigation; (iv) the obligations provide an excellent foundation for the prompt internal escalation and resolution of disputes; and (v) they may provide an independent source of performance evaluation that the participants may more readily trust and wish to rely upon.

Although performance audits can provide you with excellent information, you should consider: (i) requiring all participants to create and maintain information and records of their performance of the technology agreement, including safely and securely, with back-up copies, in accordance with the generally accepted accounting principles of the relevant jurisdiction, and that can be retrieved in an accurate and reliable form, while stipulating the location where such information and records will be inspected and copied by the auditor; (ii) having the performance audits conducted by independent third parties who are acceptable to the participants; and (iii) ensuring that the auditors will be subject to strict confidentiality arrangements concerning their investigations. Depending upon the experience and the expertise of such performance auditors, they may also be in a position to provide the participants with recommendations for improved performance and related activities to promote the success of the project. As a final matter, you should consider whether or not performance audits should be admitted as evidence, or otherwise relied upon, for the purpose of any subsequent disputes, ADR or litigation. Often, where the participants agree that performance audits should not be used or relied upon for any form of dispute resolution, they may contain more freely disclosed, practical and useful information concerning the transaction's performance and how it can be improved.

Participant-satisfaction reporting

3.2.16 In addition to performance audits discussed above, and the change-management procedures and joint-management committee structure that are subsequently discussed in this chapter, a provision that can provide important assistance in relationship management, performance evaluation and dispute mitigation or avoidance are obligations that require participants to assess and report to other participants on a regular basis their satisfaction with the overall commercial arrangements and the performance of the other participants. In the manner that is very similar to widely used customer-satisfaction surveys, such mechanisms help participants to identify, consider and address any issues of low satisfaction, and issues of developing concern about the project, very early in the development of such potential problems. Participant-satisfaction assessments can do much to facilitate the success of a transaction, including: (i) to build trust among participants; (ii) to minimise the expense and delay of disputes; and (iii) to completely involve all participants in the ongoing management and governance of the project.

Collateral services

3.2.17 Many technology transactions will require the provision of collateral services[48] that raise several important transactional issues. First, not all services carry the same risks or require the same risk-management strategies. Therefore, you should consider either rationalising or customising the risk-management provisions

---

[48] Such services may include support services, maintenance and upgrade services, call centres, system integration, software installation, data management, security arrangements, hosting, project management, network monitoring, systems or business process consulting and design, or other services that may only be peripheral to the main aspects of the transaction or project.

to reasonably reflect the collateral services. Secondly, such services may have very different operational and technical requirements, and may also require detailed description. Such important considerations are often neglected because they are overshadowed by the task of addressing the more central and germane performance obligations of the transaction. Thirdly, the interests of the participants may be best served by addressing each collateral service as a separate contractual arrangement. However, there is no "right" way and it is equally likely that collateral services will be dealt with as a separate agreement or as a schedule to the main agreement.

Future goods and services

3.2.18   In anticipation that the project may expand, or that additional goods or services will be required for the transaction, the participants should address whether or not the participants shall provide those goods or services. Those provisions may include: (i) the obligation to provide any such goods or services that may be required; (ii) the conditional right to provide whatever products or services that the participant can demonstrate substantially or materially satisfies the related operational and specification requirements (*e.g.* on a call-off basis under a framework agreement); (iii) a right of "first proposal" that stipulates a notice and proposal process within a specified time period; (iv) limits or restrictions on your discretion to select alternative providers, such as price, quality or quantity criteria; (v) obligations to procure goods or services subject to commercial availability and price competitiveness; (vi) the participant's then current provision of those goods or services to your competitors; and (vii) the willingness of the participant to provide those goods or services in accordance with either the terms of the technology agreement, or another contract that will require negotiation, preparation and settlement. You should ensure that any such provisions are dovetailed with the technology agreement's change-management provisions (see **3.2.20**).

Security obligations

3.2.19   You should consider whether or not the technology agreement should stipulate what security obligations will be required of each participant. In addition to implementing confidentiality obligations (see **2.4**) and personnel-security clearance (see **3.9.6**), you may wish participants to undertake the following requirements: (i) use a dedicated and internal-communications network; use encryption technology for all communications; (ii) require communication to be conducted through a certification authority; (iii) adhere to your organisation's security policies and requirements; (iv) maintain performance records to assist in any security audits or investigations; (v) provide participants with prompt notice of and reasonable information on any breach of security or threatened security incidents; (vi) co-operate and reasonably assist in any security audits or investigations; and (vii) full compliance with all third-party security requirements that may be required in connection with the project.

Change management

3.2.20   In order for the project and the transaction to adapt flexibly to changing circumstances during the term of the transaction, you should include change-management provisions that stipulate the process by which participants may propose changes to the project, and amendments to the agreement, for review and consideration. Those provisions typically address: (i) whether or not any scope exists for a participant to make unilateral changes to minor and non-material aspects of the technology agreement, and what relevant limitations should restrict any such right; (ii) the administrative process and protocol, including notice periods, designated management involvement, change-proposal content requirements, and all relevant time limitations; (iii) unless otherwise agreed to, the requirement that all changes to the transaction (especially substantial and material changes) require a contractual amendment and the mutual agreement of the participants; (iv) any discretionary requirements concerning change requests or proposals, such as requiring "good-faith" discussions, stipulating the ability to withhold consent unreasonably, or requiring the reasonable exercise of the participant's discretion; and (v) the role of the Joint Management Committee in the administration and process of any change management activities among the participants.

You should ensure that those provisions are dovetailed with the agreement's contract-amendment restrictions (to the extent that they differ from the change-management provisions), *force majeure* provisions, and remedial rights in the event that transaction changes are required due to a participant's failure to perform their obligations. In rare circumstances, depending upon the nature of the requested change and its relevant commercial context, there may be topics of change that the participants wish to have decided for them as a matter of dispute resolution. As a final point, all change-management arrangements should be determined from the outset of the transaction. Any delay in establishing an efficient and practical protocol to adjust the project to changing circumstances may put the success of the transaction at risk.

Performance warranty

3.2.21   One of the most frequently relied-upon provisions of any technology agreement concerning the performance of any good or service are the warranties that are provided to the consuming participant. Although such warranty provisions are often promised and presented under the guise of consumer protection, they are more often drafted as a way of protecting and limiting the liability of the provider of those goods and services by including exculpatory or limiting language along with the "warranties". Therefore, you should review all performance-warranty provisions with scrutiny and scepticism as to which participant those provisions intend to protect.

Risk allocation

3.2.21.1   In determining the extent to which a performance warranty should protect your interests, remember that such warranties support the promise that the good or the service will comply with specified requirements and characteristics. Therefore, you must also consider which participant should be responsible for the risks associated with those failed promises and obligations. When negotiating warranty provisions, consider whether or not it is reasonable to limit any promises and obligations upon which a participant has relied upon concerning the technology transaction. In fact, many warranty provisions actually erode and limit any risks and liabilities that might be associated with a failure of the related good or service to perform as otherwise promised in the technology agreement.

Scope of warranty

3.2.21.2   Since the technology agreement includes detailed obligations and responsibilities concerning the definition, performance and qualities of the good or service that is being acquired, you should ensure that the scope of any associated warranties do not conflict with or contradict those other provisions. Therefore, you should ensure that the scope of the warranty addresses both the duration of the warranty, and the particular features and characteristics of the good or service, in a manner generally consistent with the participant's other obligations under the technology agreement. For example, if the technology agreement provides extensive provisions concerning a technology product's operational end requirements and material service levels, it may be reasonable for the warranty to extend to that specified functionality. Conversely, it would be unrealistic for a warranty to have a very limited scope of application that excluded such functionality.

Remedial rights

3.2.21.3   Warranties routinely stipulate what remedies should apply in the event that the warranty is breached. However, keeping in mind which participant should benefit from the warranty and the reasonable allocation of risk concerning the subject-matter of the warranty, you should ensure that any short-term remedial obligations that are stipulated do not otherwise limit or preclude your right to any other remedy that is stipulated in the technology agreement. For example, although the provider of the good or service is routinely obligated either to repair or replace a technology product that does not comply with the warranty, you should consider what other remedy should be available to you in the event that such repairs or replacements still do not conform to the provider's warranty obligations. Furthermore, warranty breaches may also be tied to liquidated damage provisions, increased delivery inspection rights, acceptance-testing provisions and the right to secure financial damages in the event that the inability of a technology product to perform in accordance with its warranty is not achieved by a stipulated milestone date. The technology provider's obligations to repair and replace a defective technology product should also be dovetailed with the technology provider's support and maintenance obligations.

Financial benefit of warranty

3.2.21.4   As a matter of business logic and commercial common sense, a participant should not be required to pay for the support and maintenance of a technology product during that technology product's warranty period. Since the technology provider has agreed that the product will operate and function in accordance with detailed specifications and requirements, and since the warranty provides the consuming participant with the additional "promise" that the product will substantially and materially operate in accordance with those characteristics and qualities for a stipulated period of time, any failure of those covenants and warranties will constitute a breach of the technology agreement. Despite this, many technology transactions require the consuming participant to pay for the technology provider's remedial obligations to fix, maintain and repair defective technology products through separate support and maintenance payment obligations and even attempt to require the consuming participant to start payment for maintenance from the point of delivery, *i.e.* even before acceptance! If faced with such a requirement, a participant should ensure that it is exempt from all related support and maintenance payment obligations throughout the warranty period, whether as a payment blackout period or a rebate for support and maintenance fees that have been paid with respect to defective technology products.

Business-continuity planning

3.2.22   In addition to the risk-management arrangements discussed in **4.7.10**, technology agreements usually stipulate that the participants must develop and implement a business-continuity plan to ensure that the project will continue through circumstances that might otherwise delay, interfere with or discontinue the project. Such plans routinely include contingency arrangements for: (i) alternative suppliers; (ii) secure document and information storage, processing and production; (iii) IT and communications redundancy; (iv) alternative power supply; (v) personnel-replacement contingencies; (vi) financial reserves to implement the business continuity plan; and (vii) property-protection measures (including fire-retardant measures such as fire doors and sprinkler systems, earthquake-tolerant architecture and bracings, and flood protection).

Subcontractors

3.3   You will usually select a potential participant to a transaction based upon their unique credentials and specialised contributions. Therefore, the issue of whether or not, or the extent to which, others may be retained to provide the goods and services that you associate with a particular participant can be problematic. However, where the business case requires convergent expertise, and a combination of many different contributions to the success of the project, it may be extremely difficult to avoid structuring all, or parts, of the technology transaction in a manner that will exclude subcontractors. Remember that your contractual link, or nexus, will be with the prime contractor, your one-stop shop for the implementation. It will be up to that organisation to satisfactorily back-to-back its obligations downstream to its various subcontractors. Whilst, contractually, this need not concern you as you are not a party to those subcontracts, you will nonetheless want to know who the subcontractors are (their identity may influence your decision to appoint the prime contractor in the first place) and you may seek to go further by attempting to gain sight of the subcontracts so that, as a matter of due diligence, you can satisfy yourself that appropriate arrangements are in place. Therefore, you should carefully consider the following commercial and legal issues that are frequently forgotten in those situations.

Subcontractor approval

3.3.1   Considering the reasons why you selected a particular participant, it is natural that you will want selection of that participant's subcontractors. In that regard, you should consider: (i) requiring the participant to provide you with complete, accurate and current information concerning a proposed contractor; (ii) securing the right to approve, in writing, of any subcontractors that are proposed by the participant; (iii) ensuring that the subcontractor will be required to perform their portion of the transaction in the same manner, and to the same extent, as the participant, including with respect to all professional standards and service levels; (iv) ensuring that the participant remains fully and directly liable for both the performance of the subcontractor, and in any connection with other acts or omissions that may cause you harm or liability; (v) ensuring that any third parties (such as your customers) have also approved of the subcontractor where that is either contractually required or commercially prudent; and (vi) whether or not you should have any direct contractual connection with the subcontractor, whether with respect to their performance obligations, a particular rights of remedy that you may wish to have directly against the subcontractor, in accordance with the provisions of the Contracts (Rights of Third Parties) Act 1999. You should also ensure: (i) that you will not have any financial obligations to the participant's subcontractors; (ii) that you secure the participant's assurance that no representations promises, warranties, covenants or guarantees have been made in that regard; and (iii) that the participant has guaranteed the performance obligations of the subcontractor and has fully indemnified you for claims, demands, expenses, harm, liabilities and damage that you may suffer in any connection with the subcontractor's acts or omissions, whether arising in contract, tort or otherwise.

Confidentiality

3.3.2 You should consider requiring subcontractors to protect the confidentiality of your project's information in two ways. First, you should require participants to "flow down" all of their confidentiality obligations to its subcontractors in the same manner, and to the same extent, that they are obligated to protect your confidential information. Secondly, you may wish to go a step further by requiring the participant's subcontractors to enter into a written confidentiality agreement with your organisation so that you will have a direct contractual right to enforce those obligations, and to protect your confidentiality interests, against the subcontractor. Depending upon many issues related to how well you know and trust that subcontractor and their particular role in the technology transaction, you may also wish to require the subcontractor to "flow down" their obligations of confidentiality to the employees, or at least to "key persons" who will be assigned to the project. Depending upon the nature of the technology transaction, it may also be appropriate for you to require those employees to enter into a confidentiality agreement with your organisation.

Intellectual property transfer

3.3.3 Where subcontractors will create, develop, author or contribute to any knowledge assets, you should ensure that the ownership of those knowledge assets is addressed and understood among all subcontractors. For example, if it is agreed that the subcontractor shall not own the knowledge assets, then you should require all subcontract agreements and commercial arrangements to include the obligation for the subcontractor to transfer, in writing, all right, title and interest in, and to, such knowledge assets to the appropriate participant. As discussed in **1.2.2.4** and **3.12**, you should ensure that all chain-of-title issues, as well as written moral-rights waivers, related to the knowledge assets are clearly and expressly addressed in all agreements that participants may enter into with their subcontractors.

Dovetail obligations (a.k.a. "back-to-back arrangements")

3.3.4 In any situation involving subcontractors, you will want to ensure that you are not "caught in the middle of risk". That is to say, you should ensure that all of your upstream risks and obligations with a participant are flowed downstream to subcontractors, to the extent of their contribution to the transaction. That, in turn, requires very careful drafting of subcontractor agreements so that all of the participant's obligations are dovetailed in a way that does not expose you or others to performance obligations and risks that you expect, and reasonably require, others to assume. Therefore, you will have to carefully manage the timing associated with those commercial and legal arrangements. If you attempt to settle your commercial and legal arrangements with subcontractors before your upstream commercial and legal obligations are settled, you will run the very serious risk of having to accept and agree to performance obligations and risks that are not addressed in your commercial or legal arrangements with the subcontractor. Therefore, in an effort to manage subcontractor relationships strategically, and to avoid that unfortunate predicament, you should ensure that all subcontractor arrangements are not definitively settled and concluded until the upstream obligations have been agreed to. The management of that circumstance may require several strategies, including three-way discussions where the subcontractor is directly involved in discussions and negotiations with the upstream participant in a manner that reasonably facilitates such performance and risk dovetailing.

Replacement rights

3.3.5 Situations frequently arise in technology transactions where a subcontractor is in breach of its performance obligations, and all, or some, of the participants wish to terminate and replace that subcontractor as quickly as possible. Unlike the prime-contractor participants who have approached the technology transaction as an "all for one" project, subcontractors may not be regarded in the same manner, or with the same long-term commitment. Therefore, you may wish to subject the prime contractor to termination remedies that will allow you, both quickly and efficiently, to extricate a defaulting subcontractor from the project, and to require their assistance and co-operation in transitioning their role in the project to their replacement. This consideration will vary from project to project; however, there are few circumstances that are more potentially frustrating to the progress of a technology transaction than being held up by a subcontractor who cannot be readily replaced.

Multi-channel communications

3.3.6 One of the most frequently overlooked subcontractor issues concerns the subcontractor's important role in, and contribution to, the project's governance and management, change management and dispute resolution. Unless contractual mechanisms are created to involve subcontractors in the important administrative and governance aspects of the overall project, their invaluable contributions will be omitted. Therefore, you should consider the following important additions to your subcontractor arrangements: (i) make sure that subcontractors are copied in all of the transaction agreement's notice provisions, otherwise they may not have any knowledge of important administrative disputes and governance events as they occur; (ii) make sure that all subcontractors receive information concerning joint-management committee meetings and proceedings that reasonably relate to their role in the project; (iii) you may wish to include subcontractors in relevant joint-management committee meetings; (iv) you should include subcontractors in all of the agreement's dispute-resolution provisions, whether by notice, by granting them standing to participate in proceedings, or otherwise[49]; and (v) you should ensure that they are included in the technology agreement's change-management process to the extent that their input and contributions are relevant to the subject-matter of those changes or amendments. Even though subcontractors will not be a party to the governing technology agreement, it may be extremely beneficial to ensure that they have standing to participate, where appropriate, and that all of the information, management and governance aspects of the agreement will include them to the extent that promotes the objectives of the project.

License provisions

3.4 Most technology transactions will, to one extent or another, involve the licensing of technology or other knowledge assets. Because of the legally technical nature of those rights, there are many potential commercial and legal pitfalls associated with the licensing provisions of technology agreements. However, this section of the book discusses some of the most frequently misunderstood or neglected aspects of those provisions, all of which require particular attention toward the mitigation, and perhaps avoidance, of the risks associated with this aspect of the transaction.

Scope

3.4.1 It is extremely important to designate the ambit and scope of the licence rights by stipulating: (i) the time period; (ii) the territory in which the knowledge assets may be used; (iii) the limited purpose for which the knowledge assets may be used; (iv) the persons who may use the knowledge assets; (v) whether or not the licence is exclusive or non-exclusive; and (vi) any other descriptive qualities or aspects that will describe the scope and ambit of the licence (including, *e.g.* the media upon which the assets may be used). Since a licence is a granting, or conveyance, of a particular proprietary interest, the licensee will have no other rights to use the knowledge assets, except those which are expressly stated or otherwise necessarily implied by a court. Therefore, you should ensure that the granting of any license does not provide the licensee with rights that exceed what is strictly necessary for the project, or which the participants otherwise intend.

---

[49] Otherwise, if a dispute arises among participants under the agreement concerning performance obligations that the subcontractor is responsible for, the participants may not be able to involve the subcontractor in the dispute-resolution process. Of course, the parties are always free to agree subsequently to a subcontractor's participation in the arbitration process. However, if there is a dispute concerning a subcontractor's participation or standing in those proceedings, then such agreement may not be possible and the failure of the subcontractor to participate in the proceedings may be harmful to the interest of one or more of the participants.

Restrictions

3.4.2 In order to better define the licensee's limited right to use the knowledge assets, and as a complement to the licence's granting provisions, you should consider stipulating a broad range of restrictions concerning the nature and extent of the licence rights that are being granted. For example, you may wish to "carve out" a broad range of uses and activities to which the licence will not extend, including: (i) particular uses or applications; (ii) use within particular markets, or in connection with certain persons or entities; (iii) territories or jurisdictions; or (iv) even conditions that must be satisfied concerning the ongoing validity and effectiveness of the licence. The provisions stipulating the permitted uses of the knowledge assets should clearly and directly complement and support all of the use restrictions. For example, where a licence may grant the use of a knowledge asset for the personal and internal business uses of the licensee, you should also consider including a provision that prohibits the licensee from using the knowledge asset for the benefit of any other person, whether in connection with a service bureau, outsourcing or otherwise commercial arrangement.

Time

3.4.3 When considering the term of the licence, some transaction managers make the mistake of stipulating that the licence will be irrevocable and perpetual without adequately considering whether or not those legal rights reflect the commercial intention of the participants. In either case, you should ensure that an unlimited time period for use, and the irrevocable nature of those rights, remain subject to your ability to terminate the licence for the fundamental or material breach of particular issues that form the "essential bargain" of the licence, such as: (i) uses beyond the licence's scope and ambit; (ii) breaching use restrictions; (iii) breaching your confidentiality rights concerning those knowledge assets; and (iv) breaching any associated remuneration provisions.

Audit rights

3.4.4 Due to the commercially and legally important nature of the licence's scope and use restrictions, you should have a right to audit the licensee's compliance with those obligations. For example, you should have the right to verify compliance with a licence's restriction that only a certain number of users can have access to, and use of, the knowledge asset at any one time. Similarly, where the remuneration for a participant's use of the knowledge asset is based upon a volume-use royalty (concurrent user licensing), the licensor should have the right to audit those uses and verify the participant's accounting practices.

Right to copy

3.4.5 Participants may require the right to copy the knowledge assets, and to otherwise maintain and store the licensed materials in ways that will enhance their use in connection with the project. Therefore, it is common for licence provisions to grant licensees those rights, but to further require that: (i) the licensor shall own all right, title and interest to those copies; (ii) the licensee shall inform the licensor of all such copies, and how they will be stored and maintained; and (iii) the licensees should either destroy or return all such copies upon the expiration of the licence. The right to make a copy of the licence materials may also be restricted to only those copies that are: (i) necessary and required for the project; (ii) solely for the licensee's own use; strictly for back-up or disaster-recovery purposes (this right is "inalienable" under English law and as such cannot be disapplied by a contract term to the contrary)[50]; or (iii) essential for the compatibility of the other materials or technologies that are being used in connection with the project.

A moot point is whether to allow the licensee to translate the software into another language. Reverse-engineering can be prohibited under English law by wording in the contract and so translation is usually prohibited. Note, however, that the law does provide for a right to make modify software for the purposes of interoperability.[51]

Since the right to make copies is proprietary to the owner of the knowledge asset, you must ensure that none of the participants, or any other persons connected with the project, makes any copies of technology, intellectual property or other knowledge asset without the express written consent of a person authorised to give that permission. It may be prudent to provide all participants, and others who are associated with the technology transaction, with a notice and directive in that regard, and to undertake regular project audits to ensure that the project will not be delayed or interfered with in any connection with the possible infringement of third party intellectual property rights.

[50] See Copyright, Designs and Patents Act (CDPA) 1988, s.50A (introduced as a result of The UK Software regulations permit the making of back-up copies under certain circumstances. This new section allows a lawful user of a program to make any necessary back-up. This right cannot be excluded by contract. The Copyright (Computer Programs) Regulations 1992 (SI 1992/3233) took effect on January 1, 1993.

[51] Interoperability is the ability for computers and separate programs to speak to each other but decompilation may also be used to create a computing program. The UK Software Regulations have introduced a new s.50B into the CDPA which permits "decompilation" under certain circumstances. In essence, those circumstances are that decompilation is required to achieve interoperability. The addition of the new s.50B was added for the sake of competition. It is sometimes argued that the right to decompile can be excluded by contractual terms, provided that the licensor of the software has supplied sufficient information to the Licensee in order for him to achieve interoperatibility. It is argued that given the difficulty in anticipating a licensee's interoperability requirements, a purported exlusion of the right to decompile may be held to be void.

Right to modify

3.4.6   An issue that frequently arises in the course of a technology transaction is whether or not the participants require the right to modify, revise, customise, enhance, add to or otherwise change the technology or intellectual property of the licensor. If those rights are required for the technology transaction, then you should ensure that the technology agreement includes the following provisions: (i) that you are being provided with all of the information, technology know-how and other intellectual property that are necessary to undertake those modifications; (ii) that the scope of the licence expressly includes the right to make such modifications, including translation rights for both foreign languages and alternative computer software codes; (iii) that your right to make those modifications will not breach any obligations or duties that the licensor has with any third parties, whether contractual or otherwise; (iv) that those modifications will not infringe the rights of any third parties, whether intellectual property rights, industrial rights, confidentiality rights, moral rights or otherwise; (v) whether or not the licensee is obligated to notify the licensor of any such modifications; and (vi) which participant will own those modifications.

Delivery

3.5   Common among all of the commercial and legal issues associated with the delivery of a technology product, whether hardware, software, equipment or otherwise, are the two fundamental issues of responsibility and risk. One of the most frequently relied-upon performance milestones in technology transactions are those related to the shipping, delivery, inspection and transfer-of-title obligations of the participants. Therefore, the following commercial and legal issues have important implications for the entire project.

Shipping and delivery

3.5.1   Depending upon the nature of the technology product and the place of shipment, you may have to give special consideration to how the commodity is being transported, and by whom. Although those issues are ultimately ones of risk assumption, they are frequent causes of project delay. Even though another participant has assumed the risk of shipment, you may not want to risk project delays that are associated with shipment and delivery problems. Therefore, where relevant to the technology transaction, you should delve into the specific facts and arrangements that have been made concerning the shipping and delivery of the commodity being purchased. Once you have completed your due diligence in that regard, you should stipulate: (i) the time of shipping; (ii) place of shipment; (iii) shipping agent; (iv) the nature and quality of the shipping transportation method; (v) the shipping company the participant will retain; and (vi) your right to receive regular reports and information concerning the commodity's transit progress. If you assume any risks associated with shipping, you should consider: (i) reviewing the participant's shipping contract; and (ii) securing the right to enforce the participant's rights against the shipper.

Customs clearance

3.5.2 A frequently forgotten aspect of shipping and delivering technology goods across international borders is the issue of clearing those goods through customs, and at which participant's risk and expense. Depending upon the uniqueness and sophistication of the acquired technology, you should also consider retaining a customs broker or agent who has particular experience and expertise in related customs matters. Depending upon the project's particular timing requirements, you may also include provisions that stipulate any special handling requirements, address the qualifications and experience of the custom agent, and require you to be promptly notified in the event that any customs issues or delays arise. The participants should also ensure that all country-of-origin documents are provided to customs officials in full compliance with all export trade laws, regulations and treaties.

Inspection

3.5.3 A practical risk-management issue involves your right to inspect any goods as they are delivered to you. As a preliminary step to possible acceptance-testing activities, the right of inspection can be relied upon as a payment milestone, and to identify problems with the goods as quickly as possible. In some circumstances, of course, a right to inspect will not help, as there will be no way of telling whether or not the product works without installing it and turning it on.

   In situations where you include inspection rights, you may also want to consider specifying certain remedies associated with any problems that you discover upon inspection, such as: (i) the right not to accept delivery; (ii) the right of replacement within specified time periods; (iii) warehouse, storage or holding requirements until you are ready to accept delivery; (iv) the right to require repair within a specified time period; (v) the right to withhold payments until the inspection is completed and delivery accepted; and (vi) possible liquidated damages associated with inspection failures and associated transaction delays.

Installation

3.5.4 The installation of technology can be an extremely important part of the transaction process, but it is also a frequently overlooked aspect of a participant's general obligations of delivery. It is often at this stage of product delivery that performance problems or discrepancies in operational requirements can first be identified and addressed. Therefore, this step in the transaction process is very important for the early and prompt mitigation, if not avoidance, of associated risks. Often, a technology product cannot adequately be inspected or tested for acceptance purposes until it has been at least installed and capable of preliminary operations. Therefore, you should consider including provisions that: (i) require the provider of that technology to install the technology fully; (ii) require that provider to reasonably assist and co-operate in the technology's installation; (iii) define the operational environment and infrastructure that is necessary for installation, including the network, operating environment, electrical requirements, humidity and temperature parameters, and any technology connectivity or compatibility issues; (iv) define the technology's installation in sufficient operational and functional terms that are necessary for any inspection or acceptance testing procedures that will be undertaken; and (v) reasonably allocate risk associated with the failure to install that technology as required.

Configuration

3.5.5 An issue that is closely related to the installation of the technology involves the extent to which the technology must be configured (or "commissioned"), and perhaps "assembled", in order for it to operate in accordance with its operational and functional specifications. In addition to the applicability of the installation obligations discussed above, there are additional issues of technology configuration that are very closely involved in the delivery process, including: (i) configuring the technology to operate within a specified environment; (ii) the networkability of the technology; (iii) the interoperability, compatibility or connectivity of the technology to other technology, systems, software applications or otherwise; and (iv) the ability of the technology to perform certain tasks or functions that must be configured or specifically adjusted in order for the technology to operate for the purposes of inspection, acceptance testing or operability.

Title and risk

3.5.6 Once the participant's interests concerning timely and secured delivery are addressed, the next important issue that must be addressed relates to when the title, and thus the risk, to the delivered goods will pass to the purchaser. Depending upon the particular transaction, title and risk can pass to the purchaser at any point along a continuum between the good's creation, to the good's final acceptance and payment. However, when describing or drafting those obligations, be very careful how you use summary nomenclature. For example, "FOB" (free on board) only generally and vaguely refers to the transition of the goods to the shipper, and does not stipulate any particular obligations in that regard. Therefore, you will have to designate what specific terms and conditions should apply to that transit circumstance, where title and risk to the goods will transfer to you.[52] Another commonly used designation is "CIF" (cost, insurance and freight), which generally designates that the vendor will maintain title and risk until the goods are delivered to their point of stated delivery or destination.[53] In addition to being extremely careful not to confuse those designations,[54] you should also keep in mind that all shipping, delivery and insurance responsibilities, as well as the associated expenses, may readily be separated from issues concerning transfer of title and risk.

Many transaction managers simply assume that all delivery and related expense obligations are necessarily tied to the point at which title and risk will pass to the purchaser, and that is not the case. For example, you may wish to stipulate that title in the technology equipment you have just purchased will pass to you as soon as it is assembled by the manufacturer at its place of origin; however, that in no way prevents you from requiring the vendor to also be responsible for shipping, purchasing risk insurance (designating you as the sole beneficiary), clearing the good through customs and ensuring that it is delivered to your place of business.

If you are acquiring goods, your interests may be best protected by taking title to the goods as early as possible, by requiring the vendor to be entirely responsible for all aspects of delivery and by managing your risks in such a way that you do not accept any risk for the goods until they have been delivered to you, fully inspected and accepted. Conversely, the transaction may also require you to assume all of those delivery obligations and costs from the point of shipping, even though you will not secure title to the good until it has been fully installed, configured, tested and accepted.

When structuring title- and risk-transfer arrangements, you should keep in mind the following: (i) if you will own goods that will remain in the possession of others, you may wish to register your ownership of that good publicly so that the public (possible third-party purchasers) will have deemed notice of your ownership; (ii) you may wish to require the person holding the goods you own to physically separate those goods from all other goods that may be in that person's possession; (iii) your goods should be clearly marked and labelled as your sole and exclusive property, with relevant contact information clearly marked in prominent view; and (iv) you should also have a right to inspect those goods and to take possession of them upon very short notice.

---

[52] The buyer assumes risk in the goods from the point where the seller puts the goods on the mode of transportation that will bring the goods to the buyer, and the buyer is responsible for the cost of the transportation and insurance from there on, unless those costs are otherwise allocated in the transaction agreement. See *George Smith Trucking Co. v Golden Seven Enterprises Inc.* (1989) 55 D.L.R. (4th) 161 at p.174.

[53] See G.H. Fridman, *Sale of Goods in Canada* (3rd ed., Carswell, Toronto, 1986), p.480. See also the International Chamber of Commerce standard trading terms known as "INCOTERMS" at *www.iccwbo.org/incoterms*.

[54] Unfortunately, many standard-form agreements still confuse and misuse these designations, *e.g.* by describing the transfer of title and risk as either "F.O.B. destination" or "C.I.F. place of origin/shipping dock".

Trade treaty compliance

3.5.7 Increasingly, international technology transactions are subject to international trade treaties and so-called "free trade" agreements among trading nations. Since such international trade treaties and agreements have important financial, packaging and labelling, environment standards, technology standards and tax implications, all project participants should agree to co-operate and reasonably assist each other to maximise preferential treatment under any such trade rules and requirements, and to take advantage of any beneficial programmes that may be associated with such treaties and agreements.

For example, in the EU, a new technology-transfer block exemption will affect many types of technology licence agreements.[54a] The new Regulation came into effect on May 1, 2004 and aims to prevent abuse by adopting an economic analysis of the market. The block exemption creates a "safe harbour" from Art.81 of the EC Treaty.[54b] Below certain market-share thresholds (20 per cent for parties which are competitors and 30 per cent for non-competitors), technology licensing agreements can benefit from the block exemption so long as the relevant listed hardcore restrictions are avoided.

The exemption applies to a variety of types of intellectual property right (patent, know-how, software copyright) and application depends upon a number of factors, including whether the agreement restricts available customers, the right to exploit the technology or the field of use of that technology.[54c]

Acceptance testing

3.6 Acceptance-testing protocols are among the most beneficial risk-management, and project-expediting, strategies that can apply to almost all technology transactions. Whether you are involved in acquiring hardware or software, integrating systems, outsourcing any form of business or technology operation, developing technology or involved in any other "deliverable" commercial arrangement, then you should consider whether or not you require the opportunity to inspect, verify and assess whether that "deliverable" satisfies the performance obligations and requirements agreed to. By tying your acceptance to financial milestones or to other remuneration holdback rights, and by ensuring that other aspects of the technology transaction are conditional upon your verification of compliance, acceptance-testing provisions can provide you with a tremendous degree of control over the operational and financial management of the project.

[54a] See Regulation 772/2004.

[54b] Art.81 prohibits certain agreement or other arrangements which distort competition.

[54c] Note that if an agreement is held to be outside of the block exemption and therefore subject to Art.81, it does not mean that it will necessarily fall foul of the EC Treaty.

Test protocol

3.6.1   There are several administrative details concerning the acceptance-testing procedures that you will have to determine. First, you should determine at what stage the acceptance testing occurs. You may wish to conduct preliminary acceptance testing upon the installation and configuration of the technology, or it may be reasonable to wait until the entire system, network or broader infrastructure is ready to assess and verify. Secondly, you should determine who should participate in those procedures. Most often, they are a collaborative endeavour, where the technology providers can provide tremendous assistance and guidance to ensure that any misunderstandings or inadvertent operational mistakes are quickly identified and resolved. Thirdly, you should determine where the acceptance testing should occur. Some providers of technology propose that acceptance testing occur at the provider's facilities, before the technology is shipped and delivered, while most technology acquirers insist that acceptance testing occur in the operational environment where the technology will be used and relied upon in the ordinary course of business. Lastly, you should determine over what period of time and through what operational cycles the acceptance test should occur. In practical terms, that tends to be a discussion about the scope of the acceptance test and how comprehensive it should be in relation to the technology's stipulated specifications and requirements.

Scope of test

3.6.2   Depending upon the technology to be assessed, it may be reasonable to limit the scope of acceptance testing to high-level operational functionality, or perhaps to running artificial operations to gain a general sense of functionality. On the other hand, it may be more reasonable, depending upon the circumstances of the project, to assess and verify the operability of the technology in the operational context that the technology will be used on a day-to-day basis. In any event, you should determine what your reasonable and legitimate interests are in such acceptance-testing procedures, and then ensure that the scope of those procedures reasonably and adequately reflects those legitimate interests. For example, if you wish to test accounting software that generates monthly reports, it may be reasonable to verify that operability after a one-month accounting cycle has been completed. In determining the scope of acceptance procedures, you should be sensitive to the legitimate concerns of technology providers that such acceptance-testing procedures, in nature and scope, are not "trial-use" periods, or constitute unreasonable delays in their remuneration. Acceptance-testing procedures should, in all respects, fairly and reasonably allow participants to verify that they have received the "deliverable" that the other participant is contractually obligated to provide. The scope of those tests will be a matter of balancing those interests and whatever is reasonable in the circumstances of the particular project.

Participant co-operation

3.6.3   As noted above, you should consider the extent to which you involve either the technology provider, or another participant to the technology transaction, in the acceptance-testing procedures. If that "deliverable" will be relied upon by the other participants, then you may benefit from their involvement, and the right to involve those third parties should be specifically stated in the technology agreement. You should also consider the extent to which the technology provider should be directly involved in the acceptance-testing process, keeping in mind that you do not want the acceptance-testing process to be unduly influenced by that involvement or participation. Therefore, you should identify the precise benefits that the technology provider, and other participants, can bring to the acceptance-testing process, and define the scope of their involvement specifically in those terms.

Independent third party

3.6.4   Where the participants determine that testing the technology should not be left to the determination or discretion of either participant, they may wish to stipulate that the acceptance testing be undertaken by an independent third party whom they mutually agree upon. For reasons related to the time and effort needed to settle that retainer and to the expense of that retainer, the involvement of independent third parties in those circumstances is usually reserved for extremely complicated or expensive technology transactions. However, the participants may also wish to consider involving independent third parties in their deliberations without delegating the entire acceptance-testing process or discretion to them. There are many ways that technology consultants and professional advisors can play a valuable, albeit limited, role in assisting participants to verify whether or not "deliverable" obligations have been performed.

Compliance threshold

3.6.5   As I discussed earlier in this book, the definition of the subject technology is the entire foundation for your acceptance-testing rights. All that acceptance testing can do is to verify the extent to which the technology complies with the stipulated and agreed operational, functional and technical specifications and requirements. Therefore, the threshold for technology compliance must be directly based upon those agreed specifications and requirements. In that regard, all acceptance criteria should be clearly described, and be objective and empirically verifiable against those definitional specifications and requirements. In recognition that the technology may require further work, correction or augmentation subsequent to its delivery, acceptance-testing thresholds are often, as a general matter of industry custom, limited to material or substantial compliance with the agreed upon specifications and requirements. However, there may be aspects of the technology's performance that may be so important to the project that they should not be subject to any such compliance qualification, and acceptance should reasonably be based upon absolute compliance with those specifically stated, and exceptionally important, performance specifications and requirements.

Interim Acceptance

3.6.6 In large projects it will often be necessary to "sign-off" upon various elements during the course of the implementation, especially if completion of various tasks is linked to payment milestones. Whilst this is normal in order for the project to progress, thought must be given to the effect that such a sign-off might have. A sign-off constitutes acceptance, even if only an interim acceptance and therefore is the point at which the right to reject the goods or services in question is lost. From the supplier's perspective, sign-off will mean that monies can be released which will help to finance the work at hand. From the customer's perspective it will be important to retain the right to fully test (and therefore accept or reject) the finished project. As such it is normal to draft into large scale agreements of this sort a "mother of all acceptance" provision which should provide the customer with the ability to end-to-end test the fully installed and running system. Secondly, the drafting should reserve the rights of the customer to later reject something that has been accepted at an earlier stage should it turn out that the entire system does not perform as expected. As such an interim acceptance or sign-off should be stated to be without prejudice to the customer's right to later reject.

Non-compliance determination

3.6.7 The two most important issues concerning testing technology for possible non-compliance are: (i) who decides whether or not such non-compliance has occurred; and (ii) what should your remedial rights be in that event? With regard to the former, as long as all acceptance-testing criteria objectively and empirically relate to agreed performance specifications and requirements, you should retain the right to decide if those performance obligations have been complied with, as long as your exercise of that determination[55] is reasonable. Disputes concerning such determination should be subject to the dispute escalation and resolution procedures of the agreement. With regard to the latter, the most frequent remedial rights include: (i) providing a detailed written report of non-compliance; (ii) requiring the technology provider to repair such non-conformity; (iii) securing the right to retest the technology on an expedited basis; (iv) the right to require replacement or substitute technology within

---

[55] The issue of whether or not the technology operates in compliance with its functional requirements is a "determination". Whether or not you choose to accept non-compliant technology is at your discretion.

a specified time frame, and at no additional cost; and (v) possibly the right to terminate the transaction if repeated attempts at acceptance testing have failed within a stipulated time frame. Those possible remedies are in addition to any stipulated rights to hold back remuneration until the technology is accepted, and you may also wish to require the payment of liquidated damages for any loss, expense or damage that may be caused to the project due to delays associated with the repeated failure of the technology to comply with its stipulated requirements.

Reasonable time periods

3.6.8 The time period stipulated at each stage of the acceptance-testing process must be fair and reasonable, and balance your need to have the necessary time to evaluate the technology, and the remuneration interests of the technology provider. Therefore, it will be extremely helpful to stipulate: (i) the time periods in which the acceptance-testing procedures will be completed; (ii) the time period in which you will report, in writing, either compliance or non-compliance; (iii) the time period in which the technology provider will either repair or substitute the non-compliant technology; (iv) the time period in which the subsequent acceptance-testing procedures will be completed; and (v) the time period in which you will have the right to exercise any other stipulated remedial options.

Repeated non-compliance implications

3.6.9 If the technology, or other deliverable, does not comply with agreed specifications, then you should have the express right not to accept it. In those situations, the technology provider will likely be in breach of their contractual obligations. In addition to how you have otherwise structured those risks and managed such liability in the agreement, you may wish to ensure that any disputes arising in connection with the acceptance-testing procedures is dovetailed with both the joint-management committee provisions and the dispute-resolution provisions of the agreement. You should also ensure that as many practical and commercial remedial options as possible are available to you, which may include: (i) re-defining the specifications and requirements of deliverable, with a corresponding price adjustment; (ii) accepting only the compliant portion of the deliverable, if possible and practical; (iii) accepting the non-compliant deliverable with a reasonable and proportionate price adjustment; (iv) entirely terminating your arrangements with the technology provider; (v) requiring the delivery of substitute or alternative technology solutions; and (vi) even re-evaluating the entire project.

In addition to those remedial options, you will want to ensure that the technology agreement does not contain any restrictive covenants that would interfere with your commercial options, and that would continue after the arrangements are terminated in those circumstances, such as prohibiting you from retaining the services or purchasing the technology of a competitor of the defaulting participant.

Restrictive covenants

3.7   The business case for a technology transaction will often depend upon the competitive advantage that will be gained. Therefore, technology agreements may contain provisions that preserve that competitive advantage by restricting others from engaging in any conduct that either diminishes that advantage, or that is otherwise competitive with or damaging to the commercial interests of the participants in the project. Such restrictive covenants are scrutinised by courts to ensure that they are not illegal or otherwise offend public policy by unfairly restraining trade or the freedom of individuals. Case law regarding restrictive covenants and restraint of trade generally has developed as public policy has changed. It is fair to say that although broad principles can be gleaned from previous cases, each new situation will turn on its own facts. If a clause or a contract falls foul of judicial scrutiny it will be rendered void.[55a]

Generally, an agreement's restrictive covenants will be enforceable where they (according to Canadian case law, but equally relevant in the United Kingdom): (i) do not extend beyond the scope of protection that is reasonably needed to protect the legitimate interests of the protected participant[56]; (ii) the impact of the restriction on the affected participant is not unfairly onerous or arbitrary[57]; and (iii) do not otherwise offend public policy[58] or any other laws, such as competition law.

[55a] See *e.g. Esso Petroleum Co Ltd v Harper's Garage (Stourport) Ltd* (1968) A.C. 269 which laid down the judicial approach to issues of restraint; firstly to assess whether the contract was so adverse to public policy that it should be rendered void, and secondly, if not *prima facie* void, whether the individual term in question can be seen as being in some way reasonable, so as to allow the contract to stand. See also, *Faccenda Chicken Ltd v Fowler* (1987) Ch. 117 which has assessed restraint of trade provisions in the employment context.

[56] See *Cameron v Canadian Factors Corp.* [1971] S.C.R. 148; *Hecke v Cie de gestion Maskoutaine* [1972] S.C.R. 22; *Maguire v Northland Drug Co.* [1935] S.C.R. 412; *Baker v Lintott* [1981] 2 W.W.R. 385; *Ernst & Young v Stuart* (1994) 92 B.C.L.R. (2d) 335, CA; *Lyons v Multari* (2000) 50 O.R. (3d) 526 p.533, Ont. CA; *Tank Lining Corporation v Dunlop Industrial Ltd.* (1982) 140 D.L.R. (2d) 659, Ont. CA re process secrets and "know-how".

[57] For example, the covenant must not deprive the person or enterprise of a livelihood or carry on business. The restraint cannot entirely deprive a person or enterprise of all benefit of general experience and expertise outside the area of protected interests. See *Cameron v Canadian Factors Corp.*, above, n.1; *Matheson v Kelly* (1913) 15 D.L.R. 359 at pp.370–371; *Gibbons v Drew Chemical Ltd.* (1972) 8 C.P.R. (2d) 105, BCSC concerning continuing use of knowledge assets.

[58] Some cases suggest that competitive restrictions that go beyond the protected participant's proprietary interest in knowledge assets or confidential information may not be enforceable. See *Drake International Ltd. v Miller* (1975) 9 O.R. (2d) 652, HC; *Cradle Pictures (Canada) Ltd. v Penner* (1977) 3 C.P.R. (2d) 34, Ont. HC; *Arvak Management Inc. v McKee* (1983) 40 Nfld. P.E.I.R. 116; *Colonial Broadcasting System Ltd. v Russell* (1964) 48 D.L.R. (2d) 242; G.H.L. Fridman, *The Law of Contract in Canada* (4th ed., Carswell, Toronto, 1999) states (p.414) that the courts "dislike . . . covenants which are simply designed to prevent competition, that is, which are purely and simply monopolistic in character".

However, as long as those attributes are adhered to, the courts will generally uphold contracts that are "freely entered into without fraud, duress, etc.".[59]

Therefore, the way to structure restrictive covenants to reflect and protect your reasonable commercial interests is to assess the nature of your organisation's interests, and then describe those interests in objective and empirically verifiable terms. For example, rather than merely restricting a participant from selling financial software, you should more narrowly and rationally stipulate that the participant shall not sell financial software that: (i) relies on a particular operating system; (ii) is commercially more recent than two years old; (iii) has been approved by a particular standards association; (iv) is not sold in conjunction with a specific brand of hardware; and (v) has any other narrowly differentiating characteristic or quality that adequately and reasonably provides you with the commercial protection that you require.

Exclusivity

3.7.1 Perhaps the most frequently relied-upon restrictive covenants in a technology agreement are the provisions that require exclusive participation in, and full-time devotion to, the transaction. Those provisions are usually drafted in positive terms that require performance obligations to be performed exclusively for the transaction. However, such positive covenants of exclusivity may also be supported by corresponding covenants that, for greater certainty, stipulate what activities the participant will not, otherwise, be engaged in. For example, if a participant is required to develop exclusively a particular type of software for the project, you may also wish to confirm that participant's exclusive engagement by also stipulating that: they shall devote their services to the project on a "full-time" basis, and not engage in any other software-development project until the present services are completed; and/or, they shall not create, design or develop (whether directly or indirectly) such software for any other person during a stipulated time period. Also, if you are securing rights to technology, you should also consider securing the exclusive rights to the technology to ensure that the grantor of those exclusive rights does not use the technology to compete against you. A sole licence will mean that both you and the licensor may use the technology; an exclusive licence will mean that only you can use it, to the exclusion of the licensor himself. (As an aside, whilst you will often seen licences drafted using the phrase "sole and exclusive rights", the concept of a "sole and exclusive" right is not possible under English law.)

You should also consider whether or not those provisions: (i) should be stipulated as a material and fundamental term of the technology agreement; (ii) should stipulate any particular remedies for breach of such exclusivity; (iii) acknowledge and confirm the commercial and financial implications that will result from a breach; and (iv) are clearly and unambiguously drafted to ensure that they reflect the commercial intentions of the participants. Unfortunately, exclusivity rights are very

---

[59] Above, n.3, G.H.L. Fridman, *op. cit.* on the topic of enforceability of restraint of trade covenants at p.414.

often agreed to without the participants fully understanding their legal and commercial implications.

Transaction-specific

3.7.2   You should consider whether or not the restrictive covenant should be narrowly defined to apply only to the specific transaction or project that is being engaged in. Such restrictive covenants would, subject to further qualifications on the scope of the restriction, restrain participants from engaging in similar activities, transactions or projects. You should carefully define those activities so that the scope of the restriction will be clear, and to ensure that the parameters of those restrictions do not extend beyond the reasonable interests of the participants. Generally, restrictive covenants that are transaction-specific may be more enforceable because they are so directly and clearly connected to the commercial interests of the participants.

Activity restrictions

3.7.3   One way to protect your commercial interests is by restraining a participant from engaging in only selected activities that are particularly relevant to either your business or the transaction. Such activity-specific restrictions can take as many forms as there are ways for you to define your market and commercial interests. For example, instead of restricting a participant from a general activity within a stipulated time or territory, you may wish to narrow the activities that the restrictive covenant will apply to. The more you limit the application of restrictive covenants to narrowly defined and specific activities, the more you may claim to have limited those restraints to protecting your commercial interests, and the more enforceable the restrictive covenant will be. Rather than defaulting to broadly drafted restrictive covenants that are designed to catch a range of competitive activities, the enforceability of the restraint may depend upon exerting the extra effort to rationally limit the scope of that restraint to the specific activities that would actually interfere with or harm your commercial interests.

Scope of covenant

3.7.4   Regardless of the nature of the restrictive covenant, you must ensure that the scope and effect of its restrictions are fair, and that they reasonably protect the legitimate interests of the protected participants. The scope and effect of a restricted covenant can be qualified in many ways, including: (i) by the length of time that the restrictive covenant will last; (ii) by the jurisdiction or territory in which the restrictive covenant will apply; (iii) to specifically identified uses or purposes; (iv) by the particular industries, markets or other categories of possible beneficiaries of the good or service that the restraint will apply to; and (v) by any other quality or characteristic that would narrow the application of the restrictive covenant in a manner, or to an extent, that reasonably protects the legitimate interests of the protected participant. For example, rather than restraining a technology developer from engaging in any software-development activities that are, in any way, similar to those required by the project, you should consider limiting that restrictive covenant to apply: (i) only for a reasonable period of time, perhaps two years in the circumstances of the transaction; (ii) only in the United Kingdom, which is the only jurisdiction in which you carry on business; (iii) only to the insurance industry, which is 90 per cent of your market; (iv) only for applications to insurance data-management systems, which is the only type of software that you have developed; and (v) only in combination with three of your specifically identified competitors, because those are the only operating systems that your software is compatible with.

Personnel non-solicitation

3.7.5 An extremely common restrictive covenant in any technology transaction restrains participants from soliciting, or otherwise hiring or retaining, the officers or employees of other participants. You should consider the following issues when drafting those restrictive covenants: (i) whether or not the restriction is broadly drafted to prevent any form of direct or indirect solicitation activity, including advertisements or third-party search agencies; (ii) broadly draft the definition of employment services to include direct employment, consulting, independent contractor services through a personnel service or agency corporation, partnership or otherwise; (iii) whether or not the restrictive covenant is restricted to solicitation, or whether the parties should be free to retain or employ persons who independently request employment; (iv) the duration of the restrictive covenant, especially whether or not it should extend beyond the term of the technology agreement; (v) whether or not it should apply only to certain personnel whose "defection" would have a particularly detrimental commercial impact on the participant employer; (vi) whether or not a participant can be financially compensated for lost personnel, perhaps as a liquidated damage provision rather than as an outright prohibition; (vii) how such a restrictive covenant will be practically enforced, including injunctive relief or reasonable financial compensation; and (viii) whether or not the allowance for such activities should be subject to the consent of the other participants, which may or may not be unreasonably withheld.[60] Lastly, you should carefully consider the personal and professional impact that such covenants will have on the affected personnel, and ensure that any such restrictive covenants are in the best interests of the participants and the project. In that regard, the progress of the transaction and the success of the project may suffer if employee morale is detrimentally affected by such restrictive covenants.

---

[60] You should also secure the advice of specialist employment or labour counsel to consider the enforceability and viability of any such restrictive covenants.

No subcontractors

3.7.6 As previously noted in **3.3**, it is extremely common to restrain the participants from retaining the services of, or from performing their transaction obligations through, independent contractors, subcontractors and affiliated persons without a series of conditions being satisfied. Although such provisions may be generally regarded as restraints on the ability of participants to carry on business, those restrictions are specifically related to the transaction and are specifically designed to protect your legal and commercial interests in retaining the unique and special services of the participants.

No third-party benefit

3.7.7 An increasingly prevalent restrictive covenant in technology transactions restrains participants from using the project's technology, or otherwise relying upon the transaction, for the benefit of persons who are not engaged in the project. Those restrictive covenants generally prohibit participants from allowing any other persons to secure those benefits: (i) through any Application Server Provider arrangements; (ii) through any outsourcing or facilities management arrangements; (iii) by using any of the transaction's facilities in a Service Bureau arrangement; (iv) by prohibiting the participants from misappropriating or otherwise commercially exploiting the benefits of the project for their own purposes and commercial interests; and (v) by stipulating that the technology and services provided shall be used solely by the participants for their internal and personal purposes and benefit.

No-restriction clarification

3.7.8 In order to better clarify the scope and application of restrictive covenants in the technology agreement, you should consider including provisions that clarify your ability to engage in activities that may otherwise be prohibited by such restrictive covenants. First, that may be accomplished by stipulating exceptions to those restrictive covenants such as, "shall not provide those services to any bank in The United Kingdom, except to XYZ Bank". Secondly, that may be accomplished by stating the rights, activities or commercial arrangements that shall not be, in any manner or to any extent, limited, prohibited, restricted or otherwise interfered with by any provisions of the technology agreement whatsoever. Such "For greater certainty" provisions can clarify the scope of the restrictive covenant by clearly stating what important commercial activities, among others, are outside the scope of those restrictions and restraints. Considering that exclusivity provisions, restrictive covenants, confidentiality restrictions and other obligations related to the participants' devoted care and attention to the project may combine to restrain participants in ways that they may not intend, such clarification provisions can do much to avoid subsequent misunderstandings and disputes concerning those fundamental transaction issues.

Export restrictions

3.7.9 Most technology agreements restrict the ability of participants to export any technology, or related information, for any (or all) of the following reasons: (i) a participant may be subject to third-party export restrictions concerning the technology that must be contractually flowed down to all of the other project participants; (ii) to appoint exclusive technology importers in foreign jurisdictions, which such export from the United Kingdom or EU may interfere with; (iii) otherwise to control the jurisdictional integrity of the participant's markets, *e.g.* to avoid "grey market" or "parallel importation" of technology into unauthorised international markets; or (iv) to ensure that the participants comply with applicable export control restrictions that regulate the proliferation of technology that may be used for military purposes. With regard to the latter, technology agreements may require UK participants to comply with non-UK export-control laws and regulations, irrespective of what jurisdiction's law will govern the technology agreement. However, all parties to such technology agreements should carefully consider the enforceability of such foreign-export control provisions in the context of UK law.[60a] This is part of the "new era" (as it has been dubbed) of export controls in the United Kingdom led by the Export Control Act 2002, which came into force on May 1, 2004, and which has established a new legislative framework for the control of strategic goods and technology.[61]

[60a] See *e.g.* UK Trade in Goods (Control) Order (2003) (SI 2003/2765) (TGCO) which relates to military and certain paramilitary goods.

[61] For a Canadian parallel, the Foreign Extraterritorial Measures Act R.S.C. 1985, c.F-29, which, in certain circumstances, limits the ability of Canadian participants to follow certain directives of foreign entities concerning a Canadian participant's international trade activities. Considering that foreign participants may be legally compelled in their own jurisdictions to comply with the extraterritorial effect of their domestic export control laws and regulations, there may be a risk of being caught between a foreign export control rock and a domestic export freedom hard place—unless, that is, the foreign participant wishes to side-step the entire issue by simply avoiding any obligation on the Canadian participant to comply with foreign export control laws and regulations, and either: (i) require the Canadian participant to comply only with Canadian export control laws and regulations; or (ii) prohibit any export of the technology from Canada whatsoever without the prior written consent of the foreign participant. There are many commercially reasonable reasons why a foreign participant may wish to control the export of its technology from Canada that have nothing to do with complying with foreign export control laws and regulations—including those already mentioned in this section.

Human resources

3.8 As discussed earlier in this book, issues pertaining to human resources and knowledge-based skills are essential to almost any technology transaction. Whether you are building your transaction team or you have specific human-resource requirements of other participants, you can promote the success of the proposed transaction by carefully considering what human-resources and personnel obligations should be contributed to the project.

Key individuals

3.8.1 In situations where participants have promoted themselves as having particular expertise and experience, you should consider having the individuals who actually possess that expertise and experience perform the participant's obligations. Such "key person" provisions routinely stipulate that identified individuals will provide or perform the services stipulated in the agreement, and that they will devote a specified percentage of their time to the transaction. Such provisions can be very useful in a competitive bid situation where the "A team" has pitched for and won the contract, only to be replaced by the "B team" when it comes to implementation. Tying in key persons by naming them in a schedule and requiring them to remain involved in the project can overcome this problem.

Those obligations are often subject to a series of limitations, including non-solicitation restrictive covenants, and time limitations concerning the duration of their assignment. Often, the key person's responsibilities are described in terms of a job description or mandate which is usually included as a schedule to the agreement. Usual exceptions include: (i) periods of absence due to health-related matters; (ii) the right of the employer to terminate that key person for cause (or related employment suspension); and (iii) that person's resignation from their employment. In order to address those situations, replacement covenants often stipulate the specific nature of expertise and experience that is required to perform the services and that such key persons must be replaced by a reasonably competent and qualified person who is mutually acceptable. As such, an express right to interview the potential replacement will be critical.

Team composition

3.8.2 In addition to key-person provisions, the technology agreement may specify the precise nature of the expertise, experience, qualifications and skills that are required of the individuals who will be assigned to perform the participant's obligations. Rather than naming the specific individuals who will perform those services, team-composition provisions merely stipulate the qualities that will be required of the individual members of the team. Therefore, any substitution or replacement of

team members would be subject to compliance with the team's skills-set requirements. Such qualities and attributes may also be generic rather than personal, such
as requiring the team to include at least two people who have worked on two similar
project assignments. Again, if the participant has promoted itself based upon promised experience in previous assignments, you should ensure that such experience is
directly contributed to the project. You should consider whether or not any participants should have the right to require personnel replacements in the event of any
dissatisfaction with the performance, behaviour or attitude of the personnel who
have been assigned to perform the agreement. Usually, any such rights are restricted
to verifiable circumstances of such personnel's breach of specific behaviour obligations, as opposed to the mere subjective discretion of a "dissatisfied" participant.

Turnover controls

3.8.3 In situations where you have not designated key persons or other team
requirements, you should consider limiting the extent to which personnel can be
assigned to and removed from the project. Obviously, personnel gain important
project knowledge and experience over time, and it may be in the interest of the
overall transaction to reduce personnel turnover as much as possible. Therefore, you
should consider: limiting the ability of participants to remove their personnel from
the project; having the right to refer any important personnel changes to the Joint
Management Committee for consideration; making only important personnel
changes, subject to prior notice to the other participants; perhaps making any such
changes subject to the prior written consent of the other participants; and designating a specific percentage of original personnel, or skills-set threshold, that must
always be assigned to the project. Many human-resource executives and transaction
managers also believe that employee assistance programmes (EAPs), which allow
employees to address mental-health problems, financial difficulties, family disputes
and job-related stress confidentially, directly reduce employee attrition and absen-
teeism—which would benefit technology transactions greatly.

Qualifications

3.8.4 Covenants that require specific personnel qualifications can be as specific, as
there are relevant skills across all professional, business and technology industries.
However, you should reasonably assess and identify any particular professional designations, education, trade qualifications, qualities, attributes, training, expertise or
experience that you feel are required for your project's success. If you are too aggressive in those requirements, and overstate what skills are reasonably required for the
project, you may have difficulty staffing the project and retaining personnel. On the
other hand, as long as you can reasonably justify and rationally connect specific
skills sets and personnel qualities to the participant's performance obligations, you
stand a much better chance of finding suitable candidates that will remain with the
project throughout the term. The technology agreement should also stipulate that:

(i) all personnel will not be younger than the minimum employment age in the jurisdiction where the work will be performed, or in any other jurisdiction that may have extraterritorial application concerning such matters; and (ii) all personnel shall otherwise have the right to provide their services with full compliance with laws, regulations and third-party obligations (including immigration authorisation and any contractual restrictive covenants that may exist).

Security clearance

3.8.5 Technology transactions increasingly require participant personnel, especially key individuals, to have some level of security clearance, whether they have been investigated by police or other governmental agencies. The security of IT and telecommunication infrastructure is essential for business operations, and it is also essential for you to ensure that all of the persons assigned to the project will adhere to your security arrangements. Therefore, you should consider conducting a security investigation ("due diligence") on the individuals who are the most important to the success of the project, including their work history and related references and whether or not they have a criminal record, by retaining the services of a private-investigation service, or by simply asking participants what steps they have taken to ensure the trustworthiness of their personnel.

Recent high-profile lapses in security clearance in the United Kingdom, particularly in relation to those having contact with children, has highlighted the need for comprehensive vetting procedures. In the United Kingdom, the Government has set up the Criminal Records Bureau (CRB), launched in April 2002 and intended to regulate the disclosure of information about an individual's criminal record.[61a]

Confidentiality and intellectual property

3.8.6 As previously discussed, you should determine which project personnel should be subject to both: (i) confidentiality obligations; and (ii) obligations to transfer any intellectual property that they may create—especially independent contractors who will otherwise own the intellectual property that they create, and employees who create intellectual property outside of the ordinary course of their employment.[61b]

You should require all such personnel to execute and deliver the agreements. The following issues may also arise in connection with personnel-confidentiality arrangements: you may make the execution of such personnel agreements a condition of their participation in the project, and refuse to assign any personnel to the transaction who do not agree with the required confidentiality and intellectual property ownership arrangements; in order to ensure that those agreements are

---

[61a] See also Guidance on Pt I of the Information Commissioner's Code of Practice on Employment Data: Recruitment and Employee Selection and Pt V of the Police Act 1997.
[61b] See CDPA 1988, s.11(2).

enforceable, it may be prudent to pay those individuals (as legal consideration) a nominal sum for entering into such arrangements.

Rules of conduct

3.8.7 As all of the participants come together for the purposes of the project, you should ensure that they will strictly comply with all of your organisation's: workplace, health and safety rules; anti-sexual-harassment policies; and all of the relevant administrative and security arrangements concerning your premises. Remember to provide a copy of all of those administrative procedures and policies to all of the participants, and to clearly acknowledge their receipt of those policies in the agreement.

Financial arrangements

3.9 Financial issues are so important to every transaction that you should consider retaining the services of a broad range of consultants and advisors who have varying degrees of expertise in such matters. From business consultants to accountants, and from tax planners to market-research analysts, there is a wide range of financial experience and expertise to assist you. As a general financial matter, stipulate whether or not the financial practices and accounting terms used will be in accordance with a designated jurisdiction's generally accepted accounting principles that are approved and promulgated from time to time by the governing institute.[62]

Price discrimination

3.9.1 One of the most frequently occurring, and misunderstood, limitations on pricing in technology transactions are those in the price-discrimination provisions of the Enterprise Act 2002. The Act introduces criminal penalties for individuals (directors and employees) who engage in cartels, such as horizontal price fixing, market sharing or bid-rigging. The Act sits alongside the new investigatory powers of the Office of Fair Trading (OFT). The new offences will operate alongside the existing regime of civil sanctions under the Competition Act 1998. Conviction could result in up to five years' imprisonment and/or an unlimited fine. However, the OFT may grant total immunity from prosecution or a substantial reduction in fines, to whistleblowers who inform the OFT of a cartel and co-operate with the OFT in an investigation. Therefore, you should ensure that the pricing and other financial arrangements among the participants will not contravene those restrictions.

---

[62] At the European level, listed companies have to comply by January 1, 2005 with the new EC Regulation on the application of international accounting standards (EC/1606/2002) (the IAS Regulation), which came into force on September 12, 2002.

Pricing and fees

3.9.2 The remuneration provisions of the agreement must be drafted clearly and concisely. Usually, technology agreements stipulate general pricing requirements which then tend to be qualified by a broad range of exclusions and exceptions, such as: rebates; volume discounts; price escalation; bonuses; set-off for liquidated or other damages; and price adjustments that may be triggered by many possible circumstances that are stipulated in the agreement, such as service credits for unavailability. Pricing may be stated as a formula, such as a royalty rate, or as usually stipulated in "time and material" contracts that state pricing as hourly rates or other way to calculate remuneration. Pricing may also be stated as fixed and certain remuneration, such as "deliverable" transactions where a good or service is delivered for a one-time fixed price or license fee. If the pricing provisions are particularly complicated, then you should consider placing those provisions in a schedule to the transaction agreement. You should also consider whether or not the remuneration will be paid directly to the participant, or to any other third party who will collect and remit that remuneration to the participant. If that is the case, the transaction agreement should include a clear direction to pay those funds to the third party, with a corresponding exclusion of liability provisions concerning those funds after you have performed your payment obligations. You should also be cognisant of "bundled" fees where the remuneration of many aspects of the project are consolidated into an omnibus pricing arrangement—where expected component discounting and undesired component price padding may be very difficult to determine—especially where the technology transaction involves pricing for: (i) consulting fees; (ii) technology-development fees; (iii) hardware purchases; (iv) software licenses; (v) training fees—technical and user; (vi) installation fees; (vii) maintenance service fees; (viii) back-up and disaster recovery, including data-warehousing fees; and (ix) support fees for future enhancements, releases and versions of the technology.

Price escalation

3.9.3 If the technology transaction will be performed over a significant period of time, the participants may request the pricing during that term to protect it from general economic inflation, and to insulate it from the inflation of the commodities and services that they require to perform their obligations. Price-escalation rights are usually expressed as an arithmetic equation in which all of the dependent variables are cited and reproduced. For example, the following is a price-escalation formula where the escalation of price is tied to the Retail Price Index (RPI) (published by the Office of National Statistics).[62a]

Participant A and participant B agree to purchase communications equipment once a year for the next four years. If A sells B the first instalment of the

---

[62a] See *www.statistics.gov.uk*.

communications equipment on October 31, 2002 for £1,000.00, the subsequent price to be ascertained is for October 31, 2004. If the price increase for the communications equipment is to increase with the RPI, then consider the following formula:

Adjusted price	$=$	Base price	$\times$	$\dfrac{\text{Index at payment date}}{\text{Index at Base Date}}$
A	$=$	BP	$\times$	$\dfrac{Ip}{Ic}$
A	$=$	£1,000	$\times$	$\dfrac{\text{Index October 31, 2002}}{\text{Index October 31, 2004}}$
A	$=$	£1,000	$\times$	$\dfrac{160,}{130}$
A	$=$	£1,000	$\times$	1.22
A	$=$	£1,220		

If the interests of the participants require escalating the pricing based on inflationary markers, then you should ensure that you rely upon the most appropriate index, preferably an index that is published by, or otherwise available from, an independent source for that inflationary information.[63] For example, there are a broad range of indices concerning the electronics, telecommunications and IT industries that might, depending upon the nature of the particular transaction, have a particular relevance. On the other hand, you can also structure price-escalation provisions to take account of inflationary increases in the services and materials that one participant must rely upon in order to perform their obligations under the transaction agreement. Although the participants may not agree to absorb all of those price increases, the price-escalation formula may be designed to account for only a percentage of those price increases.

Note that suppliers will have a different view of the most appropriate index and will often prefer to link to an index which carries with it concepts of changes in the salaries of IT professionals, particularly where payments in a long-term contract relate to the performance of IT services. As such, you may see reference to CEL, the index promulgated by Computer Economics Limited—an independent specialist salary survey publishing company. The CEL index is based on information supplied by the industry itself relating to IT staff salaries within companies. In the run up to the year 2000, we witnessed a doubling and trebling of certain IT salaries and, as such, suppliers were keen to use such an index at that time.[63a]

---

[63] In addition to government sources for statistics, participants should consider relying on independent, private-sector sources for this information, such as an academic institution, an economics research institute or even a bank.

[63a] See *www.celre.co.uk/salaries.asp*, and also the Computer Economics Index, Average Earnings Index and the Consumer Price Index.

Whenever the issue of price escalation is raised, you can expect the issue of price reduction (or "de-escalation") to also be raised. In that regard, economies go through periods of deflation, especially with respect to particular materials and components. During those periods, participants reasonably may expect to receive the benefits of cost reductions. This issue is particularly important to technology transactions. Whether you track the price of high end severs, bandwidth, laptop computers or digital cameras, an argument can be made for accommodating the medium- to long-term trends of price de-escalation while functionality and capabilities of technology increase. Such de-escalation formulae are somewhat complicated, and they may not be applicable to many of the technology transactions that you may be engaged in. They are, however, likely to feature in large or public-sector contracts where a service provider will be obliged to pass on to the customer the benefits of savings achieved through increased efficiency and new technology installation.

Penalty/price rebates

3.9.4 There is some truth to the expression that one person's damages remedy is another person's price rebate. However, in addition to whatever other remedial provisions are included in the technology agreement, financial compensation provisions should be drafted carefully to ensure both their clarity and enforceability. Any provisions that require financial compensation, such as adjust pricing, provide for payment refunds, price rebates or otherwise, should avoid being drafted as "penalties" which will generally not be enforced by a court. Such remedial provisions should be drafted as fair and reasonable compensation and as a genuine pre-estimate of the losses that might be suffered. Since financial-compensation provisions are designed to compensate participants for minor breaches of the technology agreement, and to also motivate the participants to properly perform their obligations, such liquidated damage provisions are often included in the transaction's pricing provisions. See **4.7.5** and **4.7.6** for continued discussion on the topic of liquidated damages as financial compensation.

Bonuses/price premiums

3.9.5 As with price escalation and de-escalation, any discussion of pricing adjustments or rebates (even liquidated damages) will most likely raise the issue of performance remuneration awards and bonuses. However, since the remunerative provisions have already been tied to specific performance obligations, performance rewards and bonuses are usually tied to very specific performance events that exceed what the contract otherwise requires. In situations where there are particular service levels, or standards of performance where you would particularly benefit from exceeded performance expectations, you may wish to consider performance rewards and bonuses as additional motivation towards project success. Since service levels or other performance obligations are often expressed in terms of a range of performance specifications, where the failure to perform the minimum requirement in that range may precipitate financial compensation, the performance (or perhaps, consistent performance) of the top of that range of performance specifications may precipitate financial rewards that exceed the remuneration otherwise agreed to. Equally, a bonus will not be relevant where the customer receives no benefit or utility arising from the supplier exceeding the service level in question. In such situations, the concept of a bonus should be resisted. The participants may wish to stipulate the criteria that will either entitle (or proscribe) the ability to charge price premiums or value-added bonuses. Often, technology agreements simply prohibit participants from charging any such premiums without the prior written consent of the customer.

Payment terms

3.9.6 There are a broad range of administrative requirements concerning the payment of remuneration that should be clearly stipulated in the technology agreement. Those provisions will likely include: (i) whether or not any disputed payments should be paid to either the payee or to a third party who will hold that disputed payment in trust pending the resolution of the dispute (and to which participant's account interest on such held funds should accrue); (ii) how monies owed will be invoiced and how frequently; (iii) what information invoices should include, such as past and current amounts owing, unbilled pass-through expenses, rebated or credited amounts, price adjustments, volume discounts, set-off amounts, all applicable taxes and tax credit information; (iii) how the payments should be made, and in what form; (iv) what the interest rate is and whether or not interest will accrue on a net 30-day basis, or otherwise; (v) to whom payments should be made, whether directly, or to a third party under a direction to pay; and (vi) any other unusual terms that should apply to a particular transaction. Your payment obligations may also be subject to a myriad of other arrangements in the technology agreement, including: (i) payment milestones; (ii) right of set-off; (iii) interest payments; and (iv) any remedial/bonus obligations.

Participants may designate certain costs or expenses that the provider of the good or service will be reimbursed for. However, those payment and reimbursement obligations are usually qualified as follows: (i) the ability of the provider to incur reimbursable expenses may be subject to the participant's prior written approval; (ii) the types of recoupable costs may be specifically identified; (iii) recoupment is conditional on the extent to which the expenditure was necessary and required for the project, or otherwise provided for in the Strategic (or Work) Plan; (iv) the provider has agreed to use its reasonable efforts to minimise any such costs or expenses, including by relying upon the provider's wholesale, volume discount or other commercial relationships to do so; (v) all such costs and expenses are substantiated with reliable proof, and are subject to audit and verification; and (vi) such costs or reimbursed expenses shall be subject to any mark-up or administration fee that is payable to the provider.

Note that it is important, in terms of controlling costs and avoiding invoice "surprises" to establish clearly in the contract that incurring fees must be authorised, in advance, in writing by the party who will ultimately have to pay. As such it is good practice to insert a clause which states that the service provider will not be entitled to re-imbursement for costs incurred where such pre-authorisation has not been sought.

Payment milestones

3.9.7 A frequently relied-upon and prudent financial-management and risk-management strategy is the stipulation that remunerative payments will be spread out across, and made confidential upon, specifically designated performance events or milestones. Typically, those milestones may include the following events: (i) the technology agreement's execution and delivery; (ii) the product has been inspected and is ready to ship; (iii) the product has been shipped; (iv) the product has been delivered; (v) the services have commenced; (vi) the product has been installed; (vii) the product has been configured or adapted to a particular operational environment; (viii) the product has been tested and has been accepted; (ix) the product has achieved a specified level or attribute of functionality; (x) the first written service/progress report has been issued; (xi) the service has achieved or accomplished the "deliverable"—or any of the stipulated developmental stages of the "deliverable"; (xii) completion of an independent third party's review and assessment (audit) of material or substantial service/performance compliance; (xiii) the product's warranty has expired; or (xiv) a specific time period for the product assessment and functionality verification has been completed. The percentage of the overall price or fees that should be paid upon any stipulated milestone events will vary among technology transactions, and will greatly depend upon the importance of those events for the participants.

Payment milestones may also be stipulated as participant incentives to encourage complete and timely performance, and other payment milestones may be simply based on the passing of time, rather than on any particular event. Such payment arrangements are generally referred to as "retentions" and are generally intended to provide assurance of adequate performance over a designated period of time. In a "retention" of remuneration scenario, the participant is required to either claim that there has been a performance default by a specified date, or pay the amount being retained. Unfortunately, some performance deficiencies or failures require more time than others to be discovered.

Although all participants are concerned with cash flow, and the time value of money, participants with particular concerns about quarterly and annual revenue targets may especially resist payment-milestone structures. Such arrangements should take into account the following issues: (i) whether or not the participant requires cash-flow thresholds to perform their obligations; (ii) are the designated milestones, and allocated percentages for payment, reasonable and fair in the circumstances of the transaction? (iii) are the payment milestones defined in objective, and based upon empirically verifiable, criteria, rather than the subjective discretion of a participant? (iv) is it clear that disputes concerning such payment conditions and obligations can be promptly resolved through the technology agreement's dispute escalation and ADR provisions? (v) have you been provided with other pricing and financial benefits that would render certain payment milestones onerous upon the participants? and (vi) are there other remedial options and incentives that are more appropriate to manage and motivate participants to perform their obligations?

Currency

3.9.8 Although the technology agreement should define the governing currency of the transaction, the selection of the governing currency is a matter of which party should assume currency exchange risks. You should also ensure that there are no governing laws in the transaction's jurisdiction that require compensation to be paid in any particular currency, and whether or not there are any currency exchange control laws that would restrict your ability to export or repatriate those funds. If currencies will be exchanged in your transaction, you should also consider how those currencies will be cleared, in what time periods, and by what financial intermediaries. All of the participants should agree to that process, and ensure that they trust all of the financial institutions that will be involved in that process.

Tax

3.9.9 Tax issues have become so specialised and complex that you should retain the specialised advice of tax practitioners. Both as an essential aspect of your financial planning and as an important risk management strategy, you will need to ensure that the technology transaction is structured in the most tax-efficient and unambiguous manner possible.

Transaction structure

3.9.9.1 There are many aspects of the structure of a transaction that will be relevant to its tax treatment and which should be considered from a tax persepctive up front. These include: (i) whether or not the transaction involves affiliated or non-arms'-length parties; (ii) the extent to which the pricing of goods or services accurately and currently reflects their fair market value and reasonable market norms; (iii) ensuring that all the participants have completely and accurately disclosed all information that may be relevant to the project's tax consequences; (iv) whether multiple jurisdictions will be involved in the transaction and, if so, each participant's relationship to those jurisdictions (and whether or not each participant is UK tax resident or has a taxable branch or other presence in the United Kingdom); (v) the legal nature of each participant, whether sole trader, partnership, corporation, charity, pension fund or other tax-exempt entity, trust or otherwise; (vi) ensuring that the technology agreement truly, completely and accurately depicts the nature and scope of the technology transaction and its related financial arrangements; and (vii) whether any tax clearances may be required. In most circumstances, there is tremendous flexibility in how technology transactions can be commercially and legally structured, so you should ensure that you take full advantage of those opportunities in order to comply prudently and efficiently with all your tax obligations.

Other direct tax issues

3.9.9.2 In addition to the more global issues listed above, further corporation, income and capital gains tax considerations may include: (i) whether receipts and payments under a contract will be income or capital in nature and the possibility of deduction or set-off; (ii) whether there may be any withholding taxes, for example on royalties/licence fees; (iii) whether any targeted tax reliefs may be available, for example amortisation for certain plant, including computer hardware and software and intellectual property; and (iv) in the case of e-commerce, the place where the participants will be taxed on their profits.

VAT

3.9.9.3 *General*—A crucial point will clearly be where the supply will be taxable for VAT purposes. This may depend on whether the supply is seen as one of goods or services (or a combination of the two) and on the nature of any services. For example most services are treated as supplied where the supplier belongs, but some, including intellectual property and electronically delivered services, are treated within the EU as supplied where received. Not all services are taxable and some services associated with a technology transaction, for example financial or insurance services, may be exempt. Where different goods and/or services are provided that will have different tax treatments, the invoice should identify all remunerative obligations as separate items. Another factor will be whether or not the participants are VAT registered. This may also impact on whether the VAT on the transaction will ultimately be recoverable. The other important issue which could affect recoverability is whether any participants are VAT exempt or partially exempt.

Inclusive/exclusive price—The tax provisions of the agreement should also state whether the pricing provisions are inclusive or exclusive of taxes. This can be a particluar a problem in multiple-jurisdiction transactions, where the norm of one jurisdiction may be to quote the price inclusive of all taxes while in another jurisdiction, the practice is to quote exclusive prices. If the practice is not explicitly stated, it may lead to confusion among the participants and the possibility of one party's being out-of-pocket.

Tax audit

3.9.9.4 In anticipation that the transaction, or one of the participants, may be audited by the relevant tax authorities, technology agreements routinely require participants to co-operate both with each other and with the relevant tax authority in connection with such audits. These duties may include: (i) production and disclosure of documents and information, and, in some cases, submission for prior review by another party; (ii) availability of personnel for interviews and meetings; and (iii) co-ordinating their respective tax advisors to work together in connection with any such tax audit.

Records and retention

3.9.9.5 There are many requirements concerning the maintenance of tax records and transaction information. You should consider obliging all participants to adhere to those record and information requirements in connection with the transaction. Generally, under UK tax law, records should be preserved at least until the latest of: (i) six years from the end of the relevant accounting period; (ii) the date on which any enquiry into the relevant return is completed; or (iii) the date on which the Revenue are no longer able to open an inquiry. The records to be kept include: records of all receipts and expenses and supporting documents such as accounts, books, contracts, vouchers and receipts. The obligation may generally be satisfied by preserving the information in such records in electronic form and electronic records are also admissible in evidence in related legal proceedings. In certain circumstances, however, the original documents must be preserved, *e.g.* records of tax paid in a foreign country and vouchers in respect of tax credits. Documentation must also be kept in relation to imported or exported goods; and individuals supplying electronic services in other European states must keep records of the transactions entered into for 10 years following the date of the transaction.

Performance audit

3.9.9.6 As you structure and implement the transaction, it is extremely important to remember that your tax liability is a matter of both transaction form and performance substance. Although the agreement may stipulate a particular transaction structure, whether by business process, commercial arrangement, financial undertaking or otherwise, the issue of whether or not the participants have complied with tax laws and regulations will depend upon their actual conduct in the day-to-day implementation of, and conformance with, that transaction structure. Therefore, it may be prudent to include regular performance audits to permit the participants to examine and verify the extent to which those contractual procedures and related obligations are in fact being complied with in the ordinary course of business. If the obligations are not being complied with, then the participants will have an opportunity to identify the compliance deficiencies, rectify the situation and ensure that the actual conduct of the participants conforms with the business structures and commercial arrangements required by the agreement.

Offshore arrangements

3.9.10 If the project involves multiple jurisdictions or any offshore arrangements, then you should consider the following financial issues: (i) have those arrangements been structured to maximise tax advantages? (ii) are there any tax or other treaties that affect the flow of money between jurisdictions? (iii) will the substance of day-to-day operations comply with the legal and structural form of those arrangements? (iv) are there any exchange control regulations or restrictions on foreign currency payments? (v) who are the intermediary financial institutions? (vi) will the project require the services of a trusted third party, such as an offshore payment and settlement service, or a certification authority for secure financial transactions? and (vii) will the financial provisions of the agreement (including rights of set-off, liquidated damages, letter of credit, third-party payment guarantees, interest rate, taking security interests in the assets of the foreign participant, etc.) be enforceable in the relevant foreign jurisdiction? Depending upon your due diligence and the advice of professional advisors in those jurisdictions, you may require additional provisions in the agreement to ensure such enforceability.[64]

"Favoured nation" pricing

3.9.11 Regardless of what pricing arrangements have been otherwise agreed to, including rebate programmes and volume discounts, the paying participant often seeks assurance that the price it is paying is as favourable as the one anyone else is required to pay for those goods or services. Such "favoured nation" pricing requirements can either be specific to the provider of the subject goods and services, or they may be industry-wide, requiring the provider not to sell goods or services at prices that are greater than others who provide those goods or services. Whereas the former is an issue of provider price consistency and equal treatment, the latter is an issue of pricing competitiveness.

Since industry pricing is usually very confidential, and each transaction is unique and reflects specific pricing for each distinctive transaction, so-called "favoured nation" pricing covenants will raise the following issues: (i) whether the covenant should apply to the provider's pricing internationally, or just to the relevant juris-

---

[64] One example, of many possible, is the Canadian requirement that interest rates must be quoted as an aggregate annual rate, and not on the monthly rates that are so often quoted in US agreements (see **3.9.6**).

diction(s) of the project; (ii) to limit the comparative pricing only to those transactions and projects that are the same as (or reasonably similar or comparable to) the provider's subject transaction, having regard to the nature and scope of those goods or services, the commercial conditions under which they are provided, volume of goods or services consumed, the required time periods and the industry in which the project is being carried on; (iii) whether or not comparable pricing should take into account reasonable adjustments, such as the cost to provide those goods or services in another jurisdiction or transportation costs; (iv) whether or not the covenant should require comparable pricing (within a stipulated margin of deviation), pricing that is "at least" as favourable, or perhaps even better pricing[65]; (v) whether to provide direct audit rights for participants to assess and verify such pricing compliance, or stipulating that an independent third party shall undertake that evaluation process; (vi) requiring the pricing evaluator to provide a written report to all participants, containing only the compliance results of that assessment and no confidential pricing information; (vii) to be promptly compensated for past over-payments; (viii) to adjust the price to satisfy the "favoured nation" requirements; (ix) securing an officer's or director's certificate of price compliance after the price adjustment is implemented; (x) who pays the costs and expenses of the audit and compliance report (usually, it is shared by both participants in that protective measure unless a price discrepancy is found, in which case the defaulting participant shall pay all such costs); and (xi) the duty to the provider to promptly report, in writing, all third-party pricing policy and practice changes that occur during the term of the agreement.

Fair market value benchmarking

3.9.12 If the "favoured nation" pricing is not based on the provider's pricing conduct in the market per se but instead on the provider's pricing competitiveness, the participants will have to compare ("benchmark") the pricing policies and practices of the provider with others who provide those goods or services in the relevant market. Price-benchmarking provisions raise the following issues: (i) to undertake comparative pricing by independent evaluators who will not have a conflict of interest in the results; (ii) specifically identifying the competitors of the provider with whom pricing policies and practices will be compared; (iii) the right of the participants to make submissions to the independent evaluator; (iv) the stipulation of comparative criteria in objective and empirically verifiable terms; (v) the stipulation that only the results of the comparison shall be delivered to the participants, and not the confidential information that will be relied upon for the comparative evaluation; and (vi) the ability to direct any dispute or disagreement with the results of the independent evaluator's report to the agreement's dispute-resolution process.

---

[65] Be sure not to contravene the price discrimination provisions of the Competition Act (see **3.9.1**).

Volume discounts

3.9.13 Whether procuring goods or services, most pricing structures of technology transactions will include volume discounts. Those price discounts are usually expressed as graduated price reductions based on the aggregate purchase volume within a stipulated time period. Different categories of goods and services may also be associated with different price reductions. Usually, those price reductions are calculated as a percentage of the non-discounted price that is generally commercially offered. You should consider whether or not those price discounts are to be calculated retroactively to "the first pound paid" or whether or not they only apply to each volume tier. For example, if 100 items cost £10.00 each, but the next 100 items will cost £5.00 each, you should determine whether or not the price of £5.00 will apply to all 200 items purchased (with a price-adjustment obligation), or only to the last 100 items, for an aggregate net discount of £7.50 per item.

In Canada, it is also common for project participants who are interested in securing project-based volume discounts to aggregate their purchasing power as a "buying group" pursuant to the Competition Act.[66] Generally, properly constituted buying groups are able to co-ordinate their procurement activities to obtain the best volume discounts available for the purpose of the transaction. A buying group must be a "true" purchaser of the goods, who accepts liability for the purchases in order to qualify for volume discounts. However, members of a buying group can, as agents of the buying group, place orders, take delivery and accept rebates without having to separately document the subsequent sale from the buying group to its member participants. Therefore, when structuring the transaction, you should consider whether or not the participants should be obligated to properly constitute and maintain a buying group for the purposes of procuring the project's required goods and services.[67]

Similarly in the UK, joint buying is promoted by the UK Government in order to attempt to realise the benefits that increased purchasing power might offer. With that in mind, and at a local government level, the National Strategy for Local Government Procurement ("the Strategy") was published at the end of October 2003. The Strategy proposed the development of a network of Centres of Excellence. Backed by the Office of the Deputy Prime Minister (ODPM) nine Regional Centres of Excellence were announced on February 25, 2004. Their remits include sharing knowledge and experience and teaming together to push forwards the modernising government agenda. In practical terms this means that one local

---

[66] See the Act's Price Discrimination Enforcement Guidelines, published by the Director of the Bureau of Competition Policy. The Guidelines also state that "international volume price concessions", which are price discounts based on the purchaser's international purchase volume, are acceptable where the foreign parent of the Canadian participant contracts to purchase goods and agrees that its Canadian affiliate purchaser may pay for the goods directly.

[67] See C.S. Goldman, Q.C. and J. Bodrug, "Price Discrimination Under the Canadian Competition Act", paper presented to the American Bar Association, April 2, 1993.

authority may take the lead in its region and procure information technology services on behalf of itself and its sister authorities.

In the private sector in the UK, there is nothing to stop organisations teaming up to obtain competitive advantage through increased purchasing power, save that the provisions of the Enterprise Act (see earlier at **3.9.1**) will have relevance if such a team is adjudged to have become an unlawful cartel.

Right of set-off

3.9.14 Due to the consortia nature of technology transactions, it is extremely common for participants to both owe payments to, and own receivables from, other participants. Therefore, you should consider including a right of "set-off" in the agreement that would allow participants to simply pay the net amount of payables once any relevant receivables are deducted. Although there may be accounting and tax reasons why it may be preferable to simply make all payments owed, and to collect all receivables owed without such a right of set-off, there may be situations where a right of set-off would be more efficient and convenient for the administration of the project.

Benefit participation remuneration

3.9.15 Many technology transactions structure their remuneration, whether partially or completely, to participate in the beneficial impact of the transaction. Such benefits may include increased profitability, increased production or related efficiencies or reduced costs. Such remunerative structures require some fundamental conditions: the participants have to know, in objective and empirical terms, what their current state of affairs is with respect to whatever change or impact is being considered. Therefore, if you propose to be remunerated based on the beneficial impact of your goods or services, you will have to have a clear understanding of the current circumstances that will form the basis of the remuneration calculation. Any alternatives to that basic and simple principle will create a significant amount of risk to the financial arrangements. Unfortunately, many "benefit-sharing" arrangements use terminology like "cost savings", "cost reduction", "demonstrable benefits" and "enhanced performance of business functions" without ever either defining the status quo or stipulating how those benefits will be determined and assessed. Such arrangements also require very detailed audit rights provisions, intimate administrative and management-control provisions, the ability to involve independent third parties in all related empirical assessments and evaluations, and extremely precise financial modelling that clearly defines all of the asset, expense and revenue items that will be within the purview of the transaction. In my experience, such pricing arrangements are greatly facilitated and enhanced where the participants have undertaken a detailed assessment and analysis of their current circumstances, which can be used as the basis for evaluating all subsequent and related improvements.

When stipulating such obligations, you should consider the following issues: (i) the time period for assessment and evaluation; (ii) what aspects of impact or benefit will be evaluated, *e.g.* production cost reduction, business-process efficiency improvements, increased profitability; (iii) the evaluation process should be described, including how to control for extraneous variables that may have caused or contributed to the beneficial changes during the stipulated time period, and the "impact formula" that should be based upon the status quo; (iv) what your participation should be in the verifiable benefits, *e.g.* what percentage of the financial benefit should constitute your remuneration; and (v) for what time period should you participate in such benefits.

Payment security

3.9.16   If there are any concerns about the ability of a participant to pay remuneration under the transaction agreement, there are several ways to secure such payment obligations (see **4.10**), including: (i) third-party financial guarantees; (ii) letters of credit (see **4.9.4**); (iii) requiring payments to be paid in advance into a trust or escrow arrangement managed by a trusted third party; (iv) performance or payment bond[68]; (v) making participants jointly liable for the financial obligations of other participants; or (vi) taking security in the assets of the payer with priority over other creditors.

It will be normal to consider whether to seek a parent company guarantee for the performance of a party, and/or whether to seek a financial guarantee in addition. Sometimes it will also be necessary to provide for the substitution of an alternative guarantor where the financial standing of the parent is called into question.

Financial metrics review

3.9.17   As part of the project's change-management obligations, the participants may wish to stipulate the commercial circumstances in which the participants may reconsider the transaction's pricing and payment arrangements. The circumstances and criteria that participants often rely upon to adjust a transaction's financial metrics include: (i) inventory supply and costs; (ii) technology price changes; (iii) direct and indirect overhead costs for materials and labour; (iv) commodity market trends; (v) legal or regulatory changes that affect the project; and (vi) changes in competitive circumstances that dramatically affect comparable market rates and/or costs.

---

[68] A performance bond generally guarantees the performance of the contract, and the person granting the bond effectively indemnifies those obligations; see *Travelers Indemnity Co. v Foley Brothers (Canada) Ltd.* [1970] S.C.R. 56 and *Ellis-Don Management Services Ltd. v Canadian Surety Co.* (1991), 46 C.L.R. 226, Alta. QB. See Moelmann and Harris eds, *The Law of Performance Bonds* (American Bar Association, Chicago, 1999).

Documents and records

3.10   As discussed in **1.5.4.3**(f), there may be a broad ambit of record maintenance, data storage, information, security, reliability and electronic processing legal and regulatory requirements that may apply to the transaction. To ensure that all participants will comply with those requirements, the agreement should stipulate those statutory and regulatory requirements as obligations under the agreement. In addition to the general provision that will require the participants to comply with all applicable laws and regulations, you should consider: (i) including specific statutory and regulatory requirements that the participants should be particularly required to perform; and (ii) add specifically required undertakings, security standards, reliability qualities and procedural activities directly to the agreement's definition of the participant's performance obligations and requirements, and, where appropriate, to the stipulated service levels.

Standards

3.10.1

Regulatory

3.10.1.1   As a result of your due diligence investigations concerning what regulatory requirements of the participants may affect the transaction, you will have identified the document and record maintenance requirements that specifically apply to the project. Based on that due diligence information, you should ensure that any of those material requirements are included in the agreement as performance obligations. For example, technology outsourcing transactions in the health-care, financial services and other regulated industries are subject to very specific data-processing and record-disclosure requirements that the transaction and each participant must comply with. Your professional advisors should assist you in the incorporation and translation of such regulatory requirements (as ascertained during the due diligence process) into compliance covenants and performance obligations in the agreement.

Electronic transactions

3.10.1.2   If any part of the transaction will be conducted in electronic form, whether through the internet or otherwise, then you should ensure that the record-retention requirements of each applicable jurisdiction's e-commerce legislation is complied with. Generally, those requirements stipulate that the document- or record-retention system must provide a reasonable assurance of the document's or record's integrity. That general standard of integrity will be considered and determined in the context of the purpose for which the document or record will be used or otherwise relied upon. Such laws also generally provide that the participant's reliance on documents that were originally created in electronic form will, in part, depend upon recording the dates and times they were originally sent, received or otherwise recorded.[69]

Tax/customs

3.10.1.3   There are several record-retention standards that are required by both the Tax Act and the Money Laundering Regulations[69a] that may have a direct impact on the transaction.[70] In these circumstances, you should require the participants to comply with those requirements and standards, and either to dovetail those requirements with verification by independent auditors or require an officer or director of the participant to provide you with an officer's certificate of compliance. (It is unlikely that participants will allow you to directly audit their tax and customs records to verify compliance due to the uniquely confidential nature of that information.)

Evidence

3.10.1.4   The are several approaches to ensuring that participants will create, maintain, protect and reproduce records and information that will be admissible as evidence and proof of those facts, including: (i) procedures and activities that will support the integrity, reliability, accuracy, completeness and authenticity of that information[71]; (ii) requiring the participants to adhere to the requirements of the Civil Evidence Act 1995, such as ensuring that the record-maintenance system shall

---

[69] See G. J. H. Smith, "Internet Law and Regulation" 3rd ed. (Sweet and Maxwell, London, 2002) at Chapter 6, "Enforcement and Jurisdiction". See also L.K. Abe, *Internet and E-Commerce Agreements* (Butterworths, Toronto, 2001), at s.2.2.5(1), entitled "Will e-contracts Meet Document Retention Requirements".

[69a] See Tax Act 1988 and Money Laundering Regulations SI 1993/1993.

[70] For a detailed review of those requirements and standards, see **1.5.5.6**.

[71] In order to ensure that a user of an electronic system can rely on its commercial records as evidence in a court of law or any other tribunal, the commercial records must be considered "reliable". Although there are no definitive tests concerning electronic-record reliability for evidentiary purposes, the following aspects of data and record maintenance are important elements to determine the reliability of any electronic system: they were made in the ordinary course of business; they are part of a complete data-management system; you can provide the original data source; the data were immediately stored; routine data entry; there is a regular business reliance by users; the maintenance technology is reliable; there is reasonable record security; and the participant regularly audits and verifies the integrity of the record-management system, and the accuracy, reliability, completeness and authenticity of the records it produces for routine reliance by the participant.

not adversely affect the authenticity and integrity of any electronic documents, that all electronic documents be recorded or stored by the participants in the ordinary course of the project and related business operations, that the information remains under the control of the participants, and that the participants use reliable encryption techniques to support the integrity of electronic records; (iii) the integrity and reliability requirements of e-commerce and transactions legislation;[71a] and (iv) the electronic-document retention requirements of the Data Protection Act 1998.[71b]

GAAP requirements

3.10.1.5 The Canadian Institute of Chartered Accountants publishes guidelines concerning the operation and management of information technology entitled, "Information Technology Control Guidelines".[72] This guide provides a practical means of identifying, understanding, assessing and implementing information technology controls in all types of enterprises, and specific chapters of that publication cover the following issues: (i) responsibility for risk management and control; (ii) IT planning; information-systems acquisition; (iii) development and maintenance; (iv) computer operations and information-systems support; (v) IT security; (vi) business continuity and disaster-recovery planning; and (vii) application-based control.

At a European level, January 1, 2005 is the deadline for publicly listed companies to comply with the new EC Regulation on the application of international accounting standards (EC/1606/2002) (the IAS Regulation), which came into force on September 12, 2002. From 2005, the International Financial Reporting Standards (also referred to as the International Accounting Standards) will replace the GAAP standards.

Similarly, the EU Transparency Directive (published in March 2004) will have implications for the auditing rules for corporations within the EU. This Directive is part of a suite of legislation and is similar in many ways to the US Sarbanes-Oxley Act. The aim of the Directive is to enhance investor protection and to create a single market in financial services within the EU by 2005.

The Directive will require regular reports to be compiled in accordance with the IAS and as yet it is undecided whether GAAP principles (where equivalent) will suffice.

In a yet further similar vein, the Basel II Accord will be implemented in the EU by way of the Risk-Based Capital Directive (CAD III). The Accord has developed an advanced system that will make banks' and other financial institutions' assessments of their own investments and loans more sensitive to credit and market-

---

[71a] See Electronic Communications Act 2000.

[71b] See principle 5 of the Act, and the guidance on the Information Commissioner's website at *www.informationcommissioner.gov.uk.*

[72] *Information Technology Control Guidelines* (3rd ed., 1998), formerly entitled *Computer Control Guidelines* and first published in 1970. Also see *www.cica.ca*, and *Audit Implications of Electronic Document Management* (CICA, Toronto, 1997).

related risks. While the Accord is not mandatory and national regulators are free to choose how to apply it, the EU is taking a very rigid stance and is proposing to apply the new rules to most investment firms as well as banks.

All such compliance requirements will create challenges for many organisations and will require systems capable of compliance and of demonstrating compliance to the relevant regulatory bodies.

Audit access

3.10.2   An important aspect of any document or record-management obligation under the agreement involves the ability to verify that those obligations are being complied with. Because of the behind-the-scenes nature of such obligations, you will not likely know whether or not a participant has complied with those obligations until it is too late, and a court, administrative tribunal or regulatory authority has made an unfavourable ruling in that regard. Therefore, you should ensure that the participants have the proactive ability to ensure compliance through: (i) direct-compliance audit provisions; (ii) independent third-party compliance audit provisions; (iii) obligations of the participant to undertake their own regular compliance audit procedures; (iv) a duty of the participant to report non-compliance, and their remedial activities; (v) the delivery of an officer's or director's compliance certificate; (vi) the right to be promptly notified of any compliance investigation, review, dispute, inspection or enquiries from any governmental or regulatory authority concerning those matters; and (vii) access to all electronic records and related IT and communication systems (including disclosure of access codes, passwords and security authorisations).

If the participants require audit access to information in multiple jurisdictions, then the audit provisions of the agreement should ensure that they will have the right to access those records. Audit provisions of an agreement routinely include provisions that: (i) permit access to premises and facilities during ordinary working hours; (ii) permit access upon reasonable notice; (iii) require access to electronic records and related IT infrastructure; (iv) require the use of a "work room" in which to conduct the audit; (v) require key personnel to assist with the audit, including document production and to answer questions; (vi) whether or not the audit should be conducted by an independent third party; (vii) that the audit will not disrupt the operations of the audited participant; (vi) whether or not documents may be copied or removed from the premises; and (vii) the execution and delivery of an officer's certificate that all relevant information has been produced for the audit, and that such information is reliable, accurate, complete and timely.

General record requirements

3.10.3   There are many general obligations concerning the collection, retention, maintenance, storage and reproduction of the transaction's documentation and records that you should consider including in the agreement, including: (i) ensuring that the confidentiality obligations apply to all project documents and records; (ii) security requirements, concerning access and protection obligations; (iii) requiring regular audits and verification tests to ensure document and record integrity, reliability and compliance with all other applicable standards and quality requirements; (iv) stipulating which participant will own such documents and records, including all associated transfer and assignment obligations; (v) covenants concerning the completeness, accuracy, currency (timeliness) and truthfulness of all documents and records; (vi) retention location requirements and method of management, where applicable; (vii) related risk-management requirements, such as back-up, disaster recovery, data warehousing and systems redundancy; and (viii) any applicable document or record-export restrictions.

Term

3.11   In most technology transactions, the length of the relationship will be very closely tied to many other aspects of the transaction, including the participant's financial return on its investment, risk tolerance and on pricing. That is often expressed by the familiar adage, "The more business you give us, the better the deal we can give you". The term of the transaction is directly related to business volume, but it is an often overlooked negotiation issue for many of those interrelated, if not interdependent, commercial issues.

Length

3.11.1   As noted above, any changes to the proposed term of the transaction will have a direct impact on many other aspects of the proposed transaction. However, in addition to the term's having a reciprocal affect on pricing, investment, scope of project and change management issues, you should also keep in mind that the term of the agreement may be conditionally structured. Rather than structuring the transaction as an unalterable fixed term, you may wish to provide for a much shorter (and guaranteed) term that may be extended subject to certain performance criteria or milestones being achieved. In effect, you can use the term of the agreement to structure a phased project with very defined performance stages. Rather than committing all the participants to a medium- or long-term transaction through which they will rely on detailed change-management and dispute-resolution mechanisms to maintain their relationship, you should consider restructuring the transaction as a series of developmental phases, each of which is premised upon stipulated preconditions and continuation criteria.

Renewal rights

3.11.2 There are several ways to structure the renewal or continuation of the agreement. First, you may provide the participants with an option for renewal that will expire in a specified time period. Secondly, you may specify that the renewal shall be subject to certain criteria or performance milestones being achieved. Thirdly, you may simply state that the contract will continue for stipulated time periods unless otherwise terminated by either participant upon a stipulated notice period (or, where you require more control and if you are worried of missing a contract-termination window and rolling accidentally into the renewal period, a provision stating that the contract will automatically terminate unless renewed). Simply stating that the agreement "shall renew upon the mutual agreement of the participants" is unnecessary, since this simply reflects each participant's ordinary legal rights. However, if the participants are to meet and use their reasonable efforts to negotiate a renewal of the agreement, that obligation should be expressly stipulated with defined notice requirements and time limitations for such discussions. Otherwise, any technology-agreement renewals that are subject to further agreement concerning fundamental and material terms and conditions may not guarantee renewal, and the participants must adjust their expectations accordingly. You should create a bring-forward system for any contract-termination or renewal dates so that you will have enough time either to plan for and negotiate the renewal, or to make alternative commercial arrangements. Finally, the renewal provisions should be dovetailed with the termination transition and assistance provisions of the agreement (see **3.11.4**).

Termination

3.11.3 The ability of the participants to terminate their commercial arrangements is one of the most important aspects of the entire transaction. As a general rule, participants are very reluctant to provide termination rights, and even courts are reluctant to allow parties to rescind a technology agreement, except in the most serious of circumstances.

Breach

3.11.3.1 In order to minimise uncertainty concerning whether or not a court would allow a participant to terminate the agreement in any particular circumstance, you should specifically delineate the nature and type of performance failures that will allow the other participants to terminate the agreement. Such "termination-for-cause" provisions generally restrict the right of the parties to end their commercial relations to breaches of fundamental or material aspects of the transaction, especially those that are likely to have a substantially detrimental impact on a participant.

Although termination rights are rarely granted for minor breaches, they may expressly apply to any breach that re-occurs to the extent those repeated or continuous breaches substantially harm the project. In addition to terminating the agreement as a result of many breaches of minor matters (death by 1,000 cuts), you should consider securing the right to terminate the transaction in response to the breach of fundamental performance obligation that is specifically identified, such as failure to pay all amounts as they become due and owing, or to protect the confidentiality of information. In many situations, such grounds for termination may be tied to "events of default", which may include: (i) situations of participant insolvency, bankruptcy or any reorganisation of their assets as a part of the creditor arrangement; (ii) failure to adhere to service level requirements, in the stipulated "cure" periods; (iii) the failure to perform financial obligations; (iv) failure to adhere to the transaction's knowledge-asset provisions, including intellectual property and confidentiality; and (v) any change in the control of the participant.

Remedial period

3.11.3.2   It is extremely common for provisions that allow termination for a breach of contract to include, and be qualified by, a remedial, or "cure", period. Those provisions may permit a participant to terminate the agreement for a breach only if the defaulting party has failed to correct the breach within a stipulated time period, and upon production of reliable evidence that the breach has indeed been cured. Sometimes, such remedial periods are either restricted only to minor breaches, or their application is excluded from applying to breaches associated with: (i) financial obligations; (ii) confidentiality; (iii) intellectual property; and (iv) material performance obligations such as service levels and mission-critical technology functionality.

Note that the remedial period must be reasonable in order not to fall foul of the reasonableness test under the Unfair Contracts Terms Act 1977.[72a]

Specified events

3.11.3.3   In addition to allowing the participants to terminate in the event of a contractual breach, as discussed above, the participants may also stipulate specific circumstances that would also allow them to terminate the agreement. Those rights may include situations where: (i) there has been a change in control of any of the participants; (ii) the participant ceases to carry on business in a particular jurisdiction; (iii) a participant sells all, or substantially all, of their assets that are required for any particular business operation; (iv) any governmental or regulatory right upon which their participation is conditionally premised is terminated or with-

---

[72a] See UCTA s.13 and recent cases such as *Granville Oil and Chemicals Ltd v Davis Turner & Co Ltd* [2003] EWCA Civ 570, and *Expo Fabrics (UK) Ltd v Naughty Clothing Co Ltd* [2003] EWCA Civ 1165.

drawn; (v) the failure of a participant to achieve a particular performance criteria or standard, which is not otherwise stipulated as a performance obligation; or (vi) where specified time-limits for particular activities or events are exceeded, which are not stipulated as performance obligations.

For convenience

3.11.3.4   Although more common in public-sector technology transactions, there are circumstances in which you may want the right to simply extricate yourself from the transaction in your absolute discretion. In some situations, the exercise of such discretion may be limited to circumstances where the participant has acted reasonably in determining their organisation's best commercial and financial interests. The ability to exercise such a right may also be limited to certain stages in the transaction process, including only after a time when the participants may have recovered a reasonable return on their investment. In most cases, such rights are usually subject to a reasonable notice period, and to specific remedies that include detailed formulas to compensate the other participants for the loss of their reasonable revenue and profit expectations. As you might expect, such remedial provisions can be extremely complicated and may require the assistance of both your financial and legal advisors.

Automatic v discretionary

3.11.3.5   Just as the rights of termination should be reasonable and proportionate to the particular transaction circumstances being considered, rights of termination may be either discretionary or automatic. In most cases, the transaction's termination rights will be drafted to provide you with discretion as to whether or not you choose to exercise those rights in a particular circumstance. However, some agreements require provisions that will automatically terminate the agreement, and you should ensure that those circumstances reflect the interests and intentions of the participants.

Force majeure

3.11.3.6   As discussed in **3.2.14**, the continuation of a *force majeure* event beyond a particular period of time may provide the participants with the right to terminate the agreement. However, the rights of the participants to secure a temporary replacement, or to find alternative participants, will greatly influence the exercise of those rights. You should ensure that any termination resulting from those circumstances can be thoroughly documented and substantiated.

Transition assistance

3.11.4 Depending upon the termination circumstances, you should consider how the participants can assist each other to dismantle the transaction, and co-operate in the transition out of the project. Although you may not want to involve a participant who has materially defaulted in the performance of their obligations in any post-termination wind-down and transition arrangements, those obligations of assistance and co-operation typically include: (i) the prompt return of equipment, information or other assets; (ii) the transition of data management and other operational aspects of the transaction's obligations; (iii) public-relations and customer-transition matters; (iv) to provide prompt information concerning any equipment, technology, skills, data or other "tools" that are necessary for the required activities; and (v) co-operation with any post-termination tax, regulatory, intellectual property or other registrations, filings and reporting obligations.

Intellectual property

3.12 Perhaps the most important provisions of any technology agreement relate to intellectual property. Since the ownership of, and the rights to use, technology and other knowledge assets lie at the very heart of a technology transaction, those provisions are essential for the protection of each participant's existing and future ownership rights. Whether such provisions protect and preserve existing proprietary rights, transfer the rights to others or grant others the right to use knowledge assets, the failure to protect the interests thoroughly and comprehensively may result in risks that go far beyond the transaction or related project. Participants who inadvertently grant proprietary rights or interests to others may cause irreparable harm to their entire organisation. Therefore, intellectual property provisions must be prudently considered and carefully drafted to ensure that the commercial intentions of the participants are very clearly and accurately set out in the agreement.

Background technology ownership

3.12.1 Unless otherwise intended, the participants should ensure that their continued ownership of all right, title and interest in the knowledge assets that they will "contribute" to the project is expressly stipulated in the technology agreement. Those knowledge assets should be specifically defined and identified in the greatest detail possible. Some options for identifying such intellectual property include: (i) detailed descriptions, either included in schedules attached to the agreement or by reference to other documents, materials or publications where those knowledge assets are described; (ii) by listing specific intellectual property registrations, such as patent registration numbers; (iii) listing commercially identifiable products or services; or (iv) including a "background technology" definition in the agreement that provides reasonable information concerning such knowledge assets. Such provisions typically include the following covenants: (i) the defined "background" knowledge assets were created by the contributing participant prior to, and independent of, the project; (ii) the identified knowledge assets or background technology is the absolute, exclusive property of the participant; (iii) the other participants will not do anything to challenge, dilute, impugn or take any action contrary to those proprietary interests; (iv) the participants will not represent, or otherwise hold out, to any person that such knowledge assets are their property; and (v) the participants will assist and co-operate to protect those proprietary interests, including notifying you of any suspected breach or infringement.

New-technology ownership

3.12.2 In the event that knowledge assets will be originally created in the course of the transaction, you should stipulate which participant will own or otherwise have the right to use the knowledge assets. Such a stipulation may involve one participants having ownership of the knowledge assets with the other participants having a licence to use the assets within some specified parameters. Such provisions should be clear and unequivocal, and may stipulate that those rights are: (i) irrevocable; (ii) unconditional; (iii) unrestricted; (iv) without time-limitation; and (v) worldwide. If the creator of the knowledge assets is required to transfer and assign its ownership to another participant, and the knowledge asset exists at the time at which the technology agreement is entered into, then the participants should include a provision that expressly transfers, assigns and conveys all right, title and interest in that knowledge asset from the owner to the acquirer. Because of potential legal complications concerning the conveyance of knowledge assets that have not yet been created in the course of the transaction,[73] it may be prudent to ensure that those provisions stipulate both the participants' agreement of your exclusive-ownership interest, and that the participants will execute and deliver all agreements, documents, filings and registrations that are necessary to transfer, assign and convey all such right, title and interest once the knowledge assets are created, *i.e.* a present assignment of future intellectual property rights. You should ensure that these requirements are administratively attended to, and that the provisions are dovetailed with the "further assurance" obligations in the agreement.[73a]

---

[73] In the case of *Masterfile v World Internet* (2001) 16 C.P.R. (4th) 139, the Trial Division of the Federal Court ruled that s.13(4) of the Copyright Act, which provides that an owner of copyright may assign its ownership if it is in writing and signed by the owner, "does not contemplate assignments that may take effect at a future date".

[73a] See s.91 of the CDPA 1988.

Rights to use third-party intellectual property

3.12.3   Most technology transactions require the participant's use of knowledge assets that belong to individuals who are not a party to the agreement. Therefore, you should ensure that all third-party knowledge assets that are required for the project are clearly identified, and that each participant who will use those knowledge assets has or will obtain as part of the transaction the authority, permission and right to use those knowledge assets as specifically required by, and for the purposes of, the technology transaction. In addition to those issues being a matter of your preparatory due diligence, you should ensure that all participants agree to all related third-party knowledge-asset representations and warranties (see **3.14.3.1** and **3.14.3.2**). Furthermore, you should ensure that: (i) the risk-management provisions of the agreement appropriately allocate the risks and liabilities that may be associated with the wrongful use of third-party knowledge assets (see Chapter 4); and (ii) that any third party's knowledge assets that are required for the project will only be used by individuals who are properly licensed and authorised to do so. For example, transactions are frequently interrupted, and sometimes irreparably harmed, because one participant to the transaction brings with it the knowledge assets of a third party that the other participants either intentionally, or inadvertently, use for the project under the mistaken belief that they have proper authorisation to do so.

Joint ownership

3.12.4   The Copyright, Designs and Patents Act 1988 (at s.10) defines a "work of joint authorship" as "a work produced by the collaboration of two or more authors in which the contribution of one author is not distinct from the contribution of the other author or authors". Technology transactions often require participants to work together and create knowledge assets, but if you are contemplating joint ownership of any intellectual property rights in the United Kingdom, the short advice is: don't! The implications of joint ownership are messy and most often lead to stalemate.

Nonetheless, the ownership of the resulting intellectual property may be structured several ways, including: (i) each participant owning the part of the resulting work that they created, as a divisible proprietary interest[74]; (ii) any one of the participating creators may own all right, title and interest to the entire work; or (iii) the participant may jointly own the resulting work as either "tenants in common" or as "joint tenants". The legal and commercial implications of joint ownership are, in

---

[74] P. O'Reilley, "Allocation of Ownership of Inventions in Joint Development Agreements: The U.S. Perspective", *Les Nouvelles, Journal of the Licensing Executives Society*, Vol. XXXV, No.4, December 2000, p.168 suggests that participants should also consider dividing ownership of intellectual property by allocating and clearly demarking separate ownership interests by subject-matter, based upon each participant's field of interest.

many cases, more complex than technology managers expect or otherwise intend. Often, participants agree to joint ownership as an mechanism to permit both parties to fully use or commercially exploit the resulting work. However, in most cases, this is unnecessary and may lead to unexpected and counterproductive results. Therefore, you should thoroughly consider the legal and commercial alternatives to joint ownership in the circumstances of each transaction. For example, depending upon the circumstances of the transaction, it may be much simpler and more practical for one participant to own the resulting work exclusively while granting the other participant the "licence-back" rights discussed in **3.12.7**. Indeed, having a wide right to use, without the headache of having to police, those rights can be advantageous. If it is appropriate for the participants to jointly own the resulting work, then you should ensure that the distinction between owning the knowledge assets as either "tenants in common" or as "joint tenants" is clearly specified in the agreement.

Tenants in common

3.12.4.1 Unless otherwise specified in the agreement, English copyright law will assume that joint owners of a copyright work are tenants in common. A tenant in common does not need to obtain the consent of the other joint owners of the knowledge assets to reproduce, license or otherwise use or commercially exploit his share of the right. Tenants in common can each maintain an action for copyright infringement, and they have the right to restrain each other from any unauthorised commercial exploitation of the resulting work. Other common-law jurisdictions allow co-owners of patent and copyright to deal with their share of the rights freely.[75]

In situations of tenancy in common, the proprietary interest of an individual joint owner will, on death, pass to his/her beneficiaries, rather than to the surviving joint owner. Therefore, in those situations, the continuation of the project may require a testamentary disposition to the co-owners. By contrast to the position regarding copyright, a co-owner of a patent cannot deal with the patent (whether by licence or assignment etc.) without the consent of all co-owners.

Joint tenants

3.12.4.2 The above is the default position under English law, subject to that position being varied by contractual provision. In order to provide each joint owner with the unrestricted right to use or commercially exploit the resulting work under English copyright law, the agreement must clearly specify that such joint ownership

---

[75] Such joint ownership is similar to the principal of undivided co-ownership under Quebec civil law, which stipulates that a joint owner cannot commercially exploit knowledge assets without the consent of the other co-owner. See S. Handa, *Copyright Law in Canada* (Butterworths, Toronto, 2002), p.255; also see H.G. Richard *et al.*, eds. *Canadian Copyright Act: Annotated* (Looseleaf, Carswell, Toronto, 1993), pp.36–37.

shall be constituted as, and is intended to be, a "joint tenancy" among the co-owners. Joint tenants may each exploit knowledge assets without the consent of the other joint tenant, although there may be an obligation to account. Therefore, in situations of joint tenancy, you should also consider whether or not any restrictive covenants are required to limit a co-owner's otherwise unfettered ability to use and commercially exploit the resulting work.

Written assignment

3.12.5 Where a participant is transferring their proprietary interests in knowledge assets to another participant, you should ensure that such assignment and conveyance is in writing and signed by the owner of the proprietary right in respect of which the assignment or conveyance is made. In addition to being a legal requirement,[75a] it is also important to document such transactions properly for several reasons, including: (i) to create reliable evidence of the transaction that is admissible in court proceedings; (ii) to document the transaction accurately and completely for accounting and tax reasons; (iii) to facilitate any investigations or audits concerning such transactions by any regulatory authority; (iv) in the event that it is considered advisable to register the transfer with government authorities; and (v) for the purposes of the project's management and governance. As previously discussed, written assignments of intellectual property interests are required in situations where the knowledge assets have been created by an independent contractor or by an employee who did not create the work in the course of their employment.

Employee contributions

3.12.6 Section 11(2) of the Copyright, Designs and Patents Act 1988 provides that, "where a . . . (work) . . . is made by an employee in the course of his employment, his employer is the first owner of any copyright in the work subject to any agreement to the contrary". Therefore, in situations where knowledge assets are being created by a participant's employees, you should ensure that: (i) each employee's assignment to the project is within their mandate of employment, and perhaps their particular job description; (ii) that the person creating the knowledge assets are, in fact, employees of the participant; and (iii) no other agreement exists between such employees and participants concerning those proprietary interests.

A frequently overlooked issue concerning employee contributions to technology transactions involves each employee's "moral rights" to the knowledge assets they create.[75b] Chapter IV of the CDPA provides that all authors of a work have the right to be identified as the author of the work, the right to object to derogatory treatment of the work and the right to not have a work falsely attributed to him.

[75a] See s.90(3) of the CDPA 1988.
[75b] See ss.77, 80 and 84, respectively, of the CDPA 1988.

Although moral rights may be waived, either in whole or in part, they cannot be assigned, nor does an assignment of copyright in the work constitute a waiver of any moral rights. Therefore, depending upon the nature of the copyright work that the employee creates, you should consider requiring all employees to wholly and irrevocably waive, in writing, all moral rights that they may have in any of the knowledge assets that they create in the course of the technology transaction.[76]

License-back provisions

3.12.7 In the interest of legal simplicity and practical management, technology transactions frequently stipulate a single owner of the project's technology assets (and all associated intellectual property rights), but ensures that the other participants receive all of the rights and interest they require to use or commercially exploit those knowledge assets through "license-back provisions". Participants who obtain a contractual, rather than proprietary, right to use and commercially exploit knowledge assets can be placed in virtually the same commercial and business provision as the owner of those knowledge assets. For example, a transferee of intellectual property rights may license-back to the transferor of those rights the irrevocable, exclusive (or perhaps "sole"), unrestricted, fully paid, perpetual, worldwide right to use and commercially exploit those knowledge assets without any further or subsequent consent or permission of the owner, including, without limitation, the right to modify, revise, market, distribute, license or commercially exploit in any manner, or to any extent, whatsoever. In effect, the objective of those provisions is to place a non-owner of knowledge assets in the same business and commercial position as an owner of those knowledge assets would otherwise be. There are many variations and structural alternatives for "license-back" commercial arrangements, and you should consider which degree of authority is appropriate in the circumstances of each particular transaction.

Right to create derivative works

3.12.8 Most laws to protect the commercial or economic value of knowledge assets are based on the industrial notions of mechanical reproduction, or uses that are similar to mechanical reproduction, such as performance, publishing, adaptation or

---

[76] The continuation of an employee's moral rights may not place all technology transactions in any practical jeopardy. Section 28.2 of the Copyright Act stipulates that an author's right to the integrity of a work is infringed only if the work is to the prejudice of the honour or reputation of the author either "distorted, mutilated, or otherwise modified, or used in association with a product, service, cause, or institution". For example, it is conceivable that an extremely religious person may feel that their honour or reputation has been damaged if technology that they created were to be used in connection with an internet pornography or gambling venture.

communication. Generally, these rights may be infringed where any person engages in such activities without the consent or authorisation of the owner of those rights. Therefore, if you require the right to use knowledge assets in any way that may infringe the intellectual property rights of the owner, you should ensure that those rights are expressly and unequivocally provided for in the agreement. Frequently, technology transactions will involve the modification, enhancement, customisation or augmentation of knowledge assets that will either involve, or otherwise result in, the reproduction of a substantial part of the original knowledge asset.[76a] Any such reproductions, sometimes referred to as derivative works, should be expressly stipulated in the agreement. For example, "literary works" under the Copyright Designs and Patents Act 1988, which include "computer programs", that cannot be produced, reproduced, adapted or licensed (*i.e.* "rented out") without the express consent of the owner.

Creation-reporting requirements

3.12.9 You should ensure that all activities concerning the use and exploitation of knowledge assets for the purpose of the project are comprehensively reported and thoroughly documented. Participants should report their creation of knowledge assets, and include information concerning: (i) the employment status of the authors; (ii) the identity and contact information of the authors; (iii) a description of the nature and subject-matter of the knowledge assets; (iv) whether or not any steps have been taken to register or otherwise protect any associated intellectual property rights; (v) the application of the knowledge assets to the project; and (vi) the place and method by which records concerning those knowledge assets will be stored and maintained by the participant. Those records are extremely important for many reasons, including evidentiary purposes, the protection of your intellectual property rights, taxation, regulatory and registration requirements, and general finance and accounting matters.

Residual knowledge

3.12.10 You should ensure that you are not restricted in your ability to continue to use, and commercially exploit, the general trade knowledge, experience and expertise that you acquire in the course of the project (your "know-how"). In that regard, the agreement should make a clear distinction between confidential and proprietary knowledge assets that: (i) are distinctive and unique to the project; (ii) have been specifically created for the transaction; (iii) provide a participant with a competitive advantage; (iv) those knowledge assets that are of generic industry application; (v) those that are not unique or specific to the project; and (vi) that merely constitute the accumulation of general experience and "stock-in-trade" that all

---

[76a] See s.16 of the CDPA 1988.

organisations require to carry on their business. Those distinctions may be applied to any intellectual property, confidentiality and restrictive covenants that might otherwise unfairly and unreasonably restrict the ability of a participant to carry on their business with improved general and generic skills and abilities that ordinarily accumulate with experience.

Assistance with intellectual property protection

3.12.11   There are many ways in which you may require participants to assist you in protecting the intellectual property rights provided to you under the technology agreement, including assistance and co-operation with: (i) filings and registrations; (ii) provision of any documentation or information necessary to protect the intellectual property rights; (iii) provision of relevant information concerning the individual creators; (iv) securing written and irrevocable moral-rights waivers; (v) notice of any knowledge of third-party infringement, or breach of contractual restrictions concerning the use of your intellectual property; (vi) prosecution and defence of your intellectual property rights, and all other related juridical, regulatory or dispute resolution claims, demands, actions or proceedings; and (vii) assuming direct responsibility for all such protection in a particular jurisdiction, perhaps as your agent with power of attorney to enforce your intellectual property rights on your behalf.

Brand association

3.13   Many technology projects will require the participants to use, combine, contribute, share or create goodwill and brand identification. Whether as trade names, trade marks, logos, graphic designs, domain names or tag lines, there are many ways to associate the goodwill of the participants to achieve the project's objectives. Because your organisation's goodwill and reputation are probably among its most valuable and important assets, this frequent aspect of technology transactions is an excellent example of where commercial protections and risk-management strategies are essential. For most organisations, the risk of any potential brand damage, or even dilution, will far outweigh the potential benefits of most technology transactions.

Association benefits

3.13.1   The goodwill and reputation of a participant may be required to legitimise, or bring credibility to, the project. By associating various brands in creative ways, the project may gain tremendous trust and confidence in the relevant market. Depending on those requirements, there are many levels of "brand association" intimacy and ways to commercially structure brand inter-dependency. However, you should ensure that any commercial arrangements concerning the project's brand associations do not cause your organisation to lose control of its brand, and that your organisation's goodwill and reputation will be enhanced by any such associations.

Brand-association continuum

3.13.2   The following diagram illustrates the most commonly relied-upon branding arrangements and association structures:

Private label	Brand recognition	Brand priority	Co-branding	Joint brand

That continuum represents, from left to right, commercial arrangements that involve increasing levels of brand intimacy and dependence, from one participant's brand being "invisible", to the participants jointly owning a new but derivative brand for the project.

(a) *Private label* (also known as "white-labelling")—where the goods or services are provided to support the other participant's brand and goodwill; where the provider of the host service brands the project entirely with the other participant's name, trade marks and logos; the identity of the service provider is unknown.

(b) *Brand recognition*—where the goods or services are clearly branded for the benefit of the other participant, but where varying degrees of brand recognition are provided to the other participant, such as "powered by ABC Co.", "ABC Co. Inside", "This service made possible by ABC Co." or "In association with ABC Co."; brand recognition may also be presented as acknowledgments, expressions of gratitude and as testimonials that will contribute to the goodwill of the beneficiary.

(c) *Brand priority*—where the recognition indicates that the service of the dominant brand is dependant upon the goods or services of another participant; where the lesser of the associated brands is dominant over the better-known brand, whether by text, relative size of markings, relative positioning of markings or otherwise; such as "This XY product or service is brought to you by ABC Co.", "An ABC Co. service", "ABC Co., exclusive distributor of XY" or "ABC Co., a leading provider of XY products."

(d) *Co-branding*—this often misused term refers to the generally equal and balanced combination or association of two or more brands to create a new brand that is inherently dependent upon the goodwill of each of the contributed brands; the brands are associated depicting their respective markings in close proximity to each other, and may even be joined in some way; except for such combination and close proximity, the colouring, size, style, font and other characteristics of each brand's markings do not change in any way.

(e) *Joint Brand*—where the participants create a new brand for the project that is jointly owned by the participants or the project entity; it may have derivative characteristics or features of some participant brands, but will avoid any confusion concerning any one participant's goods or services; the new brand may rely upon common elements of each participant's markings to combine and create a new and highly distinctive brand; where the participants intend to launch a new and unique brand but provide it with a point of "brand departure" and association to get the new brand off to a good start.

Brand licensing

3.13.3 Because brand attributes (including goodwill, trade names, trademarks, logos and other markings) are probably among your organisation's most valuable and important property and assets, you should only permit others to use that property subject to a written license agreement that contains vital protections and use limitations. If you do not adhere to very technical legal requirements concerning the granting of such rights to others, your brand may lose its distinctive quality, and you may lose the legal ability to enforce your proprietary rights in those assets against others. The most frequently neglected risks concerning those matters by managers to technology transactions include: (i) thoroughly defining the brand attributes that will be licensed, including marking size, font, colours, and with artwork samples, and by intellectual property registration numbers; (ii) the licence's royalty-free or exclusive nature; (iii) the limitations on use, including the narrowly stated purpose, territory and specific application of markings; (iv) the participants shall not dispute or contest your ownership; (v) the participants shall not diminish, harm or dilute the value of the goodwill in the brand; (vi) the participants shall permit you to inspect the use of the brand to ensure license compliance; (vii) the participants shall provide very strict quality requirements for any good, service or project entity that will use the brand; (viii) the participants shall stipulate quality-control requirements and measures concerning compliance with quality requirements; (ix) the participants shall provide assistance with any third-party infringement of the brand that is associated with the project; and (x) the participants shall agree to your ability to immediately terminate the licence and discontinue any brand association in the event of any brand licence breach.

Brand management

3.13.4 Depending upon the level of brand association that is required by the transaction, you should consider stipulating the following rights and obligations concerning the ongoing management of the brand's project use: (i) ensure that the management of the licensee's performance, and any disputes arising under the brand licence, are included in the Joint Management Committee and dispute-resolution provisions of the agreement; (ii) conduct regular inspections to ensure that the proper and correct markings are being used within the scope of the licence, and that the quality requirements of the goods and services that are associated with your brand are being complied with; (iii) promptly address and resolve any breaches of the brand licence, and do not let compliance obligations slip; research the goodwill and reputational impact of the licensed brand, and determine if the base of the brand is having the desired market effect—if not, you should not allow your brand to be used for ineffective purposes; and (iv) consider how the ongoing use of your brand should be revised to accommodate changing market circumstances and ensure that the change management provisions of the agreement will allow you to proactively and flexibly consider those ubiquitous issues.

Representations and warranties

3.14 This is a portion of the technology agreement that serves several very important business and commercial functions. First, it contractually enshrines specific provisions that you have relied upon in your decision to engage in the transaction. If that information is not correct, or is misleading, then that misrepresentation of fact, and breach of those representations and warranties, will give you the right to seek compensation for any harm or damages that may be caused by that reliance. Secondly, those provisions often address other circumstances that could interfere with the project, or otherwise prevent the transaction from proceeding. Thirdly, they serve as a checklist for each party to ensure that certain fundamental conditions for proceeding with the transaction have been satisfied. Often, the presentation of such representations and warranties to another participant will precipitate constructive and important discussions, clarifications, additions and revisions that will directly reflect the participant's adjustment in their attitudes and expectations concerning those circumstances. Fourthly, and most importantly, those provisions allocate risk for the truth of their contents. Although it practically matters whether or not a particular representation or warranty is accurate and true, it may matter more that the participant making that representation or warranty is assuming the risk of and liability for any misrepresentation, inaccuracy or untrue content. Those provisions do much more than merely state what facts are true, accurate and complete. Those provisions assign responsibility and allocate risk for any failure of that truth, accuracy and completeness. That is why representations and warranties should be closely related to the results of your due diligence enquiries—to ensure that you allocate risk for the truth of circumstances that the transaction commercially relies upon.

For all of the reasons noted above, you should consider which representations and warranties require clarification or qualification, including: (i) the time period in which it was true (*e.g.* as at the Execution Date); (ii) whether it is true, or reasonably believed to be true, or true to the best of a participant's knowledge after due enquiry; (iii) whether any lack of truth should be limited to a resulting material or substantial detrimental impact on the other participant or to the project; or (iv) "except as otherwise disclosed herein".

Under English law a warranty typically allows an innocent party to claim damages if breached, whereas a full condition of contract entitles the innocent party to claim damages together with the right to terminate the contract. However the situation is actually not so clear cut and a substantial body of case law has developed to establish the extent of the grey area between the two and which shows that if a breach of a term goes to the root of a contract, a right to terminate for breach may arise.[76b]

Authority to transact

3.14.1   The participants should assure each other that they have the corporate existence, authority and permission to enter into and perform the proposed transaction. Otherwise, the agreement may be void and of no force and effect.

Corporate existence

3.14.1.1   That the participant is duly organised, incorporated, validly existing and in good standing under the laws of its jurisdiction of incorporation.

Authority

3.14.1.2   That the participant has all of the necessary rights, entitlements, power, capacity and authority to enter into and execute and perform the transaction agreement. Also, that neither the entering into of the technology agreement, nor the performance of the obligations there under shall, in any manner or to any extent, breach or violate the articles, byelaws or other constitutional documents of the participant.

Approval

3.14.1.3   That all of the required governance actions have been taken, and that the transaction, and the agreement's execution and delivery, have been fully and properly authorised and approved, and that no other approval, authorisation or consent is required in order for the participant to enter into and perform the transaction.

Regulatory and legal compliance

3.14.2   Each participant's compliance with all regulatory and legal requirements, conditions and authorisations is often a precondition of many technology transactions.

[76b] See *e.g., Hong Kong Fir Shipping Co Ltd. v Kawasaki* (1962) Q.B. 26.

Regulatory compliance

3.14.2.1   You should require assistance that each participant to the technology transaction has fully complied with all of the following regulatory requirements:

(a) all information, notices, reports and filings that are required to be made to any regulatory, governmental body, or public-sector administrative entity that is required in any connection with, and concerning, the transaction have been made on a complete and timely basis;

(b) all approvals, licences, authorisations, permissions and consents of any governmental or regulatory authority body or tribunal that is required in any connection with, and concerning, the transaction and the participant's performance obligations;

(c) no approvals, licenses, authorisations, permissions or consents of, and no other notices or filings to, any governmental or regulatory authority, body or tribunal other than those expressly stated in the technology transaction are required by the participant in any connection with, and concerning, the transaction;

(d) the participant is in full and timely compliance with, and adherence to, all governmental or regulatory authority, body or tribunal orders, policies, tariffs, rulings, consents, approvals, notice requirements, authorisations and decisions that may be required in any connection with, and concerning, the transaction.

Legal compliance

3.14.2.2   You should require assurance that the participant's performance of the transaction will not offend any laws or regulations, as follows:

(a) their respective obligations are enforceable in accordance with their terms and conditions (except as such enforceability may be limited by any applicable bankruptcy, insolvency, winding-up, or other laws affecting creditors' rights generally and by limitations on the availability of equitable remedies such as specific performance and injunction which are in the discretion of the court from which they are sought);

(b) there are no claims, litigation, actions, suits or proceedings existing, pending or, to its knowledge, threatened against or affecting it before any court, arbitrator or governmental or administrative body or agency and there are no other events or circumstances that affect the validity or enforceability of this Agreement or that would have an effect on its ability to perform its obligations hereunder; and

(c) the participant's entering into, and performance of, this transaction shall comply with, and shall not offend, breach or contravene, all applicable laws and regulations, in any applicable jurisdiction, or any order, judgment, decision, or ruling of a court or tribunal of competent jurisdiction (and perhaps, that no such orders, judgments, decisions or rulings exist whatsoever) that may be relevant to the project.

Transaction not encumbered

3.14.3   You should ensure that the transaction will not be prevented, delayed, interfered with or otherwise detrimentally affected because of any encumbrance on a participant's ability to engage in the transaction.

Intellectual property-asset ownership

3.14.3.1   A participant should warrant that it owns all right, title and interest, and has secured all rights (whether contractual or otherwise), in and to all intellectual property, assets, information (whether in tangible or intangible form) or other items that will be used in any connection with the transaction.

Non-infringement

3.14.3.2   The owner of knowledge assets to be used in connection with the transaction, whether intellectual property or otherwise, should warrant that the knowledge assets will not breach, interfere with, contravene, infringe or detrimentally affect the rights or interests of any other person whatsoever, including any contractual, equitable, statutory, industrial, intellectual property, confidentiality or moral rights.

Third-party obligations

3.14.3.3   Participants should warrant that their performance of the transaction will not interfere with, breach, contravene or otherwise be in conflict with any other obligation or duty that the participant may have to any other person, whether arising in contract, equity, statute or otherwise, and that neither the participant's entering into the technology agreement nor the participant's performance of any aspect of its transaction obligations and duties result in any: (i) mandatory activities of the participant having to be performed; (ii) the participant losing commercial rights or privileges that have been granted by third parties; (iii) cause any obligations with third parties to be accelerated; or (iv) otherwise have an impact on the participant that could interfere with its ability to engage in the transaction.

No document restriction

3.14.3.4   Participants should warrant that their performance of the transaction will not be prohibited, delayed, impaired, limited, restricted, detrimentally affected or otherwise interfered with by any estoppel, document, obligation, duty, trust deed, promise, guarantee, commercial arrangement, contract, debenture, loan agreement, general security agreement or any other instrument, contract, commercial arrangement, or other document.

No asset encumbrance

3.14.3.5   The owner of knowledge assets should warrant that use of the knowledge assets that are the subject of the transaction will not be delayed, encumbered, restricted, limited, qualified or detrimentally affected by any lien, encumbrance, security interest, contingent proprietary interest, mortgage or charge whatsoever.

No judicial interference

3.14.3.6   Each participant should warrant that they are not, in any manner or to any extent whatsoever, prohibited, limited, restricted, constrained or enjoined by any settlement agreement, decree, pronouncement, order, judgment, proceeding, tribunal decision, obligation, duty or other dispute-resolution arrangement, from entering into, and fully performing, the transaction, and that there are no actions, claims, suits, litigation, demands or proceedings that exist, are pending or threatened against the participant, whether judicial, governmental, administrative or otherwise, that could reasonably or possibly affect: (i) the validity and enforceability of the technology agreement; (ii) the ability of the participant to perform its obligations concerning the transaction; (iii) that may detrimentally affect either the participant or the project; or (iv) that is adverse, or materially adverse, to the interests of the project or any of the participants.

Performance requirements

3.14.4

Technology disclosure

3.14.4.1   All information concerning the knowledge assets that is required for the transaction has been disclosed, and it is reliable, current, accurate and complete.

Necessary skills and qualifications

3.14.4.2 The participant shall be duly qualified, trained, experienced and prepared to perform its respective obligations. Also, that the participant shall perform those obligations with reasonable diligence, care, skill, attention, professional acumen and in a prompt and timely manner. Any specific skills, training, qualifications, educational status or experience that is required of this participant should be expressly included.

Control

3.14.4.3 Where appropriate, that specifically identified persons control the participant (whether as owners or other governance arrangements), and that there shall be no change in the control of the participant, or sale of all or substantially all of its assets, during the term of the transaction, except where otherwise permitted in the agreement.

Technology operations

3.14.4.4 All knowledge assets that are required for the transaction: (i) are "Year 2000" and leap-year compliant (pre-2000 it was commonplace to include such a provision—few agreements do so now); (ii) are compliant with all electronic-record and financial requirements, including the GAAP of the specified jurisdictions, tax and custom laws and regulations, applicable evidentiary requirements, and currency conversion and calculation, *e.g.* Euro-Currency Compliant; (iii) perform in accordance with, are certified to operate in compliance with, or are otherwise consistent with the relevant and applicable industry or regulatory standards; (iv) are free of all operational defects and bugs; (v) is complete and does not require any other technology, information, personnel, products or services in order to operate and function as required and agreed; (vi) will operate, function and perform in accordance with all agreed-upon operational and technical specifications, descriptions and requirements; and (vii) do not contain any viruses, hidden routines or subroutines, expiry codes, disabling codes or systems, so-called "bombs" or "worms", or any other functionality or operating aspect that has not been accurately and completely disclosed to all participants.

Key person/employee performance

3.14.4.5 Where relevant to other covenants in the technology agreement (*e.g.* the intellectual property ownership provisions), that the participant's obligations shall exclusively be performed by the participant's employees in the ordinary course of their employment or by the key individuals designated, and not be any other individual whatsoever except as otherwise agreed to in writing among the participants.

Environmental issues

3.14.4.6 There are increasing concerns about the environmental impact of certain technology products and associated responsibilities and liabilities.[77] Therefore, the performance obligations of the agreement must take those considerations into account and include provisions that specifically address such applicable concerns. For example, the participants may wish to require technology providers either to deploy lead-free technology products, or to provide detailed information concerning lead-containing components. The participants may also wish to consider so-called "end-of-life" product-recycling obligations, and the extent to which technology products should be reusable, recyclable and returnable—with participants' reasonably assuming responsibility and liability for the collection and disposal of such "end-of-life" products. Depending upon the nature of the technology transaction, the participants may wish to include the following provisions concerning hazardous materials: (i) listing all materials that are included in the technology product that are classified as either toxic or hazardous under applicable laws and regulations; (ii) provision of accurate and complete information concerning the safe handling of all products; (iii) information concerning adverse effects on people or the environment resulting from the use of, exposure to or disposal of such products; and (iv) standards of care and responsibility to avoid and mitigate any such adverse human or environmental impact.

Public-sector provisions

3.15 If the public sector will be involved in the project, whether as government departments, regulatory bodies or crown corporations, there are several commercial and legal issues that will require your unique attention and consideration. As discussed in **2.9**, the transactional culture of the public sector is quite different from the private sector, and you will have to take into account the public-interest dimensions of the project that may lead to participant decisions of a nature and quality that are not solely based upon transaction profitability and shareholder best interests.

Documents incorporated by reference

3.15.1 Because public-sector participants rely very heavily on standard-form agreements, it is extremely common for public-sector technology agreements to incorporate by reference a series of other documents and agreements. For example, in the United Kingdom, it is commonplace for policy statements, vision documents

---

[77] See Mark O'Conor and Alix Bernard, "Two Directives You Cannot Afford to Ignore", *Computer Law and Security Report*, Vol. 20 no. 4, 2004, commenting upon new legislation regulating the environmental disposal of certain substances and the restriction of certain hazardous substances (such as lead) from the manufature of various everyday items.

and other background materials to be referred to and incorporated into contractual arrangements.[78] Therefore, you must ensure that a very careful and detailed review of all such documents and agreements is undertaken and that any inconsistencies, contradictions or unintended provisions are expressly identified and excluded in the technology agreement.

Termination for convenience

3.15.2   Notwithstanding any agreement concerning the duration of the transaction, public-sector participants often require the right to terminate the technology agreement at any time, as they may determine in their sole and absolute discretion. Although such "termination-for-convenience" provisions are often mandatory, they are almost always accompanied by remedial provisions that are designed to compensate, at least to some degree, the terminated participants for reasonably expected economic gain. In order to protect the goodwill and reputation of the terminated participants, you should also require the public-sector participant that wishes to exercise the termination for convenience right to issue a press release, or other public statement, concerning that exercise of discretion and to exonerate participants from any perceived misconduct, or possible suggestion of any fault or liability.

Intellectual property ownership

3.15.3   Although private-sector participants in technology transactions are free to determine the terms and conditions concerning their proprietary interests in the knowledge assets created for the project, public-sector participants are subject to a myriad of policies, guidelines and directives concerning whether or not they should own intellectual property in the context of any particular transaction. If you are interested in owning any intellectual property associated with a public-sector technology transaction, you must thoroughly understand all of the policies, guidelines, rules, directives and regulations concerning the exercise of a public-sector discretion in those matters.

In the United Kingdom, the Central Computer and Telecommunications Agency (CCTA, now replaced by the Office of Government Commerce) was the keeper of and regularly updated the "model agreements" for public-sector IT contracting. A common provision reflecting long-standing policy was that ownership of intellectual property rights should stay with the private-sector service provider. The service provider would grant to the public-sector body a sufficiently wide licence to use so as to nearly approximate to ownership. This policy changed with the advent of the Private Finance Initiative and the revised contractual guidance promoted by the

---

[78] For example, in relation to the "modernising agenda", see (in the local government context) the 1999 White Paper entitled "Modern Local Government in Touch with the People".

Treasury Task Force. Now it is more common for a government department or local authority to take ownership of the rights developed by the private sector for it under contract.[78a] If you want to own the knowledge assets that you create in a public-sector transaction, you should be prepared to explain and justify that objective during the transaction's negotiations.

Freedom-of-information requirements

3.15.4 Generally, freedom-of-information (a.k.a. access-to-information) legislation requires public-sector participants to make project information available to the public unless that information satisfies exceptional criteria that is statutorily stipulated.

In the United Kingdom, such provisions are new, enacted by the Freedom of Information Act 2000 (the "FOIA"). From January 1, 2005, the remaining provisions of the FOIA will be brought into force. The Act amends the Data Protection Act 1998 and the Public Records Act 1958. The Act: provides a right of access to recorded information held by public authorities; creates exemptions from the duty to disclose information; and establishes the arrangements for enforcement and appeal. The FOIA requires government departments and certain other public authorities to make certain information available to the public and to release information in response to specific requests.

Therefore, in any technology transactions involving the public sector, you should consider whether or not any technology-agreement, or other project, information should be protected from public disclosure. Requests for access to information may relate to information held by a contractor or may relate to that contractor itself. As such, a public-sector body will need a right to obtain the information from the contractor, whereas the contractor may wish to stop the public body from releasing that information if the information is of a commercial nature or relating to its commercial interests.

If you determine that such information exists (*e.g.* pricing or trade secrets), then

---

[78a] For example, federal government participants are subject to the Treasury Board of Canada's "Implementation Guide for the Policy: Title to Intellectual Property Arising Under Crown Procurement Contracts". Furthermore, the federal government's Technology Procurement Branch stipulates that:

> Section 24 of (standard form contract) DSS/MAS 9601 dictates that the title and certain intellectual property shall vest in the crown . . . if it is wished that the crown take title to computer programs and related software documentation, it is mandatory that (participants) include the following DSS/MAS 9601-7 "Canada to own foreground information" as part of (the) RFP or any resulting contract.

Treasury Board has directed that, in the absence of an explicit contractual statement to the contrary, title to intellectual property developed pursuant to a crown contract may be presumed to vest in the contractor.

the agreement should include the following provisions to promote (but not guarantee) that information's exclusion from such statutory disclosure requirements: (i) the participants agree, confirm and acknowledge that the technology agreement contains trade secrets, financial, scientific and commercial information that is confidential and proprietary to the private-sector participants; (ii) the confirmation and acknowledgement that such confidential and proprietary information is consistently treated in a highly confidential manner by the private-sector participants; (iii) agreement and confirmation that the disclosure of such confidential and proprietary information could reasonably be expected to result in, and cause, the private-sector participants significant and material financial loss, reputational harm and commercial damage that could, in turn, be reasonably expected to severely prejudice the competitive position of the private-sector participants; (iv) agreement and confirmation that the disclosure of such confidential and proprietary information could reasonably be expected to interfere with the private- sector participant's contractual obligations, and/or currently pending commercial relations and negotiations that the private-sector participant is currently engaged in; (v) the agreement and acknowledgement of the public-sector participant that it would not be in the public interest, as it relates to public health, public safety or protection of the environment to disclose any confidential information to any person whatsoever, whether pursuant to FOIA or otherwise; (vi) the public-sector participant's agreement and acknowledgement that disclosure of the private-sector participant's confidential and proprietary information shall not, and could not, under any circumstances, outweigh the significant and irreparable harm, financial loss or prejudice to the competitive position of the private-sector participants that would be caused by any such disclosure; and (vii) the participants' agreement and confirmation that the information disclosed in the course of the transaction was provided to the public-sector participant expressly in reliance upon, and in expectation of, the public-sector participant's obligations of strict confidentiality and non-disclosure, and that the confidential information would not have been provided to, or disclosed to, the public-sector participant but for the confidentiality and non-disclosure provisions hereof.

Of course, those provisions should only be stipulated where they are true and not misleading, and where you have provided the private-sector participant with the information that they reasonably require to contractually agree to such covenants, confirmations and acknowledgments concerning those facts and circumstances. In addition, since the policies of government departments and agencies, and the policies of the administrative tribunals which supervise them, generally require that exclusions from disclosure are to be as specific and as limited as possible, it will generally be in the interests of the private-sector participant to try to be as specific as possible about what information is being claimed as confidential and therefore exempt from disclosure. Of course, from the public sector body's perspective, it will be important to secure contractual rights to disclose information to comply with the FOIA and to provide that the contractor will assist the public sector body in discharging its FOIA obligations.

Regulatory requirements

3.15.5 Since a public-sector participant may be subject to regulatory policies and requirements concerning their project involvement, you should have a complete understanding of those circumstances and their implication on the technology transaction. For example, the technology agreement may have to include provisions that will assist public-sector participants to: (i) collect and report certain information to regulatory authorities on a periodic basis; (ii) undertake regular transactional audits; (iii) require other participants to participate in project reviews; and (iv) generally assist the public-sector participant complying with required administrative, management or governance requirements concerning the project.

Risk-management approach

3.15.6 Generally, the public sector is less tolerant of assuming commercial and transactional risk than the private sector is. Whereas private-sector participants work towards balancing risks and rewards in the ordinary course of a commercial transaction, the public sector is more resistant to assume any risks that may arise due to liabilities that may be caused, or contributed to, by the private-sector participants. Partly for reasons due to their mandate to protect the public interest, and partly for reasons associated with their economic power as an extremely influential consumer of technology goods and services, most technology transactions involving public-sector participants will propose that all associated risks and potential liabilities be managed in a manner that is relatively favourable to the public sector and unfavourable to the private sector. Notwithstanding recent developments in UK contracting policy in the public sector which have established broad principles that risk should sit with the party best able to deal with that risk, since there will generally be very little room for negotiation of mandatory public-sector liability limitations, private-sector participants must determine early in the negotiation process whether the risks associated with the transaction can reasonably be assumed and managed.

Miscellaneous provisions

3.16 As an important business and legal caution, never consider the following miscellaneous provisions of most technology agreements as "boilerplate" or inevitable. Each of those provisions may have significant repercussions for your transaction, and you need to thoroughly understand the relevance and application of each of those provisions to your transaction. Indeed, each of those provisions, and the subject-matter that they address, could radically and profoundly affect both the course and the outcome of your project.

Further assurances

3.16.1 In order to ensure that the objective of the transaction is achieved, the parties should agree to undertake and perform all further actions, undertakings, filings, registrations and to execute and deliver whatever other agreements and documents may be required to implement and perform the terms and conditions of the agreement. For example, such a provision is extremely important to ensure that intellectual property is properly assigned, transferred and conveyed when it is created, and to ensure that the creator will participate in all registrations and filings to protect that intellectual property to the extent required.

Relationship of participants

3.16.2 Because legal relationships carry inherently different responsibilities and potential liabilities, it is important for the technology agreement to clearly stipulate the legal nature of the relationship between the participants. In most circumstances, the legal relationship will be one of "independent contractors" as opposed to principal–agent, trustee–beneficiary, partnership or employer–employee. Therefore, the relationship provisions of a technology agreement routinely clarify those issues, and document the intention of the participants for the benefit of any judicial or arbitral review. In order to avoid any confusion in that regard, you should stipulate the following requirements, where applicable: (i) no participant shall have the right or authority to obligate or legally bind another participant, except as expressly set out in the agreement; (ii) that the agreement does not create any fiduciary obligations among the participants, unless otherwise expressly stated; and (iii) that no participant has the right to direct the manner in which other participants fulfil their obligations and duties under the agreement, except as otherwise expressly provided.

Waiver

3.16.3 In order to protect the integrity of the agreement's change-management and contract-amendment provisions, you should include a provision that stipulates that no delay or omission by a participant to exercise any right or power under the agreement will impair or surrender any such right or power, or otherwise be construed as a waiver of those rights or powers. Furthermore, such provisions routinely stipulate that all waivers among participants must be in writing and signed by the participant waiving such rights or powers. By including those provisions, you will avoid any inadvertent loss of a right or power under the agreement that you did not intend to surrender merely by your failure to exercise that right or power.

As such, in communications between the parties it may be wise to adopt a legend, such as the following:

"This letter/email etc. is without prejudice to the parties and their rights. It is subject to contract and is not intended to affect existing contractual obligations or create new contractual obligations until agreed by the parties in accordance with the contractual change control procedures."

Amendments

3.16.4   Because you will devote considerable resources to properly planning, structuring, negotiating and implementing the transaction, you should ensure that any changes to those commercial arrangements or contractual obligations are thoroughly considered and properly documented. Therefore, you should consider stipulating that the agreement may not be altered, revised or amended in any way without a written agreement to do so, which is executed and delivered by the participants through their authorised representatives. Although the change-management provisions of the agreement will provide the administrative procedure and protocol by which those amendments may be proposed, considered and agreed to, the amendment provisions stipulate the general rule that the participants cannot alter their obligations under the agreement through any verbal arrangements that are not expressed in writing and signed by the participants.

Governing law

3.16.5   Depending upon whether or not the project will be connected with more than one jurisdiction, and the jurisdictional affiliation of the participants, the issue of which jurisdiction's law will govern and interpret the agreement are very important. Generally, the participants are free to choose which jurisdiction's law will govern the agreement, as long as the choice does not offend public policy, such as where the participants are "forum shopping" to avoid the application of laws that would otherwise apply to the transaction. In most cases, participants select the law of a jurisdiction that has a substantial connection with the technology transaction, and which is convenient for the participants. The agreement should clearly and simply stipulate what jurisdiction's law will be relied upon to govern and interpret the participants' obligations, duties and responsibilities.

Other laws

3.16.5.1   In situations in which the participants are from different jurisdictions, they frequently wish to select the laws of an independent jurisdiction to govern the transaction. For example, participants to a transaction between the US and France may wish to choose English law to govern the transaction to ensure legal neutrality. Although both England and France are members of the EU, England's laws are also based on common-law traditions that are similar to those in the US.

If the transaction will be subject to the laws of any jurisdiction that you are not familiar with, you should secure independent legal advice from practitioners who are professionally qualified to practise law in that jurisdiction. In that regard, if any aspects of the agreement are problematic under the law of the governing jurisdiction, you should secure written legal advice concerning those issues, to assist you in the further negotiation and resolution of those matters to reflect the commercial interests of all participants. As a final matter in that regard, you should be especially vigilant against professional advisors who willingly provide you with advice concerning how the transaction will be governed under the laws of other jurisdictions where they are not qualified. Most laws and their interpretation differ greatly between jurisdictions, and you should never assume the homogeneity of laws, regulations, government policy or trade custom across jurisdictional boundaries.

The Brussels Convention of 1968 on Jurisdiction and Enforcement of Judgments in Civil and Criminal Matters states that an aggrieved party should sue a defendant in the state in which that defendant is domiciled[78b] (see Art.2). Note that this general rule can be varied by written agreement to the contrary.

Avoid multiple choices

3.16.5.2   Some technology agreements stipulate that different transactional obligations shall be governed by the laws of different jurisdictions. For example, it is infrequently proposed that the participant's contractual obligations will generally be governed by one jurisdiction's law, whereas the duties and responsibilities with respect to the transaction's intellectual property matters will be governed by another jurisdiction's law. However, such provisions may lead to a tremendous degree of legal uncertainty concerning how a court would apply and interpret such unusual requirements. The lack of certainty that such provisions may create may also make it difficult to either perform or manage the agreement on a practical commercial basis.

Governing law exclusions

3.16.5.3   Although the pervasive norm is to stipulate that the agreement shall be governed by, and interpreted in accordance with, the laws of a single jurisdiction, it is common to exclude the application of particular laws to the transaction. Subject to public-policy concerns, courts may enforce several types of exceptions to the application of a jurisdiction's governing law. First, you should consider excluding conflicts of laws rules that are a part of the laws of the jurisdiction that you have selected, but which could also be relied upon by a court to override the participant's contractual choice of law to select governing laws of a jurisdiction that the participants did not intend. However, as long as the selection of particular jurisdiction's laws to govern the agreement is clear and unequivocal, the practical risk of a court's

---

[78b]   See Art.2.

having to clarify those intentions of the participants by relying upon such conflicts of laws rules may be quite remote. However, many technology managers request that exclusion out of an abundance of caution. Secondly, there may be a broad range of international treaties, conventions and agreements that have been incorporated into the domestic laws of the jurisdiction that you have selected, and which you may wish to exclude as a matter of legal governance and interpretation. For example, Canada participated in the creation of the United Nations' Convention on Contracts for the International Sales of Goods (CISG), which provides a range of consumer protection arrangements. The province of Ontario adopted those measures into its domestic law by enacting the International Sale of Goods Act,[79] which provides that such arrangements shall govern certain commercial transactions unless the participants to those transactions otherwise expressly agree to exclude those statutory arrangements.[80] Note that the UK has not yet ratified the CISG.

Venue

3.16.6   A transactional matter that is closely associated with the participant's choice of governing law is the issue of what jurisdiction's court will resolve transaction disputes, and each participant's agreement to be subject to such judicial authority. The participants should consider whether the judicial authority will be exclusive or non-exclusive, and whether or not they should agree to possible governance by courts of more than one jurisdiction—the selection of which may be at the discretion of any participant, or subject to criteria concerning where the dispute would be more convenient to resolve, based upon the location of evidence, witnesses and the potential litigants. Lastly, participants who are outside of that judicial venue should be required to accept service of any proceedings, and the judicial authority of, those courts.

Publicity

3.16.7   If information concerning the transaction is, for any reason, sensitive and requires controlled distribution, you should include a provision requiring the participants to mutually agree to any information that is released concerning the transaction, including public statements, press conferences, press releases or other public-relations matters associated with the project. Such provisions also frequently require the participants to: (i) work together and co-operate with a separately

---

[79] The federal government of Canada declared, in accordance with Art.93 of that Convention, that the Convention extend to the government of Ontario, and the Ontario government brought the Convention into force pursuant to the International Sale of Goods Act, R.S.O. 1990, c.I-10, and brought it into force in Ontario, May 1, 1992.

[80] Above, n.1, s.6 of that Act permits parties to a contract to exclude the application of that Convention by "expressly providing in the contract . . . that the Convention does not apply to it".

retained public-relations firm with expertise in those matters; and (ii) to comply with stipulated restrictions concerning any regulatory or statutory restrictions concerning the dissemination of information, such as public-company-disclosure requirements or regulatory requirements concerning prior notification to governmental or administrative bodies.

Gifts and gratuities

3.16.8   The laws of many jurisdictions prohibit the use of so-called "gifts" or "gratuities" to select participants, or otherwise enter into commercial arrangements with other individuals. Whether these legal restrictions manifest themselves as anti-bribery, conflict of interest, bid rigging, undisclosed benefits to an agent of a principal, or other legal prohibitions or restrictions, technology agreements routinely include provisions that: (i) prohibit any such conduct, whether in general terms or with explicit reference to particular restrictions; and (ii) require the participants to represent, warrant and covenant that they have not engaged in any such practices.

In UK agreements it is common to refer to the Prevention of Corruption Acts 1889–1916 and to provide that committing an offence under these Acts or otherwise committing fraud will give rise to an immediate right to terminate the agreement.

Assignment restrictions

3.16.9   Where you wish to ensure that each participant shall remain a party to the agreement, and directly engaged in the project, you should prohibit the ability of the participants to assign their obligations, rights and duties under the agreement to any other person. Qualifications on the ability of participants to assign those obligations to others may include: (i) the prior written consent of all other participants, which may be unreasonably withheld or otherwise exercised in the sole and absolute discretion of each participant; (ii) permitted assignment only to affiliates of the participants, or other expressly identified potential assignees; (iii) expressly stated assignee criteria, such as the location of the assignee, valuation, skills, experience, personnel or other performance criteria; (iv) the condition that the assignor remain fully and directly liable for all such assigned obligations, rights and duties, whether as a guarantor of the assignee or otherwise; (v) the condition that another third-party guarantee the performance of the assignee, whether as a guarantor, surety or otherwise; (vi) that the assignee will fully assume all of the performance obligations, risks, duties and responsibilities of the assignor; and (vii) the complete and accurate disclosure to the participants of all relevant information concerning the proposed assignee so that those approving the assignment can conduct a reasonable due diligence investigation of the proposed assignee. Bankruptcy law of various jurisdictions may interfere with, or not allow, assignment to third parties without consent of the other participant. Therefore, you may wish to secure the specialist advice of insolvency counsel if those issues are of particular concern to the transaction.

Change of control

3.16.10   Since the issue of who controls each participant is so closely related to the governance and the identity of each participant and to the nature of the relationship among participants, you should consider stipulating that any change in the control of any other participants will constitute grounds for either termination of the transaction, or that participant's continued involvement in the project. Those provisions may include the following: (i) that the change of control should be broadly defined to mean either majority ownership or any other form of actual, or *de facto*, control; (ii) that such circumstances may apply only where the subject participant will be controlled by a competitor of any other participant; (iii) requiring that each participant provide reasonably prompt, complete and accurate notice of any change in the control to the other participants; (iv) that any sale, transfer or other conveyance of all, or substantially all, of the assets of the participant (or those business assets that are designated for project use) shall constitute a change of control of the participant's business and operations; and (v) any conditions upon which any continued involvement of a participant in the project shall be permitted.

Successors

3.16.11   Technology agreements routinely stipulate that: (i) the agreement shall ensure for the benefit of any successors, heirs, estate or trustees of any participant; (ii) the agreement shall bind all such successors and permitted assignees; or (iii) that the agreement shall be terminable by any participant upon the dissolution or death of any other participant.

Compliance with laws

3.16.12   As discussed throughout this book, it is extremely important to include a general provision in the agreement that requires the participants to adhere to and fully comply with: (i) all applicable laws, regulations and governmental policies and published guidelines; (ii) all applicable judgements, orders, rulings, administrative decisions and arbitral decisions of any court or other body of competent jurisdiction; and (iii) all specifically identified and stipulated legal or trade-association performance requirements or standards. A matter for debate will be whether this obligation applies merely to legislation existing at the date of execution of the agreement, or to subsequent enactments that modify and replace the existing legislation. Some agreements will be drafted so as to include all present and future laws but allow for relief for the affected party where the new laws discriminate in a specific way against that party.

Contract execution and delivery

3.16.13 In situations where the participants will not be able to execute and deliver the same copy of the agreement, you can arrange for the participants to execute and deliver the agreement in counterpart by expressly stipulating that each participant may sign separate copies of the agreement and provide each of the other participants with an originally executed copy. Similarly, where appropriate, the participants may also agree to the execution of facsimile copies, or to express their assent to the agreement by affixing or authorising the issuance of an electronic or digital signature.[81]

The validity and effectiveness of an electronic signature in the UK is regulated by the Electronic Communications Act 2000[81a] which is, in the UK Government's view, the legislation required to implement the requirements of Directive 1999/93 on a Community Framework for Electronic Signatures. [81b]

Under this Act, an electronic signature is so much of anything in electronic form as:

(a) is incorporated into or otherwise logically associated with any electronic communication or electronic data; and

(b) purports to be so incorporated or associated for the purposes of being used in establishing the authenticity of the communication or data, the integrity of the communication or date, or both.[81c]

Notice

3.16.14 Since most technology agreements require the participants to communicate and provide important information to each other on an ongoing basis, the agreement should stipulate detailed procedures and information both to facilitate notice and to define legally when notice is provided and received among the participants. Those provisions should: (i) define what communications shall be subject to the notice provisions, including all notices, requests, approvals, consents, exchange of information and all other communications; (ii) stipulate that all notices shall be in writing, including any other acceptable electronic forms; (iii) the method of delivery, including email, facsimile, regular mail, courier or delivery service, telex or registered mail; (iv) the title and complete address of the recipient, since notices should be delivered to a registered office where appropriate to avoid problems of personnel change-over; (v) all required telex, facsimile, email, telephone and other contact

---

[81] Ensure that all electronic or digital signatures comply with the legal requirements of the governing jurisdiction.

[81a] See s.7.

[81b] There remains debate as to whether the UK Government has sufficiently implemented the Directive.

[81c] See s.7(2).

information that supports the address of the recipient; (vi) to whom notices should be copied; (vii) whether or not the participants must confirm delivery and receipt of notices by telephone (or voice mail); (viii) that participants shall notify each other of any address changes, and the time period in which the new address shall take effect after such notice; (ix) the time period after notices are sent that they shall be deemed to have been received; (x) whether or not notices shall be copied to any relevant third parties, such as subcontractors, guarantors, sureties or affiliated entities; and (xi) that each participant shall be solely responsible for the cost and expense of all notices that they send.

Survival

3.16.15   To ensure that certain obligations of the participants shall continue after and survive any expiry or termination of the agreement, you should include a provision stipulating which of those obligations shall survive in full force and effect. Such surviving obligations typically include: (i) intellectual property rights; (ii) confidentiality; (iii) limitation of liability; (iv) indemnities; (v) specific remedial provisions and consequences of termination; (vi) dispute resolution, including choice of law, venue and ADR provisions; (vii) all relevant interpretative provisions, such as severability, definitions and entire agreement; and (viii) the survival provisions— otherwise, the entire effort to stipulate the survival of all such provisions may turn out to have been in vain.

Entire Agreement

3.16.16   This Clause sets out the boundaries of an agreement. It states that the agreement contains all the terms of the agreement between the parties and that in entering the contract neither party has relied on any representations. The purpose is to prevent the implication of any additional terms based upon, for example, statements printed in sales literature or oral statements made by the negotiation team.

   This clause should ensure that, as a matter of commercial certainty, all obligations are recorded in the agreement. However, notwithstanding the presence of such a clause, it is not unheard of for courts to rule that other documents should be taken into consideration when interpreting a contract.[81d]

[81d] See *e.g. Thomas Witter Ltd. v TBP Industries* [1996] 2 All E.R. 573 which held that exclusion of liability for fraudulent misrepresentation could never be reasonable. This has meant that the convention for drafting entire agreement clauses is to expressly state that the agreement, referenced documents and other schedules and annexes represent the entire agreement of the parties, "save for fraudulent misrepresentation".

Chapter 4

Risk-management strategies

"A prince must play the animal well . . . He must be a fox, therefore, to recognise the traps, and a lion to frighten the wolves."—Niccolo Machiavelli, *The Prince*

Checklist IV: Reasonably managing risk

4.1 Relationship management
- ☐ Project-management committee
- ☐ Performance information reporting
- ☐ Choosing battles
- ☐ Controlling project personnel turnover
- ☐ Project morale

4.2 Proactive risk-management strategies
- ☐ Performance requirements
- ☐ Breach reporting
- ☐ Record-keeping
- ☐ Monitor participant performance
  - ○ Verification/audit
  - ○ Participant records
  - ○ Follow-up

4.3 Exclusion of liability

4.4 Limitation of liability
- ☐ Exemplary damages
- ☐ Economic expectations
- ☐ Indirect, incidental and consequential damages
- ☐ Third-party damages
  - ○ Third-party damages
  - ○ Third-party beneficiaries

4.5 Performance disclaimers

4.6 Indemnification of liability

4.7 Access to specified remedies
- ☐ Repair and replace
- ☐ Performance adjustment
- ☐ Service credits
- ☐ Price adjustments
- ☐ Liquidated damages
  - ○ Enforceability issues
  - ○ No penalty
  - ○ Quantum
  - ○ Fair and reasonable
- ☐ Access to alternative services/products
- ☐ Equitable relief
- ☐ Time requirements
- ☐ Enforceability enhancements
- ☐ Contingency planning
  - ○ Contingency and emergency-response plan
  - ○ Disaster-recovery and back-up systems
  - ○ Redundancy
  - ○ Supplier arrangements
  - ○ Source code escrow
  - ○ Government agencies

    ○ Succession planning

    ○ Contingency audits

4.8 Dispute resolution

    ☐ Internal escalation

    ☐ Alternative dispute resolution

       ○ Expert consultation

       ○ Mediation

       ○ Arbitration

    ☐ Litigation issues

4.9 Third-party risk-deferral strategies

    ☐ Additional parties

    ☐ Risk assumption

    ☐ Insurance

    ☐ Letters of Credit

    ☐ Performance bond

    ☐ Professional opinions

    ☐ Trusted third parties

4.10 Financial arrangements

    ☐ Payment adjustments

       ○ Payment advances

       ○ Payment retention

       ○ Payment milestones

       ○ Remuneration rates and adjustments

    ☐ Payments in escrow

    ☐ Security interests

4.11 Planning for termination and extrication

    ☐ Document the reliance

    ☐ Transition plan

    ☐ Transition services

    ☐ Competitor assistance

    ☐ Separate contract

    ☐ Joint Management Committee

The next step in the sequential progression of planning, structuring, negotiating and implementing a successful technology transaction requires the participants to consider and analyse all the transaction's commercial arrangements in the context of, and as a part of, a risk-management strategy that practically and effectively minimises, if not avoids, project delays, participant disputes and potential liabilities that may arise. In my experience, the most effective risk-management strategies require the blending of a very broad spectrum of participant obligations, administrative requirements and governance duties, all of which are designed to identify and address proactively the most frequent and serious dangers for project delay, dispute and liability. The goal is to get the deal done in a manner that protects participant relationships, maximises the chances of project success and minimises disputes and liabilities.

Just as Chapter 3 was devoted to recognising the pitfalls and transactional traps of Machiavelli's fox, this chapter is devoted to helping create Machiavelli's risk-management lion to frighten the project's liability wolves.

Relationship management

4.1 Many technology managers make the mistake of regarding participant relationships as an operational and administrative matter, rather than as an essential risk-management strategy. Since most transactional delays, disputes and liabilities arise either directly or indirectly as a result of poor commercial relationships, there are several strategies that you should consider to improve participant communication, trust and co-operation.

Project-management committee

4.1.1 Perhaps one of the most important relationship-building structures that you can create is the project's Joint Management Committee, which typically comprises one or two management representatives of each participant. By requiring regular meetings and stipulating reporting obligations, Joint Management Committees can provide the following transaction and relationship management assistance: (i) facilitating communication and building trust among managers who are likely to establish a personal rapport; (ii) identifying concerns before they have time to escalate into problems and potential disputes; (iii) creating a management forum for internal dispute resolution; (iv) creating an administrative and governance mechanism for project management; (v) engendering a sense of equal participation in the project among all participants; and (vi) creating a sense of management accountability and direct project involvement among the participants.

Technology agreements routinely stipulate the membership of the Joint Management Committee, how often it will meet, the subject-matter of its mandate, whether or not minutes of its meetings will be recorded, its dispute-resolution involvement and authority, circumstances in which it will be required to involve each participant's executive management, and whether or not it will have any authority to amend the technology agreement. Even if the technology joint venture or project corporation has a board of directors, you should also consider establishing a Joint Management Committee as an essential first line of governance and operational management among the participants.

Performance information reporting

4.1.2 In an effort to identify and resolve potential transaction problems before they become disputes, you should require each participant to monitor and regularly report upon their performance of the transaction. In particular, such performance reports should focus on operational difficulties, delays or deficiencies at their very earliest emergence so that the participants, whether through the Joint Management Committee or otherwise, can discuss and address the issues constructively and in a spirit of resolution. Through the discipline of tracking, reporting and reacting to transaction difficulties as they arise, the participants will be better prepared to address and resolve such matters proactively. All technology transactions, from technology procurement to outsourcing services, will face project challenges; they are inevitable and should be expected. It is the administrative anticipation of these matters and the way they are proactively managed that can make the difference between project success and failure.

Choosing battles

4.1.3   Once a technology transaction is launched and in need of management supervision on a day-to-day basis, it is easy to be overwhelmed by the minutiae of the project's operations and temporarily lose sight of the project's overall objectives. Therefore, both as a matter of management efficiency and relationship preservation, you should ensure that the transaction managers chose their battles carefully and with judgment, taking into account the business objectives that originally brought the participants together. This discipline can be entrenched in the technology agreement by making a distinction between minor issues of concern and material issues of importance in various provisions, including: (i) topics of discussion for Joint Management Committee meetings; (ii) performance-reporting obligations; (iii) change management and requirements and procedure; (iv) structuring the internal-disputes resolution protocol; (v) identifying which matters will be the subject of either mediation or arbitration; (vi) various remedial provisions concerning each participant's performance obligations; and (vii) distinguishing between material and minor obligations, such as in the service-level definitions. For example, dispute escalation and resolution provisions frequently require disputes to be elevated to very senior executives representing each participant so that even the most difficult and serious transactional disputes will be considered by executives who will have a much broader perspective of how to balance the interests of the project against the interests of each participant concerning the subject-matter of the dispute.

Controlling project personnel turnover

4.1.4   Since the quality of communication and trust among participants will greatly depend upon the personal rapport between each participant's representatives, it is not surprising that personnel turnover may have a detrimental impact on participant relations. Therefore, in order to foster and protect the direct connection between personal relationships and the ability of the participants to avoid transaction delays, disputes and liabilities, you should consider including restrictions or other controls on the ability of participants to remove or re-assign personnel from the project. In addition to stipulating requirements in key-person provisions previously discussed, you should consider other strategies to reduce personnel turnover, such as: (i) restricting the ability of other participants to replace or reassign project personnel, perhaps on a "percentage per year limit" basis; (ii) require participants to consult and discuss personnel reassignments; (iii) require the consent of participants to replace or re-assign strategic personnel who are not otherwise defined as key personnel; (iv) provide retention incentives, such as salary increase, project-completion bonuses or professional development enhancements; (vi) make employee-assistance programmes ("EAPs") available to project personnel; (vi) directly involve your organisation's human-resource professionals in developing strategies to mitigate such turnover; and (vii) stipulating a minimum term of project assignment that personnel would subscribe to.

Project morale

4.1.5 Although most transaction managers will readily acknowledge that personnel and project morale is one of the most important ingredients to a technology project's success, issues concerning this are rarely addressed in technology agreements. However, considering the vital relationship between project morale and the success of your risk-management strategy, you should consider the following agreement provisions: (i) require the participants to engage personnel in the management of the project by regularly seeking the advice and recommendations of personnel concerning transaction and project improvements, whether via personnel interviews, questionnaires or anonymous surveys; (ii) organise regular business or social-project gatherings where relevant personnel will have an informal opportunity to meet and discuss project matters of concern to them; (iii) continually monitor the morale of project personnel, whether through anonymous surveys or other consultations; (iv) ensure that the compensation structures and levels are appropriate and reasonable for the transaction, and that all personnel remuneration has been adjusted to any unique or unusual circumstances of the transaction; and (v) to keep all personnel reasonably informed, on a timely basis, of all management issues that are related to their project involvement. Lastly, depending upon the nature of the transaction, human-resource advisors with particular expertise in these matters can be extremely helpful in identifying any particular personnel requirements and obligations that should be included in the agreement.

Proactive risk-management strategies

4.2 By understanding the most frequent causes for transactional delay, disputes and liabilities, and by extrapolating those to transactional issues in a manner that allows you to address those matters in the agreement, you can directly address these concerns in administratively practical and commercially relevant ways.

Performance requirements

4.2.1 In my experience, the vast majority of transaction disputes and the litigation of technology agreements are connected, in some way, to the participants' failure to define their respective performance requirements adequately. Therefore, the risk-management significance of thoroughly defining those obligations in the agreement is obvious. Conversely, any failure to completely define the operational, functional and technical requirements and specifications of their performance obligations will create a directly proportional gap and deficiency in your risk-management strategy. This matter is so germane to the project's entire risk profile that you should heed this warning: If you are not in a position to manage such dangerous transaction risks by adequately defining each participant's performance obligations, you should consider whether or not you are ready to engage in the proposed transaction or project at all. If each participant's performance obligations cannot be adequately defined, then it may be more appropriate and prudent for your organisation first to identify and define the performance requirements and specifications, and then proceed with the next phase of the intended project.

Stepping back to engage in a preliminary project to define transactional needs and requirements is a very common and essential risk-management strategy. Transaction managers often separate "define it and build it" projects into two distinct and separate transactions, where their needs and requirements are fully defined independently of the participant who will "build it". Once the relevant performance obligations are defined, all the commercial and risk-management aspects of the "build it" phase of the transaction can be negotiated and settled in the informed context of the defined performance obligations. When considering the risks and merits of whether or not the transaction's performance requirements are adequately defined, you should consider the harm of delaying the project for that purpose and the associated risk-management benefits.

Breach reporting

4.2.2   In order to minimise the occasions on which small problems could have been proactively addressed and prevented from becoming causes of project delay, dispute and liability, the agreement should require participants both to audit the performance of their obligations and to report any delays, difficulties or deficiencies as promptly as possible. Self-monitoring procedures are also excellent quality-control and continuous-improvement measures. Often, participants make the mistake of not reporting their deficient performance for fear that such information will be used against them in a claim for breach of contract or other dispute. However, by stipulating cure periods, constructive (non-punitive) remedial action, and by reserving any causes of monetary damages to continuing or material performance failures, the agreement can include a range of provisions that induce participants to report difficulties and act quickly and responsibly to minimise project failures. Once the participants decide on this strategy, you should ensure that all provisions of the technology agreement promote and foster such proactive measures.

Record-keeping

4.2.3   An important aspect of any risk-management strategy is the recording and maintenance of reliable information concerning the performance of each participant's obligations. A significant number of any transaction's serious problems could be easily mitigated, if not avoided, if certain information were documented and readily available to transaction managers for proactive identification and resolution. Depending upon how the transaction's information is organised and presented, it may be relatively easy to identify a broad range of emerging situations long before they become problematic. Therefore, the agreement should stipulate: (i) what information concerning the transaction will be recorded and maintained; (ii) how, and at what location, will the information be recorded; (iii) what reports and records will be produced concerning the information, and how regularly; (iv) which participants will be entitled to receive and review the information; (v) require that all such records shall be accurate, complete and current; (vi) whether or not an independent third party, who may be retained to monitor the progress of the project, should be the recipient of such information; (vii) whether or not the participants will be able to rely on that information to resolve disputes; and (viii) all other record-keeping, integrity and reliability standards obligations that are otherwise discussed in Chapter 3.

Monitor participant performance

4.2.4 In addition to clearly defining each participant's performance obligations, and requiring each participant to maintain performance records, and to report any delays or deficiencies in their performance, it is also very important to monitor the performance of other participants to ensure their compliance with performance obligations on an ongoing basis. Regardless of the rights and duties that are created in any technology agreement, one of the most frequent failures of risk-management strategies, and reasons for project liability, arise because the participants did not keep track of the other participants' performance on a regular and timely basis. Therefore, you should consider the following provisions to promote the ongoing awareness of all participants in the project's implementation, performance and development.

Verification/audit

4.2.4.1 Technology agreements routinely provide participants with the right to audit and inspect the books and records of participants concerning their performance and compliance with the agreement. Those audits may be subject to: (i) being undertaken by an independent third party, which would be subject to confidentiality arrangements; (ii) restrict the auditor to disclose only the results of such audit to interested third parties, and not the confidential raw data of the audit; (iii) reasonable prior notice; (iv) only inspecting information that is directly relevant to the agreement, and to no other aspect of the participants' business; (v) to restrictions concerning your right to make copies of any such records or books; (vi) to your non-interference in the commercial operations of the participant, and perhaps only undertaking such audits and inspection during ordinary business hours; and (vii) a limited number of times in which any such audit or inspection may be undertaken within a stipulated time period. You should also stipulate your entitlement to rely upon such information as evidence of their truth and accuracy, and that you will have the right to rely on this information in any dispute-resolution proceedings concerning the subject-matter to which such information may relate.

Participant records

4.2.4.2 As a matter of transaction management, participants should be required to maintain accurate, complete and current records of all communications, materials and documents concerning each participant's performance of their obligations. That may take the form of retention and storage for emails, memoranda, correspondence, meeting notes, progress reports, presentations and similar third-party communications. You should appoint a manager with the responsibility for reviewing and monitoring these materials, and ensure that any information that is relevant to any project delays, disputes or liabilities is escalated to the attention of either the transaction's managers or the Joint Management Committee. Very often, information concerning fundamental project problems and performance deficiencies are communicated among participants at operational levels that do not have the routine scrutiny of the transaction's management. Therefore, it is essential to create an information-gathering and reporting protocol so that the information may be acted on promptly and efficiently as a matter of both project administration and risk management.

Follow-up

4.2.4.3 Obviously, the participants may be inundated with a tremendous amount of valuable information to assist them proactively to resolve potential transaction problems. However, none of that information will have any risk-management benefit if the participants do not act promptly on the information in a decisive manner. Therefore, the agreement should stipulate that parties should disclose any information that they have concerning another participant's performance obligations, and promptly act upon any circumstance that could reasonably be expected to cause project delays, disputes or liabilities. As with the adage "cook or get out of the kitchen", it may be unfair for participants to rely on information concerning performance deficiencies that they have known about for an extended period of time. A participant's response obligations may include: (i) confirming the truth, timeliness, completeness or accuracy of such information; (ii) raising the information as a matter for Joint Management Committee discussion; and (iii) undertaking further internal investigations concerning the source and reliability of such information.

Exclusions of liability

4.3 All commercial transactions find a balance between risk and reward for both participants engaged in the transaction, and technology transactions are no exception. That balance is, in part, a measure of both the levels of risk tolerance that are unique to each participant and the commercial norms and trade customs that are common within technology industries.

There are several types of liability that most participants to technology transac-

204

tions routinely determine are not acceptable or even tolerable risks to assume or to be subject to during the project. Over time, that common perspective develops into a broad range of normative transactional expectations related to pricing, preventative governance strategies, alternative dispute resolution and the complete exclusion of certain potential risks and liabilities from the project. Without liability exclusions, the entire risk–reward balance would greatly shift, and many other aspects of the agreement would have to be revised to re-define this balance, including the project's financial arrangements which ultimately compensates participants for the commercial risks that they accept in any technology transaction.

Limitation of liability

4.4 Regardless of whether or not the technology agreement excludes all or any of the risks and potential liabilities discussed in **4.3** above, the participants should consider limiting the amount of any such risks and potential liabilities that have not been expressly excluded.

The strategies that are frequently used to limit each participant's liability under technology agreements include: (i) considering whether participants should have mutual and reciprocal liability protection, with identical rights of risk limitation, or whether participants should be subject to different limitation provisions that uniquely address each participant's involvement in, and responsibility for, the technology project; (ii) what liability limits should apply on a "per occurrence" or "per year" basis, and what liability limits should apply "in the aggregate, for all occurrences"; (iii) whether or not the maximum liability and risk should be stated as a fixed amount; (iv) whether or not the maximum liability and risk should be stated as a formula, such as the amount of revenues during a stipulated time period or another "transaction value" calculation; (v) stipulating different liability limitations for different causes of action and sources of liability; (vi) excluding other remedial provisions from the liability limitations, such as liquidated damages, price adjustments or other financial remedies; (vii) whether or not the indemnity provisions of the agreement should be either subject to or excluded from the limitation of liability provisions; and (viii) whether or not any causes of action and sources of liability should be exempted from such limitations, such as negligence, wilful misconduct, personal injury or loss of life, property damage or breach of confidentiality and intellectual property provisions.

When drafting limitation of liability clauses for agreements governed by English law, one must be mindful of certain statutory provisions which (essentially) force the draftsman's hand. First, it is not permitted to limit or exclude liability for death or personal injury and, secondly, the Unfair Contract Terms Act 1977 prohibits exclusions or limitations of liability under s.12 of the Sale of Goods Act and s.2 of the Supply of Goods and Services Act.

Having dealt with the unexcludeable elements above, it is then common practice to draft a limitation of liability clause in a number of separate parts, the aim being to save some of the provisions if one element is adjudged unenforceable. As such, you will normally see a separate limit for property lost because insurance for property losses is generally cheaper to obtain and simpler to negotiate than insurance cover in respect of other liabilities.

Figures for limits of liability should reflect quantifiable potential loss to the parties. As such, contract value is relevant but not the only factor. Risk, agreement subject-matter and political environment are merely some of the additional factors which should affect the limits set.

Exemplary damages

4.4.1   Under English law, the courts take a dim view of clauses which would award damages to one part, effectively penalising the other party, the argument running that it would be unconscionable for a party to demand damages which outweigh any losses actually suffered.[81e]

In some other common-law jurisdictions, however, and most notably in Canada, participants frequently exclude the application of exemplary or punitive damages from technology agreements. Punitive damages may be awarded by a court against a wrongdoer for exceptionally egregious conduct. The inherent ability of a court to award such damages are not compensatory but are a way of punishing a participant. Much like the imposition of a fine for conduct worthy of punishment in a criminal court, exemplary or punitive damages are often justified on the basis that they are a deterrence against conduct that is worthy of penal sanction. The variety of conduct that may precipitate exemplary or punitive damages has included "malicious", "oppressive", "vicious", "grossly fraudulent", "callous" and "disgraceful".[82] Although technology agreements routinely exclude those damages from the risks that participants may be exposed to, the participants may wish to further agree that they shall not apply to the court, or otherwise, seek such relief.

Economic expectations

4.4.2   There are commercial transactions where a defaulting participant would be liable to compensate the injured participant for damages associated with lost business or other economic opportunities, inability to commercially exploit intellectual property or information, lost profits, business interruption and for preventing the injured participant from achieving a reasonably expected or anticipated level of commercial and financial success. Although such damages are generally qualified by principles of foreseeability and the proximity of the damages to the event(s) causing such harm, technology agreements routinely (almost without exception) exclude any such consequential or incidental damages, even if the injured participants have advised

[81e] See, *e.g. Dunlop Pneumatic Tyre Co v New Garage and Motor Co* (1915) A.C. 79.
[82] See S.M. Waddams, *The Law of Damages* (2nd ed., Canada Law Book Inc., Toronto, 2001), para.11.210, p.11–9, n.46.

the defaulting participant of the likelihood of such foreseeable and proximate damages arising. There are several reasons for the pervasive norm of excluding all economic expectation liability from technology transactions, including: (i) practically, it is a likely and prominent risk since technology is very frequently required for the very heart of a participant's operations and business activities, and would as frequently precipitate those damages; (ii) depending upon the injured participant's business, such damages may be enormous, and most importantly far exceed the relative benefit of the transaction for the defaulting participant; and (iii) the markets for most technologies cannot absorb or tolerate the pricing structures that would be required to compensate a technology provider fairly and reasonably for such risks and liabilities. With regard to the latter issue, there are many inexpensive technologies that are mission-critical to the operation of large businesses; their failure to operate properly could cause immeasurable damage to these businesses' future commercial opportunities and profits. Many industry pundits have argued that commerce as we know it, technologically dependent as it is, would grind to a halt if even a small percentage of such technology were priced to reflect such liability exposure.

Indirect, incidental and consequential damages

4.4.3 Sometimes it is easier to describe what something is by describing what it is not—and this is the case with indirect, incidental and consequential risks and liabilities that may arise in the course of a technology project.

Generally, transactional risks and liabilities are governed by the principle "restitution in integrum"—to make the plaintiff whole. That principle may be categorised into two distinct aspects: restoring to the plaintiff what has been lost, and the plaintiff's expectations for what would have been gained. The first aspect of that principle seeks to restore plaintiffs for sums spent, debts incurred and the cost of such restitution. Usually, these risks are associated with replacement costs and damages, out-of-pocket expenses and liabilities incurred to put the plaintiff in the position that it would have been in if the default had not occurred. The second aspect of that principle seeks to compensate plaintiffs for their lost expectations and for the reliance that they placed on the lost opportunity had the transaction been successful. S.M. Waddens has described these two principles of liability in the following way: ". . . compensation may be usefully regarded as containing two elements: a substitute for loss of the value of the property and a substitute for the loss of the opportunity to use it."[83]

Although technology agreements generally accept some level of risk, and liability exposure, for direct damages, they very often exclude all other damages or potential liability that do not adhere to the strict and narrow compensatory principle of direct restitutive damages. Such exclusionary provisions are often simply drafted as a covenant that no participant shall be liable to any other participant for

[83] S.M. Waddams, *The Law of Damages* (2nd ed., Canada Law Book, Toronto, 2001), p.1–1, para.1.20.

any indirect, incidental or consequential liability, costs or damages, regardless of how such liability may arise, whether for breach of contract, in tort (negligence), in equity, or as a result of any other form of action or source of liability.

Under English law, the object of damages for breach of contract is to put the wronged party in the position it would have been in if the contract had been performed according to its terms. Loss can be recovered, under the rule in the leading case: *Hadley v Baxendale*[83a], under two limbs, as described below. Generally, loss can be recovered if it was of a kind within the reasonable contemplation of the parties at the time at which the contract was entered into.

The distinction between the first and second limbs of *Hadley* is important because much of the case law on the meaning to be given to clauses excluding liability for indirect or consequential loss makes use of the distinction. It is also important because it is necessary to understand what is recoverable as a "direct" loss under the first limb in order to fix a sensible financial limit of liability.

The first limb of *Hadley* refers to loss naturally flowing, in the ordinary course of things, from the breach. Under this limb, the necessary knowledge to support "reasonable contemplation" is imputed to the parties. The second limb requires actual knowledge. This is loss of such a type as may reasonably be supposed, because of special circumstances known at least to the breaching party, to have been within the contemplation of the parties, at the time of signature of the contract, as the probable result of the breach.

In relation to losses such as costs of obtaining replacement systems, costs caused by delays and inconvenience of having non-operational software and loss of anticipated savings, there does not appear to be any legal principle saying that these will always be considered to be indirect in nature. An initial hurdle will need to be surmounted when considering whether, at the time of the contract, these types of loss were in the reasonable contemplation of the parties. If not, the losses will not be recoverable. But if they were, then the losses could be either direct or indirect in nature, depending upon the circumstances.

As *Hadley* suggests, indirect or consequential losses are losses other than direct loss arising naturally from a breach of contract. The case law has recognised a wide variety of loss arising directly and naturally from a breach and therefore not barred by any contractual exclusion of indirect/consequential loss. These have included, for example, extra costs incurred by reason of men and materials being kept on site without work[84]; inflation costs related to delays in carrying out the work[85]; costs of hardware required to be purchased due to deficient performance of software[86].

A series of recent decisions[87] have made clear that the expression "consequential loss" will be interpreted restrictively against the party relying on it if not further

---

[83a] (1854) 9 Exch. 341.

[84] See *Croudace Construction Ltd v Cawoods Concrete Products Ltd* [1978] 2 Lloyd's Rep 55.

[85] *ibid.*

[86] *Kwikfit Insurance Services Ltd v Bull Information Systems Limited*, unreported, June 23, 2000.

[87] Including *British Sugar plc v James Robertson & Sons Ltd* (1996) R.P.C. 281.

defined. It has also been established that loss of profit can be direct or indirect, depending on the circumstances of the loss.

Clauses by which the supplier excludes consequential loss altogether give rise to two principal issues. First, what do the parties mean by "consequential loss"? And secondly, is the exclusion reasonable under the Unfair Contract Terms Act? In principle, it is permissible for parties to a commercial agreement to exclude liability for indirect or other consequential loss, and the Court of Appeal dicta in *Watford v Sanderson*[88] provided strong support for this (recognising that there as a commercially reasonable allocation of risk).

Depending upon the nature of the technology transaction, you may go further to address specific types of such non-direct damages and for which participants will clearly and expressly not be liable, including: (i) any detrimental effect on a participant's goodwill or reputation, including any loss of market confidence or harm to a participant's commercial brand; (ii) catastrophic events or disasters that may be associated with a particular cause, such as technology that is used in connection with large communication networks, air-traffic control, mass transportation systems, nuclear-power generation or health care; and (iii) any liability, loss, harm, risk, damage, injury, cost or expense whatsoever that is not direct, and directly proximate, to the cause.

Third-party damages

4.4.4

Third-party damages

4.4.4.1 Participants may wish to limit their liability in connection with the agreement to only those damages that have been incurred by a participant to the transaction (*i.e.* a person who is a party to the technology agreement), and to exclude any liability or responsibility for any harm or damages that any other person (generally referred to as "third parties") has suffered in any connection with the project. Such exclusions are principally designed to prevent participants from flowing through damages and liabilities that they incur to third parties (*i.e.* third-party damages) to the other participants. Therefore, such liability exclusions allocate the liability and risk for each participant's third-party arrangements to each prospective participant, and precludes the attribution of those liabilities and risks to the other participants. Obviously, no agreement in a contract among participants can bind individuals who are not a party to that contract, and prevent third parties from taking legal action against the participants where they have a cause of action. However, such third-party liability exclusions may be an effective strategy to reduce each participant's liability and risk exposure to other participants under the technology agreement.

---

[88] *Watford Electronics Limited v Sanderson CFL Ltd* (2002) F.S.R. 19.

Third-party beneficiaries

4.4.4.2 Many technology agreements expressly exclude the right of persons who are not participants to the technology agreement, or participants in the project, from enforcing any rights, duties or obligations concerning the technology transaction. As such, a routine clause in technology agreements is to disapply the provisions of the Contracts (Rights of Third Parties) Act 1999. Such exclusions typically stipulate the following: (i) an agreement and acknowledgment of direct and personal obligation and duty of the transaction participants; (ii) a disclaimer and denial of any duty, obligation or responsibility concerning non-participants and any detrimental reliance they may have concerning the project; (iii) an agreement and confirmation that only participants who are expressly agreed to shall have the right and entitlement to enforce (or otherwise make a claim concerning) the technology agreement, or any other duties and obligations of participants, concerning the technology agreement and the project; (v) that no rights, duties, obligations, property, benefits or confidential information is being held by any project participant for, or on behalf of, any other person whether in trust, as an agent, or otherwise; and (vi) that the participants shall have no obligation, responsibility, duty, liability or other risk whatsoever to any persons who are not participants to the agreement, and that the project participants have not been expressly authorised, agreed to or otherwise recognised as "third-party beneficiaries" of the technology agreement or project.

Performance disclaimers

4.5 There are many important ways to qualify and narrow the technology agreement's liability provisions to exclude circumstances and risks that should not fairly be attributed to a defaulting party. Although a participant may agree to a maximum amount of potential liability in connection with the project, circumstances for which a participant should not be responsible or liable may include: (i) any good, service or information concerning the project that the participant did not provide; (ii) any good, equipment, technology or data that is either connected with, networked to, used in conjunction with, or attached to the participant's products that was not provided by the participant; (iii) any alteration, customisation, modification, enhancement, revision or other change to any part or aspect of any good, service or information that was either made by a person other than the participant or without the participant's prior consent; (iv) circumstances concerning the care, maintenance, protection and safety of the good or information after it is no longer under the custody or control of the participant; (v) to the extent that any part or aspect of such liability or risk was caused, or otherwise contributed to, by any failure of the non-defaulting participant to perform any duty, obligation or responsibility, *e.g.* breach of contract, tort (negligence) or failure to perform either a statutory or equitable duty; (vi) events of *force majeure*, that are defined separately in the technology agreement; and (vii) to the extent that any part or aspect of such liability or risk was caused, or otherwise contributed to, by any person other than the participant.

Indemnification of liability

4.6 In addition to managing the project's risks by either limiting or excluding certain liabilities, technology agreements frequently identify aspects of the transaction for which one participant should assume most or all of the risk. The allocation of stipulated risks are usually set out in provisions where the participant assuming such risks and liability indemnifies (and "saves harmless") the other participants from the risks.

Indemnification provisions have several important aspects, including: (i) which participants, or other interested individuals, should be indemnified, *e.g.* participants, individuals benefiting from the project, affiliated individuals, directors, officers and employees; (ii) for what causes of liability, or subject-matter should participants be indemnified, *e.g.* breach (material or substantial) of confidentiality or intellectual property obligations, personal injury or death, breach of applicable regulatory requirements, fraudulent misrepresentation or any harm or liability that a participant may cause to a third party, such as infringing another person's intellectual property or confidentiality rights; (iii) the scope of the indemnity as to time, geographic territory or specific causes of action, *e.g.* restricting the scope of an intellectual property indemnification to copyright and trade-mark claims and actions in England for two years; (iv) restricting the indemnification to losses and liabilities that are finally determined and awarded by a court (or arbitrator) of competent jurisdiction; (v) whether or not indemnified participants should have the right to participate, whether as observers or otherwise, in any claims, actions, proceedings or litigation concerning third-party sources of risk and liability; (vi) whether or not the indemnity should include the injured participant's costs and expenses (including reasonable legal fees) associated with the cause of the indemnified liability and risk; (vii) whether or not the indemnity should extend to interest and punitive damages that may be awarded against the indemnified participant; (viii) the duty of the indemnified participant to mitigate any risks and liabilities that it may suffer; (ix) whether or not any indemnities should be subject to any liability restrictions or limitations; and (x) whether or not any third parties should guarantee, or be a party to, such indemnification, such as the indemnifying participant's parent company, or any prime or subcontractors.

Depending upon the nature and scope of the transaction's indemnities, it may be reasonable to qualify those rights in accordance with the following conditions: (i) that a participant shall not be indemnified to the extent that it has caused or contributed to the liability, *e.g.* modified or used technology in an unpermitted manner, or for an unauthorised purpose; (ii) that the indemnified participant "promptly" notifies the indemnifying participant of the claim, action or subject proceeding; (iii) that the indemnified participant shall fully co-operate with, and assist (at which participant's cost and expense?) the indemnifying participant in connection with the response to, or defence of, such risk, including providing accurate, complete and timely information concerning any such matters; (iv) the stipulation that the indemnifying participant shall have the sole control of the response to or defence of such risk; (v) that the indemnified participant shall have no right to settle any such claims without the prior written consent of the indemnifying participant; (vi) that the indemnifying participant shall be subrogated to the rights and defences of the indemnified participant; and (vii) that the indemnified party shall make no admissions which might adversely prejudice the indemnifying party's ability to settle the claim.

Access to specified remedies

4.7 Transaction managers often associate the remedial provisions of a technology agreement with the transaction's demise. On the contrary, there are a broad range of remedies in response to performance deficiencies that actually promote continued performance, minimise the adversarial implications of non-performance and practically address those circumstances to promote the viability of the project.

Repair and replace

4.7.1 If the technology good or service does not operate in accordance with its requirements, the technology agreement may simply provide for either that good's repair or replacement or that service's re-performance. Usually, technology agreements stipulate a limited time period in which the technology provider must be notified of non-compliance, which then triggers a corresponding time period for the performance of repair, replace or re-performance obligations. You should consider securing the rights to supervise such repair, replacement or re-performance obligations with additional rights of inspection and supervision, and you may wish to require the participant to provide you with the most recent version, release or model of any replacement technology since the agreement was entered into.

Performance adjustment

4.7.2 Another practical strategy to respond to performance deficiencies is for the participants to reassess the nature of those obligations, and to accommodate the performance deficiencies by simply revising the participant's performance obligations. In that regard, performance stipulations and service levels may turn out to be more practically onerous than the participants originally anticipated, and it may be reasonable for the participants to adjust their expectations realistically and rationally and redefine the agreement's performance obligations. Even if that strategy is implemented in conjunction with other remedial options, it may significantly contribute to establishing goodwill and trust among the participants early in the project.

Service credits

4.7.3 Where performance deficiencies can be compensated, whether in whole or in part, by price adjustments, technology providers may be more willing to accept the adjustments if they are structured as service credits against the future acquisition of additional goods or services. You should consider what your pricing protections should be for the redemption of the credits, *e.g.* whether or not they can be redeemed in connection with any other discount or promotional arrangement then existing at the time at which the payment credit is redeemed. The strategy of compensation by providing the injured party with service or payment credits may have valuable benefits for technology providers if they can still book the original revenues under generally accepted accounting principles. Such remedies both compensate injured participants and create commercial incentives for future transactions.

Price adjustments

4.7.4 If the technology good or service is deficient to such an extent that its value, reflected by pricing, was greatly over-estimated by the participants, then it may be reasonable for the parties to adjust that pricing to correspond to the technology products' or services' actual functionality or quality. Conceptually, such price adjustments are neither pricing discounts nor rebates. Instead, the adjustments are ordinarily considered to be amendments to the agreement whereby the actual price of the product or service is changed to a more appropriate and realistic level. In order to avoid any potential tax, audit, price discrimination or other possible problems, the parties should ensure that all price adjustments are accurately and completely documented, and that they are not otherwise depicted in any misleading or misrepresentative manner. For example, if a technology product originally cost £100 and was subject to a 30 per cent price discount, the final price would be £70. If the price was subsequently adjusted down to £80 due to a performance deficiency, with the same 30 per cent discount, the new price would be £56. Subject to the advice of your accountants, tax counsel and competition-law counsel (re price discrimination), it may be misleading not to actually adjust the price, and keep the price at £100, and to offer the participant a 44 per cent price discount (which no other purchaser would otherwise be entitled to in similar commercial circumstances).

Liquidated damages

4.7.5 Technology agreements routinely secure performance obligations by stipulating that a defaulting participant shall be required to pay a certain fixed sum of money. Unless such provisions are structured as genuine pre-estimates of damages, they may not be regarded by a court as remedial provisions, and the enforceability of such provisions may be problematic. You should ensure that such provisions are, to whatever extent possible in the circumstances of the transaction, structured and drafted in a manner that promotes their enforceability. As long as the participants approach such remedial rights on a reasonable and rational basis that does not create unfair or unconscionable results, liquidated damage provisions provide a mechanism to avoid delays associated with compensation disputes and the cost of litigation to otherwise determine the appropriate remedies for the circumstances that are specifically addressed by such provisions.[89] Liquidated damage provisions can provide commercial and remedial predictability in the event of a mishap, and they can motivate transaction performance due to the knowledge of agreed consequences.

Enforceability issues

4.7.5.1 Because the law generally seeks adequately to compensate participants who have been injured in the course of a commercial transaction, the courts are reluctant to enforce any additional rights that penalise the participant at fault beyond that defaulting participant's remedial obligations. Therefore, provisions that penalise a participant for any particular acts or omissions in addition to the injured participant's ordinary remedial rights may not be enforceable. However, provisions that provide for the payment of money as a genuine pre-estimate of damages that may be suffered, and therefore create a remedial debt, may be enforceable as "liquidated damages". However, a court must determine whether or not any such payment is in fact a penalty or a liquidated damage provision, without regard to how the participants may have merely described those rights in the agreement.[90]

No penalty

4.7.5.2 (a) *Quantum*—The enforceability of liquidated damage provisions may be promoted where: (i) the stipulated damage amount should not be "extravagant and

---

[89] See again *Dunlop Pneumatic Tyre Co v New Garage and Motor Co* (1915) A.C. 79. See also S.M. Waddams, The *Law of Damages* (2nd ed., Canada Law Book Inc., Toronto, 1991); J. Berryman, *Remedies: Issues and Perspectives* (Carswell, Toronto, 1991); and J. Berryman, T. Cromwell *et al.*, *Remedies: Cases and Materials* (Emond Montgomery Publications, Toronto, 1988).

[90] See again *Dunlop Pneumatic Tyre Co v New Garage and Motor Co* (1915) A.C. 79. Use of such terms will not be conclusive of itself; the courts will look at all the surrounding circumstances to decide whether a "liquidated damage" is, in fact, a "penalty". Courts will not hesitate to disregard provisions that merely stipulate such payments are payable "as liquidated damages and not as a penalty", see *Federal Business Development Bank v Eldridge* (1986) 76 N.B.R. (2d) 399, CA, and *Huffman v Spalding* (1989) 57 D.L.R. (4th) 589, 56 Man.R. (2d) 317, CA. Therefore, the agreement must look beyond the mere contractual description of such provisions and promote the enforceability of those obligations by satisfying the common law criteria for "liquidated damages".

unconscionable" in comparison with the potential loss that could conceivably result from the breach; (ii) the amount payable relatively corresponds to the seriousness of the events, rather than stipulated as a single amount that is payable regardless of the seriousness of the particular occurrence; (iii) the amount stipulated is a genuine pre-estimation of the damages that will be caused as a consequence of the performance failure, especially where those damages may not be easily calculated; and (iv) the calculation for such amounts are related to, if not based upon, remedial and compensatory objectives.

(b) *Bonus balance*—The enforceability of a liquidated damage provision may be promoted by structuring liquidated damage provisions to correspond directly to the technology agreement's bonus provisions, so that the incentive aspects of the transaction are relatively balanced against the disincentive aspects of the provision. For example, where a participant is entitled to a £100 bonus for each extra good sold, it may be prudent to stipulate that the same participant will not exceed £100 of liquidated damages for each good that is not sold below the minimum threshold targets.

(c) *Debt credit*—You may wish to structure the liquidated damage "debt" as a credit against the future procurement of goods or services from the defaulting participant, in order to minimise any unintended punitive impact on the defaulting party.

(d) *Accelerated payments*—Many technology agreements, including technology-lease agreements, include provisions that require all amounts due during the term of the transaction to become due and payable upon a breach of the technology agreement. Such payments may constitute a genuine estimate of damages when the plaintiff has fully performed its obligations and there is no opportunity to mitigate the loss.[91] Such provisions may also be more likely to be considered restitutive, and not penalising, where the participants agree that such payments are liquidated damages for depreciation, administrative and consequential damages for the interrupted completion of the transaction.[92]

Quantum

4.7.5.3 The enforceability of liquidated damage covenants may also be promoted by stipulating the formula, or at least the methodology, by which such stipulated amounts were calculated to compensate the injured participant fairly. Alternatively, the participants should at least provide a written explanation of how such a pre-estimate of damages was arrived at, and to document the compensatory intention of the participants for evidentiary purposes.

---

[91] Jamie Cassels, *Remedies: The Law of Damages* (Irwin Law, Quicklaw, Toronto, 2000), p.419; see *Neonette Sign Co. v Stankovic* (1961), 66 B.C.L.R. 269, CA; *Neon Signs Ltd. v Henze* (1989) 105 A.R. 343, CA; *Claude Neon Ltd. v KDJ Enterprises Ltd.* (1995) 136 Sask.R. 66, QB.

[92] ibid., *Claude Neon Ltd. v KDJ Enterprises*, at p.70.

Fair and reasonable

4.7.5.4   The enforceability of liquidated damage clauses will also depend upon their reasonableness and fairness in the commercial circumstances of the transaction. For example, various cases have struck down such clauses where they have had the effect of putting the injured participant in a better position than it would have been if the contract had been performed, and if the benefit of the provision far exceeds the proportionality of the benefit that would have been secured if the obligation had been fulfilled.[93] Generally, the courts will take a broad view as to whether or not such provisions are fair and reasonable in the circumstances of the transaction, and the courts will not enforce any such provisions that they determine to be unconscionable or an "injustice".[94]

Access to alternative services/products

4.7.6   A practical remedy that is often overlooked is the ability for an injured party to procure replacement services or products from alternative providers. Although such remedial rights may be commercially threatening to the incumbent provider, you may stipulate those rights subject to the following: (i) the expiration of a reasonable cure period; (ii) the exhaustion of other provider remedies, such as the duty to repair or replace; (iii) stipulating the temporary nature of the substitution, subject to the provider's ability to subsequently perform; (iv) issues of technological compatibility, interoperability and other environmental requirements and specifications; (v) that the procurement and case of such third-party services and products will not diminish or qualify the effect of the incumbent provider's performance obligations or technology performance warranties; and (vi) the extent to which the defaulting provider should be responsible for all costs and expenses associated with such substituted and alternative services and products.

Equitable relief

4.7.7   An extremely important remedial option for technology agreements involves the ability of the participants to request a court to order the defaulting participant to either do, or to refrain from doing, a particular duty or obligation in connection with the transaction. In addition to my comments concerning injunctive relief at **2.5.3**, you should ensure that all such remedial provisions are drafted in a manner that will facilitate the court's exercise of discretion to grant such relief. Since all such remedies are

---

[93] *Canadian Acceptance Corp. Ltd. v Regent Park Boucher Shop Ltd.* (1969) 3 D.L.R. (3d) 304, Man. CA; *RCA Victor Company Ltd. v Pelletier* (1968) 68 D.L.R. (2d) 13, CA; *Unilease Inc. v York Steel Construction Ltd.* (1970) 83 D.L.R. (3d) 275, 18 O.R. (2d) 559, CA; *Meunier v Cloutier* (1984) 9 D.L.R. (4th) 486 at p.492.

[94] See *Bridge v Campbell Discount Co. Ltd.* [1962] A.C. 600, HL *per* Lord Denning.

within the "equitable" jurisdiction of a court, the court's discretion to provide the remedies may be enhanced if: (i) the order being sought is capable of being enforced by the court issuing that relief; (ii) if there is an equitable relationship among the participants concerning which the relief is sought, such as a fiduciary duty to protect a participant's confidential information; (iii) your application for equitable relief is not tainted by any wrongdoing or unconscionable behaviour on your part; (iv) the extent to which the participants have relied upon such provisions as an inducement to enter into the technology agreement; (v) where monetary compensation will not be an adequate remedy; (vi) where an immediate and irreparable harm can be prevented; and (vii) there is a fair, real and substantial justification for the relief's being requested.

The decision of whether to grant the participants any equitable relief, whether an injunction or a specific performance or otherwise, will remain entirely within the court's discretion. Therefore, the most that participants can do in a technology agreement to promote the availability of equitable relief is to agree and acknowledge the factual criteria that genuinely exist, and upon which the court may rely (or at least be cognisant of) in determining whether or not the circumstances surrounding such a claim reasonably warrant the granting of equitable relief. As a final matter, a participant's agreement not to object to, defend against or otherwise oppose an application for equitable relief may not be of much practical significance if the court calls upon that participant to address the factual circumstances in which an application for equitable relief is made. However, it is arguable that such provisions may restrict the ability of a participant to oppose such applications independently of the court's request for their involvement and participation.

Time requirements

4.7.8 An important aspect of any risk-management strategy is the time limitations and requirements that are stipulated for a participant's performance obligations. For example, time periods associated with curing a performance deficiency, notice of breach, obligations to repair or replace, performance reporting and the effectiveness of specific remedies should all stipulate time requirements that are reasonable and practical for the participants to comply with. Too short a period may, as previously discussed in Chapter 3, result in the clause's being held unreasonable.[95]

The practicality of such time requirements will also, in part, depend upon: (i) any time-zone differences between the participants; (ii) whether or not weekends and public holidays should be taken into account; (iii) whether or not the participants should be afforded a reasonable time to consider their legal and commercial position before the "remedial clock" commences; and (iv) the agreement's administrative timing requirements concerning notice obligations, change-management requirements and dispute-resolution protocols.

---

[95] See UCTA s.13 and recent cases such as *Granville Oil and Chemicals Ltd v Davis Turner & Co Ltd* [2003] EWCA Civ 570 , and *Expo Fabrics (UK) Ltd v Naughty Clothing Co Ltd* [2003] EWCA Civ 1165.

Enforceability enhancements

4.7.9 As previously discussed, a technology agreement's risk-management provisions may be closely supervised and narrowly interpreted by a court to ensure that the intentions of the participants are fairly and reasonably complied with. Given the importance of the risk-management strategies that are employed for your transaction, and the judicial scrutiny that those provisions are subject to, it may be prudent for the participants to consider the fairness and reasonableness of the agreement's remedial provisions, including whether or not the agreement should stipulate the following: (i) that the provisions are fair and reasonable in the commercial circumstances of the transaction; (ii) that the risk-management duties, limitations, exemptions and obligations are reasonably reflected in the pricing and remuneration obligations among the participants; (iii) that the participants have secured, and relied upon, independent legal advice concerning their remedial obligations; (iv) the express denial and disclaimer by the participants that there are any circumstances (whether commercial or otherwise) that may, in any manner or to any extent whatsoever, render the agreement an undue hardship, unconscionable, or otherwise oppressive; (v) that the risk-management and remedial provisions and agreements have been an inducement which the participants have relied upon in entering into the agreement; and (vi) that the technology agreement has been negotiated, at arm's length and without duress, among participants who have determined that entering into the agreement, as a whole, is in their best and beneficial interest. Where the technology transaction involves the participation of individuals, you may also wish to secure a written certificate from those participants that they have secured of independent legal advice concerning the technology agreement.

Contingency planning

4.7.10 One of the most important and practical strategies either to avoid or mitigate risk in a technology transaction involves planning for such contingencies in a manner and to an extent that will allow you to act quickly, minimise mistakes due to management error, and secure "fail-safe" operational arrangements to allow the project to avoid delays and disruptions. Where appropriate, you should consider forming a Contingent Planning Committee that will be responsible for formally developing risk-management strategies, and for managing their implementation and ongoing readiness in the event that they must be relied upon.

Contingency and emergency-response plan

4.7.10.1 The first step in developing a risk-management strategy to address potentially harming contingencies is to formulate a contingency strategy that

218

addresses the following issues: (i) the identification of contingency risks and possible external events that may reasonably interfere with the progress of the transaction, including possible *force majeure* events, breaches of security, corporate espionage, the loss of key personnel; and (ii) the failure of any participants to perform their obligations, duties and responsibilities in connection with the transaction. Secondly, your contingency plan should take into account what resources you will require to address any such performance threats, such as budget allocation, personnel and management supervision. Thirdly, you should ensure that the contingency plans and "strategic response options" that you propose will be integrated in a complimentary and supportive manner to ensure that all of the procedures and contingency arrangements stipulated in the plan will work together in a uniform manner. Usually, contingency plans are prepared in writing and are formally approved by each participant's executive management, including any risk-management committees of your organisation's board of directors. All contingency plans should be frequently reviewed and reconsidered in the context of changing commercial and other circumstances, and the Contingent Planning Committee should frequently ensure that the contingency demands of the project do not outpace the project's contingency plans. As a final matter, comprehensive contingency plans may provide additional risk-management benefits, such as: (i) reduced insurance premiums; (ii) a forum for regular risk-management assessment and planning; (iii) securing the risk-management attention and responsibility of executive management; and (iv) avoiding extemporaneous "crisis management" decisions that often contribute to, rather than mitigate, the potential harm of the contingency being addressed.

Disaster-recovery and back-up systems

4.7.10.2 One of the most common and effective contingency strategies is the implementation of disaster-recovery and back-up systems. Such arrangements may take a variety of forms, including: (i) data warehousing; (ii) alternative power generation; (iii) redundant systems for environmental conditions such as temperature, humidity and air ventilation; (iv) the use of fire doors, fire-retardant materials and sprinkler systems; (v) earthquake-resistant architecture; (vi) purchasing or leasing offsite (perhaps out of region) redundant computer hardware and equipment; (vii) the duplication and location of data-processing and storage devices from the project's primary location, both "hot sites" that are currently active and "cold sites" that are dormant until required, *e.g.* to an offsite storage facility that is secure; and (viii) retaining a third-party service provider to make whatever technology systems, communications facilities and personnel available to carry on the project's operations in the event that such is required by any contingency. Of course, such disaster-recovery and back-up systems and services should be commercially settled, legally binding and prepared for implementation at the outset of the project.

Redundancy

4.7.10.3 Perhaps a simpler form of securing disaster-recovery and back-up systems involves the ongoing operation of redundant systems, including data-processing, communications and related computer hardware and equipment. Whether that redundancy is structured as a distributive computing and network architecture, telecommunications triangulation, so-called "parallel processing" or insuring that separate "mirror sites" can, at any time, step into perform identical and parallel services, multiple systems with over-capacity and redundant functionality can contribute a great deal to the project's contingency strategy.

Supplier arrangements

4.7.10.4 In a manner similar to the arrangements discussed in **4.7.6**, the participants should work closely with all of their suppliers to ensure that any product or service-supply interruptions are addressed within the project's contingency plans. In addition to proactively identifying, and perhaps retaining, alternative suppliers, you should also consider whether or not any of the project's suppliers should agree to allocate and reserve a particular percentage of their goods or services for your benefit in the event of a relevant contingency. For example, you should consider whether or not a satellite communications services provider should also commit to ensuring that at least a minimum percentage of their satellite's communication capacity will be reserved for and devoted to the project in the event of a contingency that places excess demand on those communication services from other customers.

Source code escrow

4.7.10.5 Software transactions often anticipate project difficulties that may arise in connection with either the failure of the licensor to properly maintain and support the software, or the licensor's losing ownership and control of the software source code due to insolvency or bankruptcy proceedings. To address these and related contingencies, participants often require the licensor to place the software's source code in escrow with a third party for release to the licensee in the event of any such contingency. However, such arrangements are fraught with many potential pitfalls and legal complications, and you should ensure that such arrangements address the following issues: (i) that all three participants in the escrow arrangement (the licensor, licensee and escrow agent) are all a party to the source code escrow agreement[95a]; (ii) that a default of the licensor to maintain the escrow arrangement is a default of the licensor's obligations, which will trigger the release of the source code to the licensee; (iii) whether or not participants may require an independent third party to inspect the

---

[95a] See, *e.g. www.ncc.co.uk*, the website for the National Computing Centre, arguably the United Kingdom's largest escrow agent.

escrowed deposits; (iv) the simplicity of the release event (*e.g.* written notice from a participant), and the escrow agent's duty of enquiry and verification of a release event's occurrence; (v) that the version of the source code being held in escrow is completely updated in a prompt manner; (vi) that the escrow arrangement is enforceable under the debtor–creditor and bankruptcy laws of the jurisdiction where the source code is being held, despite whatever the governing law of the source code escrow contract is; (vii) that no simpler and direct commercial arrangements between the participants were possible, such as licensing the source code to participants from the outset, or providing the licensee with the source code but contractually restricting the use of the source code to a stipulated contingency event; and (viii) that the source code is maintained in a protected and secure environment by extremely trustworthy third parties.

Government agencies

4.7.10.6   Because many of the contingencies that may have to be addressed will involve circumstances of civil unrest or economic infrastructure (such as power failures, transportation disruption or declaration of environmental disaster areas), you should ensure that the project's contingency plans include practices and procedures that complement the emergency-response practices and activities of the public sector. Therefore, you should consider all contingency plans in the context of publicly available emergency response plans and strategies of the central and local government departments in the jurisdictions where the project will be carried on. Furthermore, you should ensure that all third parties who will provide you or the project with contingency services and relief have also undertaken that public-sector "response plan" analysis.

Succession planning

4.7.10.7   Since the project's management, and other key personnel, are usually material factors to the success of a technology transaction, the loss of personnel for any reason is a contingency that requires risk-management and response planning. Therefore, you should ensure that each participant's contingency plan includes a personnel succession component. Because emergency circumstances may also be associated with personnel attrition, you should ensure that all succeeding managers and personnel are also apprised of the project's contingency plans well in advance, and that they are trained and prepared to both manage and work in those circumstances should the need arise.

Contingency audits

4.7.10.8   You should ensure that the appropriateness, practicality and efficiency of your contingency plans are regularly tested and verified. Such assessments may involve the expertise of experienced contingency planning and emergency-response professionals, and it may also require you to test your contingency systems on a frequent basis. In addition to testing your contingency plans through mock exercises and test drills, such audit and verification activities also enable you to train the project's personnel in the prompt and efficient implementation and performance of the arrangements. Contingency plans on paper are important, but the proven ability to implement those plans is vital.[96]

Dispute resolution

4.8   The primary objective of any technology agreement's dispute-resolution provisions is to keep the dispute away from lawyers to the greatest extent possible. That is a lofty and honourable goal, and it is achievable—if you structure a dispute-resolution process that expedites the resolution process, facilitates communication and co-operation among the participants, and requires the participants to exhaust all reasonable business opportunities to settle their differences.

Internal escalation

4.8.1   The agreement should provide a process by which project problems and disputes among the participants can be identified and promptly brought to the attention of the other participants for review and consideration.

The diagram on p.223 shows, in pictorial form, an example escalation procedure within a technology agreement.

Perhaps the most efficient structure to facilitate this process is by directing all of those matters to the Joint Management Committee. Since the Joint Management Committee is primarily "operational" in nature, it is well positioned to administratively address those matters and to seek the assistance and co-operation of all participants to find a practical, relevant and commercially reasonable solution to project problems and disputes as they may arise. Although joint-management committees are rarely authorised to commit the participants to a proposed dispute solution, they will have the operational and administrative capability to recommend cogent solutions. If the Joint Management Committee is unable to recommend a solution, there are two additional levels of internal escalation that you should consider. First, the matter may be brought to the attention of each participant's senior project manager for review and consideration. Since the transaction managers will have a broader appreciation of the business case and the project's objectives, there may be opportunities for reasonable trade-offs to settle disputes that are not apparent to the members of the Joint Management Committee. In the event that the project's transaction managers are unable to settle a dispute, the matter may be elevated to very senior executives within each participant's organisation for review and consideration. That level of executive management will be able to take into account strategic issues concerning the participant's relationships that extend beyond the project, and the best inter-

---

[96] See, *e.g.* the review of July 13, 2004 of the Turnbull guidance on internal control and risk management, undertaken by the Financial Reporting Council.

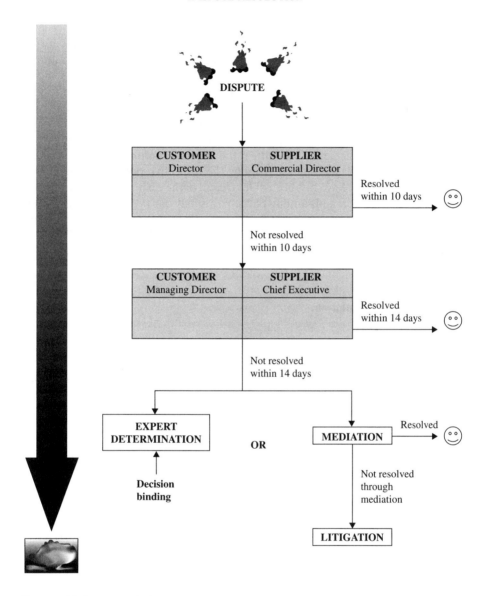

Chart provided courtesy of Bird & Bird.

ests of their organisation, that will not be readily apparent to the technology managers, and that can be taken into account in resolving the dispute.

In my experience, almost all project problems and disputes can be resolved through internal escalation procedures that require: (i) the prompt identification of problems and disputes; (ii) the disclosure of all relevant information concerning those matters to all interested participants; and (iii) tight time requirements for dispute notice, resolution and determination that the dispute has either been resolved or cannot be resolved. You should also consider whether or not formal minutes or written notes are kept concerning all meetings and discussions among participants to resolve disputes, and whether or not any of these records should be admissible as evidence in any subsequent arbitral or court proceedings. Such records, as well as any correspondence or memoranda concerning the interests or positions of the participants, can assist and expedite subsequent levels of internal-dispute resolution. In that regard, it is extremely helpful to senior executives to have the Joint Management Committee and the transaction managers prepare executive summaries describing the dispute, the respective positions of each participant, and why they have not been able to resolve the dispute. As a final matter, disputed claims and demands among participants may constitute contingent liabilities for accounting purposes, and you should ensure that all dispute-resolution procedures require each participant to provide their Chief Financial Officer with notice of, and reasonable information concerning, the dispute at the earliest possible opportunity.

Alternative dispute resolution

4.8.2 Where the participants have not been able to resolve a dispute between them, and they do not wish the matter to be litigated, they should consider a broad range of ADR mechanisms that are frequently relied upon in technology transactions. ADR procedures can provide significant benefits that directly pertain to technology transactions. First, most technology transactions have onerous time constraints; the participants can agree to an expedited time frame to resolve the dispute. Secondly, the resolution of technology-transaction disputes may require technologically complex or commercially complicated matters. In such situations, the participants can select an arbitrator who has particular experience and expertise in the subject matter of the dispute. Thirdly, unlike judicial proceedings, ADR proceedings are private and may be subject to strict confidentiality requirements among the participants. Lastly, participants in international technology transactions can select an arbitrator and arbitral venue that is independent of and neutral to each of the participant's jurisdictional affiliations.

Expert consultation

4.8.2.1 One of the most informal ways to involve others to help the participants to settle a dispute involves the selection of persons with particular expertise or experience in the subject-matter of the dispute to consult, advise, propose and recommend ways in which the interests of the participants can be met, or minimally compromised, to settle a dispute. Often, participants may be involved in disputes concerning issues and interests that are unfamiliar to them, and where they do not have the time to create solutions to common industry problems that they have little experience in dealing with. In such situations, independent and trusted advisors who have considerable business, legal, technological or other experience and expertise in the disputed matter may help to resolve the dispute by: (i) creative problem-solving based on their subject-matter experience; (ii) advise the participants of industry norms and customary trade practices for such matters, which may help the participants either to adjust their perspective on the dispute or create resolution opportunities; (iii) facilitate resolution through conciliatory meetings and discussion of the problems; (iv) identify relevant information that one of the participants was unaware of, and which had contributed to the dispute; and (v) provide the impartial and interested creative abilities of an experienced and knowledgeable person who can see beyond the dispute towards a solution. Even if that process does not lead to a dispute settlement, it is fast, inexpensive and the participants will likely become much better informed about the dispute and the position of each participant.

Mediation

4.8.2.2 Non-binding mediation involves a process in which the participants agree to continue their dispute-settlement discussions with the assistance of an independent mediator in the interests of: (i) helping the participants to identify and communicate their interests; (ii) calm emotionally charged relationships to facilitate communication; (iii) organise the dispute into time-line priorities, subject-matter categories and into interests of graduated importance; and (iv) guide the settlement-discussion process along constructive avenues of interest compromise and solution options. Good mediators, like psychiatrists, are skilled listeners and creative thinkers who rely on diplomacy to guide the participants to solutions that the participants will feel they (not the mediator) created. Although the issue of control over the mediation process is important, mediations are frequently conducted within a defined process of presentation, rebuttal, question asking and information disclosure. You should consider whether or not you wish your legal advisors or business consultants to participate in the mediation process, and whether or not the mediator should be entitled to request further research or information concerning the subject-matter of the dispute. Unlike lawyers in a litigation process, mediators promote direct communication between the participants, have a non-adversarial relationship with each participant, and are involved to help the participants to arrive at a solution that they created, rather than impose a solution on them. In my experience, a technology-transaction mediation will benefit if the mediator has legal and/or business experience in both the subject-matter of the dispute and the relevant technology sector.

Arbitration

4.8.2.3 If the participants select binding arbitration to resolve their disputes, the following issues should be addressed: (i) what aspects of the transaction will be subject to dispute resolution by arbitration, *e.g.* the participants may wish to exclude certain critical aspects of their business from arbitration in favour of formal judicial proceedings and determination such as intellectual property owner-ship, or confidentiality matters; (ii) what rules of procedure will govern the proceed-ings, and with what level of procedural formality, *e.g.* international rules such as the UNCITRAL Arbitration Rules,[97] the International Council of Commercial Arbitration Rules,[98] or the International Chamber of Commerce Rules,[99] a trade association's rules (*e.g.* American Arbitration Association[1]), or the domestic arbi-tration legislation of an appropriate jurisdiction, such as the Arbitration Act 1996; (iii) what arbitral institution, or which person, should arbitrate the dispute, and how they will be selected, *e.g.* some multinational technology providers prefer to name a selection of possible arbitrators in the technology agreement; (iv) whether or not the dispute should be resolved by a single arbitrator or a panel of arbitra-tors—which will usually depend upon the level of desired proceedings formality, and the ADR budget; (v) whether the arbitral institution and the arbitration rules should differ depending upon the subject-matter of the dispute, *e.g.* although you may decide to generally arbitrate dispute according to a particular set of procedu-ral rules, such as resolving internet domain name disputes through organisations like eResolution,[2] the CPR Institute,[3] or The Internet Corporation for Assigned Names and Numbers (ICANN)[4]; (vi) whether or not there are any procedural aspects of the arbitration rules that you have selected that should be revised by mutual agreement to tailor the administrative aspects of any potential arbitration to the project's and participants' particular circumstances; (vii) the location of the arbitration, and whether the participants have jurisdictional neutrality concerns, or otherwise require a cost-effective and convenient forum in which to conduct the proceedings; (viii) what time requirements should apply to commence and conduct the arbitration, and for what subject-matter of the transaction; (ix) what privacy and confidentiality obligations should govern the proceedings; (x) whether or not there are any third parties who should also commit to participate in (or perhaps fund) any arbitration proceedings, *e.g.* affiliated companies, guarantors, suppliers or subcontractors; (xi) what information and documents should any notice com-mencing arbitration contain; (xii) whether or not the decision of the arbitrator is final, or on what grounds the arbitration award may be appealed (and to the juris-diction of which court); (xiii) the nature of the evidence that may be relied upon, *e.g.* whether the oral hearing should be conducted solely as the basis of documen-tary and affidavit evidence and the submissions of counsel, or whether or not the proceedings should include live testimony that counsel can cross-examine; (xiv)

---

[97] See *www.uncitral.org.*

[98] See *www.arbitration-icca.org.*

[99] See *www.iccwbo.org.*

[1] See *www.adr.org.*

[2] See *www.eresolution.ca/services.*

[3] See *www.cpradr.org.*

[4] See *www.icann.org/udrp.*

whether or not the decision of the arbitrator shall be issued with written reasons; (xv) the substantive law that will govern the arbitrator, including the law of evidence; (xvi) whether or not the arbitrator is permitted to select and appoint his or her own expert advisor or witness concerning the subject-matter of the dispute; and (xvii) how each participant's expenses and costs (including legal fees) of the arbitration will be borne, *e.g.* by each participant for their own expenses and costs, or as awarded by the arbitrator.

There are, of course, risks associated with arbitrating technology-transaction disputes. First, depending upon the venue and formality of proceedings, arbitrations can be very expensive. Secondly, many transaction managers feel that binding arbitration will subject critical aspects of their business to a process of determination that may not include the procedural "checks and balances" that judicial systems provide. Thirdly, it is always difficult for participants to negotiate and settle ADR matters while they are structuring and settling a "relationship-building" technology transaction. Like engaged couples discussing a prenuptial agreement, detailed discussions concerning binding ADR should be sensitively handled in a manner that does not damage the commercial relationship that the participants are building during the transaction's negotiations.

Litigation issues

4.8.3   Although litigation, once begun, will proceed based on rules of procedure that exist within the jurisdiction where the action is commenced, and outside of the technology agreement, there are a few aspects of litigation that the participants can agree upon from the outset. In addition to choice of law and courts of a particular jurisdiction, the participants may also consider the following issues: (i) whether or not the participants wish to exclude a trial by jury (an issue which is relevant outside Canada and England); (ii) whether or not the participants must exhaust the internal dispute mechanisms; and (iii) if the jurisdiction of the courts selected by the participants is exclusive or non-exclusive.

Third-party risk-deferral strategies

4.9

Additional parties

4.9.1   One of the easiest ways to either share risk or to "deepen the pocket" of a participant who may have transaction liabilities is to simply add a person as a party to the technology agreement. Either as a named party, or because they are, by definition, included as a participant, additional parties should (whether directly, by counterpart or by amending agreement adding them) execute and deliver the technology agreement, and ensure that the agreement expresses that person's clear and unequivocal intention to be a party to the agreement.

Risk assumption

4.9.2   A frequent strategy of risk management is one of liability diversification, where a third party will guarantee the performance of a participant and agree to be jointly and/or severably liable for the acts or omissions of that participant. Whether the third parties are parent companies, prime contractors or other interested parties, the assumption of liability by a third party raises the following issues: (i) the requirement for the third party to execute and deliver a separate form of guarantee or other binding obligation to assume such liability; (ii) whether or not the participants must exhaust their remedies against the defaulting participant before they are entitled to recourse against the guarantor; (iii) the degree to which the guarantors should be kept apprised of developing problems and disputes among the participants; (iv) the need to either join the guarantor in the actions against the defaulting party or otherwise allow the guarantor to participate in any actions or proceedings against the defaulting party; (v) the need to undertake due diligence investigations of the guarantor, and the disclosure of accurate, complete and current information concerning the guarantor; and (vi) whether or not the guarantee raises any tax issues, *e.g.* what consideration or benefit has been given in exchange for the guarantee. Often referred to as "deep-pocket" arrangements, the goal of such third-party risk allocations is to ensure that a defaulting party will be able to pay the injured participant the damages and expenses that a court may award. The best risk-management and compensatory structures in the technology agreement are useless if the defaulting party cannot pay the tab (see discussion of parent company guarantees in **3.9.16**).

Insurance

4.9.3   Insurance coverage can mitigate the financial impact of a broad range of risks, including infringement of intellectual property, "Enterprise Risk Management",[5] employee sabotage of information systems, and the economic impact of failed or deficient performance obligations. If insurance coverage is appropriate for your project, you should consider securing the advice and assistance of a specialised insurance consultant or qualified agent to assist you to find the best-suited insurance product. You should also consider the following issues concerning the obligation of the participants to secure insurance coverage: (i) what risks are to be covered; (ii) what is the appropriate amount of coverage; (iii) whether the participants should have the right to approve of the insurance carrier, or stipulate the jurisdiction in which it must

---

[5] See "Enterprise Risk Management: Implementing New Solutions", an Executive Briefing by Marsh Putnam Mercer (Marsh & McLennan Companies) at *www.mmc.com*.

carry on business; (iv) whether or not the participants who will benefit from such coverage should be the named insured (*i.e.* sole loss payee) or co-named insured (*i.e.* co-loss payee) under the insurance policy; (v) whether the technology agreement should stipulate that such insurance policy shall contain terms and conditions, including exclusions and qualifications, that are generally consistent with industry practice for such insurance coverage; (vi) whether the participants should be provided with a copy of the entire insurance policy and have the right to review and approve the terms and conditions of the insurance policy to ensure that no unusual or unacceptable provisions, exclusions or qualifications are included; (vii) that the insured participant shall maintain the insurance policy, in good standing and with fully-paid premiums, for a stipulated term; (viii) whether or not the insurance company should be required to notify you of any non-payment or any other default of the insured participant under the policy; (ix) whether or not you should have the right to pay outstanding premiums to the insurance company, and require the defaulting participant to reimburse you promptly for those payments; and (x) whether or not the obligations to provide separate policies for separately identified risks, with separate coverage amounts, should be stipulated in the technology agreement.

Letters of Credit

4.9.4   An important management strategy for financial risks associated with international technology transactions involves the issuance of a "Letter of Credit" by a financial institution to secure a participant's payment obligations. Simply defined, a Letter of Credit is an undertaking by a financial institution to pay a sum of money to the person to whom the payment is owed upon a particular circumstance, or upon a stipulated precondition being satisfied. In the context of a technology transaction, participants often rely upon Letters of Credit to require the financial institution rather than the other party to the transaction to pay the amount owed upon reasonable evidence of performance, such as acknowledgment that the technology has been delivered to the purchaser. The use of Letters of Credit to manage potential financial risks is more prominent in international technology transactions, where the participants have not established transactional trust based on a prior course of dealing, where there are currency-exchange control restrictions, where there is a risk of regulatory or "political" interference with a participant's payment obligations, or where it may be difficult to enforce either a participant's payment obligations or related securing interests. If the Letter of Credit is irrevocable, the financial institution will not have any right to retract it, or to otherwise avoid the payment obligations stipulated in the Letter of Credit. In international technology transactions, Letters of Credit are commonly used to guarantee a specific amount of ready cash to initiate and carry on a specific project.[6] The terms and conditions of Letters of Credit vary greatly, despite the efforts of various international organisations to standardise the

---

[6]   Often termed "bankers' commercial credits" from the English perspective. See Gutteridge and Megrah, *The Law of Bankers' Commercial Credits 2001.*

documents.[7] Letters of Credit should not be overlooked as an efficient method of ensuring the performance of payment obligations from a trusted financial institution where the project warrants this consideration. As with other financial mechanisms to manage risks associated with technology transactions, your use of a Letter of Credit is likely to require the specialised assistance of professional advisors.

Performance bond

4.9.5 A performance bond is provided by a third party to guarantee that the participant will perform the terms and conditions of the technology agreement. Because performance bonds generally allow the third-party issuer the right of election to make its own arrangements for completion of the performance obligations (to mitigate the loss caused by the default), there is no reason why performance bonds should not be used for a broad range of technology transactions. Usually, strict time-limits will apply for making a claim or pursuing an action under a performance bond, although courts will, on occasion, grant relief where a claim has been made outside the stipulated time. It is also possible to agree an extension.[8]

A third party will only be liable to perform its obligations under the performance bond if all the express conditions are met, and the participant making a claim under a performance bond has not engaged in any bad-faith conduct or deliberate misrepresentation.[9] Perhaps the most important distinguishing characteristic of a performance bond is that the third party secures the right to perform the obligation (in order to mitigate its financial obligations) that the participant failed to perform. Therefore, important operational and commercial issues will arise under any performance bond concerning the third party's discretion and authority to determine how the defaulted obligations will be performed.

Professional opinions

4.9.6 Business leaders, technology managers and lawyers all appreciate that our legal system has not kept pace with the impact of technology on our commercial

[7] See the International Chamber of Commerce's attempt to standardise LOC terminology and practice through its publication, "Uniform Customs and Practice for Documentary Credits", *ICC Publishing Publication 400 revised ed.* (1984), and see the ICC's "Uniform Rules for Contract Guarantees" and "Uniform Rules for Demand Guarantees", *ICC Publishing Publication 500* (1994).

[8] See, *e.g.* the *Uniform Rules for Demand Guarantees (URDG) of 1992*, published by the International Chamber of Commerce (No. 458) which allow for extensions, provided that all the parties agree.

[9] See *Ferrara v National Surety Co.* [1917] 1 W.W.R. 719, SCC and *Dashchuk Lumber Ltd. v Proman Projects Ltd.* (1985) 20 C.C.L.I. 120, QB, affirmed (1987), 27 C.C.L.I. 12, Sask. CA and *Elance Steel Fabricating Co. v Falk Brothers Industries Ltd.* [1987] 6 W.W.R. 679, Sask. CA, affirmed [1990] 1 W.W.R. 29, SCC.

activities. Technology transactions, which industrial laws were not created to address, are more susceptible to legal uncertainty and commercial unpredictability than other business sectors. As new legislation is enacted and case law concerning technology, the internet and intellectual property rapidly develop, these uncertainties and lack of commercial predictability create transactional risks. Controversies concerning how existing laws apply to technology transactions can directly affect the business expectations of participants in profound ways, whether they are related to tax, intellectual property, contract, electronic commerce, communications, new media, globalisation or other issues that are directly related to your project. Therefore, as a risk-mitigation strategy, you should consider engaging your professional advisors to provide you with detailed advice and opinions concerning: (i) the impact that those issues may have on the project; (ii) the nature and extent of your rights and obligations under newly created laws and regulations; (iii) how the transaction may be structured to either avoid or reduce any risks that may be associated with those uncertainties; (iv) how the risks are commonly addressed by others who engage in similar technology transactions, both in terms of commercial strategy and general industry practice; and (v) any other circumstances that they may be aware of concerning the likelihood of risks arising from such issues, *e.g.* the direction of developing common-law, pending legislation, government or regulatory policies concerning the interpretation or application of relevant laws, and the frequency with which such risks actually arise in the ordinary course of business. Although professional advice and opinions will not resolve whatever risks of uncertainty may exist concerning the project, you will be in a much better position to assess those risks and their implications for the project if you are fully informed about and thoroughly understand how these issues relate to the transaction. A complete understanding of such issues is essential to planning and structuring the transaction in a manner that will, efficiently and to the greatest extent possible, mitigate potential project risks.

Trusted third parties

4.9.7   There are many ways in which individuals who are unrelated to the technology transaction but whom all participants trust ("Trusted Third Parties" or "TTPs") can help to either mitigate or avoid project risks. Common TTP strategies that are implemented for technology transactions include: (i) requiring participants to make advance payments to TTPs, who will hold those funds either in trust or in escrow until they become due and payable; (ii) assigning or conveying intellectual property to a TTP who will hold title therein until certain preconditions have been satisfied that would then allow the conveyance of title to proceed from the TTP to the ultimate transferee; (iii) where trade secrets or other confidential information that is required for the project may be disclosed to some, but not all, of the participants and is required to be kept in a safe and secure manner; and (iv) to create source code escrow arrangements where the TTP is required to release that software source code for a participant's use in specified circumstances, such as breaching software support and maintenance obligations, or upon an event of bankruptcy or insolvency.

When structuring trusted third-party arrangements, there are several important legal and commercial issues to consider, including: (i) the legal structure of the arrangements, and the obligations that the structures may create, *e.g.* trust and escrow arrangements carry legally onerous obligations which should be fully understood by all of the participants; (ii) whether or not the arrangements require multiparty agreements, *e.g.* in a source code arrangement, whether or not the licensor, escrow agent and licensee should each be a party to the source code escrow agreement; (iii) the financial obligations of the arrangements, which may incur service fees that should be in proportion to the value of the technology transaction; (iv) the tax implications of the arrangements, especially where intellectual property is conveyed to a TTP; (v) dovetailing material terms and conditions of the technology agreement with any such TTP agreements; and (vi) ensuring that there are no jurisdictional conflicts between the agreement and the TTP arrangements, *e.g.* where the trust laws or bankruptcy laws of one jurisdiction may conflict with the laws that govern the agreement. With regard to the latter issue, where the technology transaction will involve TTP arrangements in jurisdictions outside the jurisdiction of the transaction, you should consider securing legal advice concerning the enforceability of those out-of-jurisdiction arrangements.

Financial arrangements

4.10

Payment adjustments

4.10.1   There are several ways in which to adjust a technology transaction's payment obligations as a remedial strategy. First, a participant's payment obligations may be reasonably adjusted to reflect the impact of a default or performance deficiency. Secondly, the participants may agree on an interim price that is based on expected quality and performance criteria that may be adjusted later to reasonably reflect the true value of the good or service, which can only be accurately assessed at a later date. Thirdly, as discussed in **3.9.3**, the agreement may provide that any breach or default of the agreement shall accelerate all payment obligations throughout the entire term of the transaction. Such payment-acceleration provisions are common remedies in many technology transactions, including leasing arrangements. Lastly, payments that are based on performance milestones, and that are conditional upon the occurrence of specific events, can also be adjusted in the event that the milestones and conditions are not met, *e.g.* by increasing the percentage of the ultimate payment hold-back amount, or setting off "late-performance" liquidated damages against subsequent milestone payments or otherwise.

Payment advances

4.10.1.1 In order to promote project cash flow, and to minimise the risk of late or defaulted payments, participants frequently agree to advance payments in several ways, including: (i) as a retainer, to be held in trust against the delivery of future services; (ii) as a credit against future payments; and (iii) as an initial payment, to permit the participant to purchase goods and services that are required to commence the project. The payments may also be paid directly to the payee or to a TTP, who will hold and pay out those funds to the payee subject to terms and conditions that all three parties have agreed to. In many situations, advance payments are associated with price reductions to give a reasonable reflection of the "time value" of money.

Payment retention

4.10.1.2 Regardless of any other payment arrangements agreed to by the participants, you may consider holding back a stipulated percentage of the aggregate price or fees until the project has been completed or mission-critical accomplishments have been achieved. Unlike payment milestones that are discussed in **4.10.1.3** below, retention provisions are structured as final payments of a significant percentage of the transaction's aggregate payment obligations. All payment-retention provisions should clearly define the conditions upon which those funds will be paid to the payee, to minimise any disputes concerning each participant's respective payment and retention rights. Participants should also consider the accounting and tax issues associated with the payer's payment-retention rights, especially concerning the payee's ability to rely on (*i.e.* book) contingent revenue that remains subject to preconditions, and that the payee is not otherwise entitled to receive merely by executing and delivering the agreement.

Payment milestones

4.10.1.3 Further to the technology agreement's provisions discussed in **3.9.7**, payment milestones should also be considered an important part of the project's financial risk-management strategies. While participant CFOs may require regulated payments as a matter of financial management, project managers may also require payment-milestone preconditions as a matter of risk management, performance incentive and prudent project governance. By matching the occurrence of performance requirements with payment obligations, the payee secures a cash flow that corresponds to its activities, and the payer secures protection from throwing good money after bad if the payee is not performing its obligations. When structuring payment milestones as a part of the project's financial-management arrangements, it is important to define the payment preconditions so that their occurrence can be objectively verified and payment-disputes minimised. Often considered as "graduated retention" provisions, the participants should consider the accounting and tax implications for such payment arrangements, including revenue-recognition implications.

Remuneration rates and adjustments

4.10.1.4 Remuneration rates may be adjusted either positively or negatively to either reflect deficient performance or to reward performance that exceeds a participant's expectations. Where there is disagreement among the participants at the outset of the technology transaction concerning remuneration rates, such adjustment provisions may be relied upon to assure a provider of technology goods or services that its desired remuneration rate will be paid on the condition that certain performance conditions are satisfied. Rather than having to consider the enforceability criteria of liquidated damages, remuneration rate-adjustment provisions usually understate initial remuneration rates so that they may be positively adjusted. Although disputes concerning remuneration rate-adjustments will be minimised where the adjustment criteria are objectively defined and verifiable, such criteria are often subjectively described in terms of "customer satisfaction" and participant quality assessment. This is an excellent way to control financial risk where the provider of technology goods and services is very confident of the quality of its performance, and the participant acquiring those goods and services has some trepidation concerning such performance.

Payments in escrow

4.10.2 When a payment obligation is dependent upon a particular occurrence and the payee is concerned that payment may be withheld once the required obligation is fully performed, the participants should consider advancing the payment to an independent third party, who will hold the funds in escrow for and on behalf of the payee. In these circumstances, as with software escrow arrangements, all three parties should enter into an escrow agreement which stipulates the terms and conditions upon which the funds will both be held in escrow and released upon a well defined triggering event. The most frequent commercial problem to address for such arrangements arises where the payee informs the escrow agent that the trigger event has been performed, but where the payer disputes such performance and insists that the funds should not be released from escrow. In order to avoid placing the escrow agent in a position of discretion concerning the release of the payment, the escrow agreement often makes the release of funds from escrow conditional upon written notice, with a sworn affidavit, from the payee that the triggering event has been fully performed—in much the same way that notice is provided to a technology provider when "acceptance testing" technology. In this way, the escrow agent may release the funds in reliance upon the written, and sworn, representation of the payee that it is entitled to receive the funds. Such escrow arrangements often also include alternative dispute resolution mechanisms that allow either participant to submit the matter to ADR for a period of time before the funds are released from escrow, and to require the escrow agent to hold the funds pending the determination of the ADR proceedings.

Security interests

4.10.3   There are many situations in which the financial difficulties of a participant may directly affect the outcome of the project. For example, if a participant is impecunious, insolvent or is petitioned into bankruptcy, the project may suffer due to both a loss of participant contribution, or the potential loss of access to particular assets that the participant was obliged to contribute to the project. Therefore, in any transaction that does not contemplate the payment of participants during the term of a technology transaction, or where there are any concerns about the financial solvency of a participant, you should consider securing the financial obligations of all participants by taking a security interest in their assets. Usually, such security interests are created by a separate agreement, such as a general security agreement, which will contain detailed terms and conditions concerning the granting of such security and the right of the secured participant to realise upon those security interests in specified circumstances. As a secured creditor, as opposed to an unsecured trade creditor, you will have a broad range of rights concerning the protection of your financial interests, including the benefit of a public registry that will put others on notice of your security interests in the assets. If there are any financial or other circumstances that are unusual in this regard, you should seek the advice of professional advisors who have specialist knowledge and expertise in matters related to debtor–creditor arrangements, insolvency and bankruptcy law. Depending upon the particular financial circumstances of each participant, there are a broad range of security arrangements and transaction structures that can accommodate these circumstances and reasonably protect other participants against the risks of a participant's financial default or failure.

Planning for termination and extrication

4.11   Where technology transactions create a commercial relationship over a substantial period of time, the participants may assume a risk of business dependency and losing the flexible ability to engage in other commercial arrangements. Thus, the inability to extricate themselves from the transaction relationship is itself an important project risk that should be anticipated and strategically managed from the outset of the transaction.

Document the reliance

4.11.1 Perhaps the first step in recognising the risk of transaction dependency on a particular participant's contribution to the transaction is to describe and analyse that dependency fully in terms of the impact that its absence would have on the project. Replacement or substitution alternatives can only be considered in the context of such project impact. With this first step, the project's management team can determine what resources should be invested to create a strategic plan that accounts for those circumstances, and how the remaining participants should address the transition to contribution alternatives should the need arise.

Transition plan

4.11.2 Once the impact of any particular contribution's conclusion has been assessed, the participants will be in a position to develop a transition plan that will take the project to the contingency arrangements that will mitigate those risks. Such transition plans are routinely included in the performance obligations of the technology agreement, to ensure that a participant whose contribution to the project is concluding will assist, and co-operate with, all other participants to facilitate the implementation of the contingency arrangements. As such, it is useful to write in an obligation to produce an "exit plan" as one of the key early deliverables in the life of a project.

In both the legal and commercial senses, a transition plan stipulates the obligations of a withdrawing participant to promote a smooth and seamless transition to the contingency arrangements, whether those arrangements contemplate a new participant, the winding down of the entire project, the distribution of a participant's obligations among the remaining project members, or otherwise. Considering that transition circumstances are among the most fertile ground for the emergence of conflicts and disputes, by stipulating detailed obligations of assistance and co-operation among withdrawing participants, transition plans should be regarded as a very important aspect of the project's conflict-management strategy.

Transition plans often include detailed operational provisions, including: (i) personnel requirements that may decline on a graduated basis over time; (ii) the contribution (whether by lease, licence or otherwise) of technology and equipment, with prescribed "switch-over" time lines; (iii) advisory and consulting services to transfer project knowledge to new participants, and to address connectivity, network and interoperability circumstances; (iv) assistance with public-sector, regulatory media or public-relations matters concerning the goodwill of the project; (v) ongoing management participation; and (vi) general obligations of reasonable assistance, good-faith co-operation, and diligent conduct that will minimise or mitigate any detrimental impact delays associated with the planned transition.

At the same time, sight must not be lost of the march of time. Since the original contract was let, technology, core requirements and background policy and legislative requirements will no doubt have moved on. As such, a retendering of an existing contract will not merely involve dusting down the requirements specification from several years ago. Rather, careful analysis will be necessary to identify your new requirements, as these will now have changed, not least because of the impact of your current service provider.

Transition services

4.11.3 The ambit of transition services may be as broad as any service arrangement, but the terms and conditions, and types of services, that transaction agreements typically address include: (i) reasonably detailed descriptions of the transition services, including the technical and operational scope of such obligations; (ii) provisions concerning a reasonable notice period before the transition services will begin; (iii) the duration of the transition services, and over what time periods they will be diminished or conclude; (iv) which transition services will be mandatory and which will be optional; (v) whether or not the transition services will be provided as a part of the transaction agreement or as a part of a separate contractual arrangement; (vi) whether the provider of the transition services will be separately remunerated (and at what fee/rates), or the transition services included in the provider's current project compensation; (vii) who will be responsible for the provider's out-of-pocket costs and expenses, and how these will be shared among the remaining participants; (viii) whether the withdrawing participant must provide the transition services directly, or whether they can subcontract those obligations to others; (ix) issues related to the transfer of a project knowledge to replacement participants, and all the related complications concerning the disclosure of confidential and proprietary information; (x) obligations to assist in the management and transition of relationships between incumbent suppliers and customers, and the replacement participant; and (xi) participation in future project disputes and ADR procedures where the withdrawing participant either has information concerning such matters or may otherwise help in resolving the dispute.

Competitor assistance

4.11.4 Since project participants are selected based upon their respective experience, expertise and competitive advantages, the replacement participant may be a competitor of the withdrawing participant. Therefore, the scope of the transition plan and the nature of the transition services may be compromised and limited by the reluctance of a withdrawing participant to assist, and co-operate with, a competitor. However, the following provisions are often included in the transition-services section of a transaction agreement to address such reasonable concerns: (i) all pricing and financial information concerning the respective participation in the project by each of the withdrawing participants and the new participant shall be kept strictly confidential and shall not be disclosed; (ii) the transfer of project knowledge to the new participant shall be subject to the withdrawing participant's confidentiality and proprietary interests, including any information that provides the withdrawing participant with competitive advantages outside of the project; (iii) the possible use of an independent third party to hold information in strict confidence, while releasing only aggregated information or data-analysis results that are strictly required by the new participant for project use; (iv) non-solicitation-restrictive covenants to protect the integrity of all participants' employment relationships; and (v) from time to time, the possible use of non-competition covenants that are structured, in both scope and impact, to offer reasonable protection of the commercial and business interests of both the withdrawing participant and the new participant.

Separate contract

4.11.5   As noted above, the issue of whether or not the transition services should be provided pursuant to a separate contract, as a distinct commercial arrangement, often arises. First, since the transition services are not project-specific, participants often feel that they are outside of the technology transaction, and should be separately addressed. Secondly, the withdrawing participant may prefer to provide such advisory or consultative services in accordance with the standard terms and conditions which they rely on to provide such services in the ordinary course of their business. Thirdly, there may be a broad number of distinct terms and conditions associated with the transition services, such as specific performance obligations, pricing, expense responsibility and risk management provisions. Lastly, as discussed above, there may be several important preconditions concerning the provision of the transition services, such as those related to the protection of the withdrawing participant's confidential and proprietary information.

If the participants determine that it is in the best interests of the project to stipulate the provision of transition services in a separate contract, the participants should consider discussing and settling all the material provisions of the arrangements as part of the technology transaction, and to append the contractual obligations as a schedule to the technology agreement. The more comprehensive such arrangements are under the agreement, the less opportunity there will be for disputes to arise among the participants in circumstances that are often contentious, and perhaps even adversarial. As such, it is not uncommon for the parties to agree an "unwind" or "exit" agreement at the same time as the main agreement is concluded.

Joint Management Committee

4.11.6   Regardless of whether or not the transition services are provided pursuant to the technology agreement or a separate contract, an important strategy to manage the risks associated with the provision of transition services is the required involvement of the Joint Management Committee as a management, governance and dispute-resolution mechanism. As with other performance obligations, the provision of transition services is fraught with potential conflicts and opportunities for misunderstanding—perhaps even more so, considering that those services are being performed in a context of participants' extrication from the project. Also, since the timing requirements of transition services are usually critical to the seamless continuance or wind-down of the project, the benefits of involving the Joint Management Committee may be even more crucial to the success of the project.

Chapter 5

Transaction balance and judgment

"Success tends to go not to the person who is error-free, because he also tends to be risk-averse. Rather, it goes to the person who recognises that life is pretty much a percentage business."—Donald Rumsfeld[10]

5.0   The "percentage business" of a technology transaction is the risk that the intended benefits of your project may be diminished by the project's possible losses or liabilities. In the commercial world's "risk-reward" justification for profit, the only way to maximise investment return is to do two things: maximise the project's reward and minimise the project's risks. If either part of this equation is neglected, the business underpinning of the technology transaction may be jeopardised. Transaction decisions that are based on balancing the expected reward against the possible risks should be fully informed on both sides of the equation. Project managers must equally appreciate and understand what the transaction's benefits are likely to be, and what the transaction's risks are likely to be.

When planning and implementing a successful technology transaction, it is essential to exercise prudent and reasonable commercial judgment both to maximise the opportunities for reward ("upside"), and to minimise the potential risks ("downside") of the transaction. In my experience, the cornerstone of this judgment is finding an acceptable balance between being commercially aggressive while exercising reasonable risk-management strategies that are proportionate to the transaction. Technology transactions that are too greatly burdened with risk-management bureaucracy may have the same detrimental impact on the project as commercially aggressive transactions that entirely disregard transactional risks.

Commercial mythology is replete with cautionary tales of both lawyers who encumber technology transactions with unnecessarily burdensome and unrealistic risk concerns, and cowboy project managers who ignore obvious and threatening transaction risks and fail to exercise prudent caution. Unfortunately, for all too many technology transactions, that mythology has some foundation in truth, and it provides a much-needed lesson. Because of the tension between these extremes, project teams all too frequently fail to find a reasonable balance

[10] Cited in *The Executive's Quotation Book* (James Charlton ed., CCH Canada Limited, Toronto, 1983, 1993), p.87.

between commercially aggressive obligations and reasonable ways to manage the corresponding risks in practical ways. Regardless of one's perspective on the commercial mythology, the success of most technology transactions will hang in the balance of reasonably addressing transactional risks to achieve the required business objectives efficiently.

Regardless of how commercially aggressive any technology transaction is, each participant will have their own tolerance for risk and opportunity to structure the transaction's risks to an acceptable level of tolerance. Through reasonable planning, due diligence and commercial arrangements, such risks can be deconstructed into practical business procedures and commercial strategies to achieve this balance. By following the transaction process and methodology of this book, from preparation and planning, through the preliminary steps of engagement, through the commercial negotiation and formulation of key business and legal issues, through the design and implementation of reasonable risk-management strategies, and through planning for the eventual conclusion of the technology transaction, project managers should gain both a macro and micro perspective of how possible risks can be reverse-engineered to specific transactional issues and concerns that arise throughout the chronological stages of the project.

As the Introduction described, the commercial and legal considerations of a technology transaction do not exist independently of each other. Each has an independent and a reciprocal relationship with the other, where each directly affects the other with proportional consequences. If certain business issues and procedures are ignored, the omission may have legal consequences. If important legal issues are ignored, then there may be direct and reciprocal business consequences. In a very practical business sense, technology transactions should be considered as a synthesis between the transaction's commercial imperatives and the reasonable management practices that will promote its success and minimise its risks. In my experience, project managers who fail to understand the reciprocal and commensurate relationship between those aspects of a technology transaction are far more likely to experience project difficulties, delays and even failure, either because the business risks have eroded the transaction's commercial benefits or because the transaction's risks have been over-managed to the point of stifling entrepreneurship.

Again, the overall objective is to get the deal done within an acceptable risk tolerance. There is absolutely no doubt that over-managing the potential risks of a technology transaction can be just as detrimental to the project as ignoring the risks. By understanding, in realistic and practical terms, what the project's risks really are, you will be able to exercise reasonable business judgment in a way that will provide you with a balanced approach to expedite your transaction to achieve its business case successfully.

The following eight principles may provide you with some guidance in achieving a balanced technology transaction.

1. What are the transaction's rewards, and what are the transaction's risks? The answers to both questions should be equally well informed. For example, in a technology-procurement transaction, you might ask, "What are the tech-

nology's benefits, and what are the risks associated with the technology, including its price?" In a technology-development transaction, you might ask, "What are the commercial opportunities for the new technology, and what is the downside of participating in the project with those collaborators?"

2. Assess the transaction's rewards and benefits in a realistic and unexaggerated way. Where project managers become too committed and dependent upon the desired outcome of a technology transaction, they may exaggerate the rewards and minimise the risks. Also, where the compensation of project personnel is based only on the reward side of the transaction ledger (*e.g.* revenue, profit, technology performance) without regard for the risk side of the ledger, they may make project decisions that are in their remunerative best interests, but not necessarily in the best risk-management interests of either their employer or the project. Emotional attachments to the transaction's rewards can cloud one's judgment concerning risk tolerance.

3. Be fully informed about the transaction's risks and potential liabilities. Do not be intimidated by them, so that they can be realistically and practically assessed in the context of the proposed transaction.

4. Once the transaction's risks are identified and assessed, develop transactional structures and commercial strategies to avoid, mitigate, manage or otherwise compensate for those risks. Often, creative changes to the transaction's business arrangements, the participant's legal obligations or even the way in which the participants deal with third parties can manage risk down to very acceptable levels of risk tolerance.

5. You should require your professional advisors to participate actively and creatively in developing business options and commercial and legal strategies, both to maximise the transaction's rewards and to minimise its risks. If your professional advisors do not have the business acumen, professional specialisation or transactional experience to fully participate in and successfully contribute to these aspects of the technology transaction, get new professional advisors.

6. In finding the balance between required reward and acceptable risk, be prepared to compromise and respect the reasonable interests of the other participants. You should especially avoid uncompromising positions that do not affect your interests concerning either the transaction's rewards or risks. Avoid the pitfall of not being able to see the wood for the trees, of missing balance in the reward–risk because of unrelated and less important individual positions.

7. Communicate your transactional interests to the other participants, including your reward expectations and your risk tolerances. All participants should be engaged in an open, co-operative and respectful dialogue concerning the other participants' transactional requirements and limitations.

8. Have the ability and be prepared to walk away from the technology transaction and the project. If necessary, create project alternatives and transaction options to avoid engaging in a technology transaction that you "have" to do. To negotiate a transaction otherwise is like negotiating when commercially cornered. If you are not free to determine whether or not the proposed rewards do not justify the potential risks, and if the transaction is not in the best interests of the participant you represent, then you will have little power to avoid an exploitative transaction. In my experience, there is a direct and proportional relationship between the ability of a participant to walk away from a proposed transaction and the beneficial outcome of the transaction. It is absolutely true that the best commercial deals are secured by those who need them least. Luckily, few technology transactions occur while one of the participants is being held commercially hostage—but when it does happen, it is not pretty.

The following are some of the statements that experienced technology transactions professionals most like to hear from project managers as they work to find a balanced approach:

1. I understand the concerns; so now I need all the structural, commercial and legal options you can come up with to address the concerns and move the transaction forward.

2. We are in this for the long haul, so let's discuss the problem with them frankly, understand their interests concerning this issue, get it resolved and move on to the next issue.

3. Look, if they say, "That's the deal," then why won't they put it in the contract?

As this book discusses, technology transactions are like icebergs—only 10 per cent of the transaction is visible to the other participants. Most of the reasons why technology projects are successful has to do with the other 90 per cent of the transaction: the planning, due diligence, strategy sessions on commercial issues, risk-tolerance analysis, and problem solving that participants cannot see from the surface of the project. Again, like an iceberg, it is the submerged part of the technology transaction that is the most dangerous if ignored and not respected.

Among the most dangerous things that project managers can say about their technology transactions are the following:

1. I admit it is a serious problem, but I doubt they will ever discover it. Let's just ignore it—I think they will too.

2. Why don't we define the product and the services after we sign the contract, and once we get to know each other a little better (also known as "safely kicking the problem into the long grass").

3. Don't be ridiculous, they wouldn't do that. That will never happen.

A successful technology transaction has nothing to do with chance, but everything to do with preparation, diligent work and attention to detail. From the macro considerations of the project's business case, participant relationships and project administration to the micro concerns of the project's very detailed commercial arrangements and document drafting, technology transactions involve a very broad array of commercial, legal, regulatory, administrative and management issues that will require the organisation, planning and strategic implementation discussed in this book.

Index